T0343877

Decentralized Music

This book offers a thorough exploration of the potential of blockchain and AI technologies to transform musical practices. Including contributions from leading researchers in music, arts, and technology, it addresses central notions of agency, authorship, ontology, provenance, and ownership in music.

Together, the chapters of this book, often navigating the intersections of post-digital and posthumanist thought, challenge conventional centralized mechanisms of music creation and dissemination, advocating for new forms of musical expression.

Stressing the need for the artistic community to engage with blockchain and AI, this volume is essential reading for artists, musicians, researchers, and policymakers curious to know more about the implications of these technologies for the future of music.

Paulo de Assis is an artist researcher operating at the intersection of music performance, composition, critical thought, and contemporary philosophy. Active as pianist, researcher, and author, he wrote *Logic of Experimentation— Rethinking Music Performance through Artistic Research* (Leuven, 2018). Recent artistic research projects include experimental performance practices on music by Beethoven, Schumann, Nietzsche, and Luigi Nono.

Adam Łukawski is a pioneering music composer and computer programmer, innovating at the nexus of computer-assisted music composition and posthumanist artistic research. His work, deeply engaged with aleatoric and generative methods, explores the integration of AI and blockchain technologies for creating novel compositional frameworks and enhancing musical interactivity.

Decentralized Music
Exploring Blockchain for Artistic Research

Edited by
Paulo de Assis
Adam Łukawski

CRC Press
Taylor & Francis Group
Boca Raton London New York

CRC Press is an imprint of the
Taylor & Francis Group, an **informa** business

First edition published 2025
by CRC Press
2385 NW Executive Center Drive, Suite 320, Boca Raton FL 33431

and by CRC Press
4 Park Square, Milton Park, Abingdon, Oxon, OX14 4RN

CRC Press is an imprint of Taylor & Francis Group, LLC

© 2025 selection and editorial matter, Paulo de Assis and Adam Łukawski; individual chapters, the contributors

Reasonable efforts have been made to publish reliable data and information, but the author and publisher cannot assume responsibility for the validity of all materials or the consequences of their use. The authors and publishers have attempted to trace the copyright holders of all material reproduced in this publication and apologize to copyright holders if permission to publish in this form has not been obtained. If any copyright material has not been acknowledged please write and let us know so we may rectify in any future reprint.

Except as permitted under U.S. Copyright Law, no part of this book may be reprinted, reproduced, transmitted, or utilized in any form by any electronic, mechanical, or other means, now known or hereafter invented, including photocopying, microfilming, and recording, or in any information storage or retrieval system, without written permission from the publishers.

For permission to photocopy or use material electronically from this work, access www.copyright. com or contact the Copyright Clearance Center, Inc. (CCC), 222 Rosewood Drive, Danvers, MA 01923, 978-750-8400. For works that are not available on CCC please contact mpkbookspermissions@tandf. co.uk

Trademark notice: Product or corporate names may be trademarks or registered trademarks and are used only for identification and explanation without intent to infringe.

Library of Congress Cataloging-in-Publication Data
Names: Łukawski, Adam, 1997- editor. | Assis, Paulo de, editor.
Title: Decentralized music : exploring blockchain for artistic research / edited by Adam Łukawski and Paulo De Assis.
Description: First edition. | Boca Raton, FL : CRC Press, 2024. |
Includes bibliographical references and index. |
Identifiers: LCCN 2024006297 (print) | LCCN 2024006298 (ebook) |
ISBN 9781032601618 (hardback) | ISBN 9781032602400 (paperback) |
ISBN 9781003458227 (ebook)
Subjects: LCSH: Music--Computer network resources. | Dissemination of music--Technological innovations. | Composition (Music)--Collaboration. | Blockchains (Databases) | NFTs (Tokens)
Classification: LCC ML74.7 .D43 2024 (print) | LCC ML74.7 (ebook) | DDC 780.285--dc23/eng/20240327
LC record available at https://lccn.loc.gov/2024006297
LC ebook record available at https://lccn.loc.gov/2024006298

ISBN: 978-1-032-60161-8 (hbk)
ISBN: 978-1-032-60240-0 (pbk)
ISBN: 978-1-003-45822-7 (ebk)

DOI: 10.1201/9781003458227

Typeset in Palatino
by SPi Technologies India Pvt Ltd (Straive)

Contents

Contributors

Paulo de Assis has developed an international profile as a prolific researcher who combines musical practice (as a pianist of the classical repertoire and experimental performer), musicological expertise on 20th-century Western art music, publishing experience (as author and editor), and wide-ranging transdisciplinary interests in contemporary philosophy and epistemology. He was the PI of a prestigious European Research Council Grant (2013–2018), the founder and Chair of the international conference series Deleuze and Artistic Research (DARE), and the editor of the book series Artistic Research at Rowman & Littlefield International (London/New York). He is regularly invited for keynote speeches, evaluation committees, review panels, PhD external examinations, masterclasses, and performances. He is President of the Panel Arts, Design and Architecture at the Swiss National Science Foundation. He wrote *Logic of Experimentation—Rethinking Music Performance through Artistic Research* (Leuven 2018). As an editor, he published fourteen volumes, including *Artistic Research: Charting a Field in Expansion* (Rowman & Littlefield International), *Machinic Assemblages of Desire* (LUP, 2021), *Virtual Works—Actual Things. Essays in Music Ontology* (LUP, 2018), *Futures of the Contemporary* (LUP, 2017), *The Dark Precursor: Deleuze and Artistic Research* (LUP, 2017), *Emmanuel Nunes. Escritos e Entrevistas* (Casa da Música, 2011), *Luigi Nono. Escritos* (Casa da Música, 2013), and *'Pierre Boulez. Escritos Seletos'* (Casa da Música, 2012).

    Academia.edu: paulodeassis.academia.edu/research

    Research Catalogue: www.researchcatalogue.net/profile/?person= 46970

Diane Drubay has been working towards the transformation of museums and the arts internationally since 2007 through various communities, conferences, and change programs. Founder of WeAreMuseums, a community-powered think tank on the future of museums good for people and the Planet. Diane Drubay is a visual artist nudging for nature-awareness and better futures. She is a Web3 futures explorer and main advisor for the arts and culture for the Tezos ecosystem and for the artist-led gallery alterHEN.

Einar Torfi Einarsson is Professor at the Music Department of the Iceland University of the Arts. He received his PhD in Composition from the University of Huddersfield, where he was supervised by Aaron Cassidy. Previously he studied composition at Reykjavik College of Music,

Conservatory of Amsterdam and University of Music and Performing Arts in Graz. He also studied in masterclass and private setting with Salvatore Sciarrino, Brian Ferneyhough, Beat Furrer, and Peter Ablinger. His music has been awarded several prizes and been performed and broadcast throughout Europe by ensembles such as Klangforum Wien, ELISION Ensemble, Ensemble Intercontemporain. His research interests lie in the interplay of poststructuralist philosophy and notation, and in inter- and post-disciplinary art. In 2013–2014 he was a post-doc Research Fellow at the Orpheus Institute in Belgium. His research has been published in *Perspectives of New Music* and by Leuven University Press.

Website: www.einartorfieinarsson.com

Kosmas Giannoutakis (*1985 in Thessaloniki, Greece) studied piano and percussion performance, composition, and computer music in Greece, Germany, and Austria. He is a PhD candidate in Electronic Arts at the Rensselaer Polytechnic Institute, where he investigates the emerging field of decentralization, which is crucial for understanding and navigating the incipient musicalities in the labyrinthine era of algorithmic automation. His artist output includes a wide range of acoustic and electroacoustic music genres such as acousmatic music, film music, robotic and interactive sound installations, audiovisual game performances, algorithmic and computer-generated compositions, concert installations, live-electronics, live coding, telematic performances, systematic processes of collaborative composition and Machine-Learning generated media. His works have been presented and received awards at numerous international festivals and conferences.

Website: http://www.kosmasgiannoutakis.eu/

Adam Łukawski is a pioneering music composer and computer programmer, innovating at the nexus of computer-assisted music composition and posthuman artistic research. His work, deeply engaged with aleatoric and generative methods, explores the integration of AI and blockchain technologies for creating novel compositional frameworks and enhancing musical interactivity. He is a doctoral fellow in the MetamusicX research group at the Orpheus Institute in Ghent and a PhD candidate at the Academy of Creative and Performing Arts of Leiden University. As a lecturer, he participates in numerous international scientific and artistic events and teaches a Master's elective course 'Posthuman Creativity Labs: Artificial Intelligence and Blockchain in Music' at Conservatorium van Amsterdam. Since 2023, he has been a member of the expert group of the Polish Ministry of Education and Sciences (MEiN) advising on the use of AI in education. As a computer programmer, Adam Łukawski gained experience working for several start-ups and at the Polish Information Processing Society. He studied Music

Composition at Conservatorium van Amsterdam and at Guildhall School of Music & Drama in London.
Website: www.adamlukawski.com

Catherine Mulligan is currently Professor of Computer Science at the Instituto Superior Técnico at the University of Lisbon and Director of the newly established lab called DCentral. She is a regular presenter on emerging technologies in media and at events with previous speaking engagements at GSMA Mobile World Congress, ITU, OECD, Chatham House, UK Parliament, BBC TV/Radio and World Service. She is a sought-after technology advisor for NGOs, governments, start-ups, and corporations. Cathy has had a long interest and track record in applying digital technology to achieve sustainability outcomes, including a Master's in Engineering for Sustainable Development from the University of Cambridge (2006). She completed her PhD at Cambridge on *The Communications Industries in the Era of Convergence*, and led projects in India, Malaysia, Singapore, London, and the EU as well as participating in high-level policy discussions across NGOs, the UN, the OECD, and the European Commission. She was a member of the UNSG's High Level Panel for Digital Cooperation during 2019 and is a current member of the World Economic Forum's Data Policy Global Futures Council. Cathy is an Honorary Senior Researcher at UCL within the Department of Computer Science and also leads the MBA Elective 'Digital Transformation – Leading Real-World Change' at Imperial College Business School. She was previously the Co-Director of the Imperial College Centre for Cryptocurrency Research and Engineering and led a number of high-impact grants in the Digital Economy across the world, including India, Malaysia, EU, Australia, and the UK; her research approach is deep understanding of the end-user communities who lead the co-creation process.

Marcus O'Dair is a writer, consultant, and academic interested in creativity and innovation management, particularly from a whole systems perspective. With a PhD in collective authorship, he has been carrying out research into what is now called Web3 since setting up the Blockchain for Creative Industries research cluster at Middlesex University in 2016. Marcus is currently Associate Dean of Knowledge Exchange at University of the Arts London (UAL), consistently named the best university in the world for undergraduate art and design education. In this role he leads knowledge exchange for 200 academics, working with partners from Nike to IBM. He has been awarded over a million pounds in funding for his own academic work. Marcus is a Fellow of Enterprise Educators UK and a Senior Fellow of the Higher Education Academy. As well as journal articles, book chapters, and

reports, Marcus is the author of *Distributed Creativity: How Blockchain Will Transform the Creative Economy* (Palgrave 2019).
Website: www.marcusodair.com

Claudio J. Tessone is Professor of Blockchain and Distributed Ledger Technologies at the Informatics Department, University of Zurich. He is co-founder and Chairman of the UZH Blockchain Center. He holds a PhD in Physics (on complex systems) and an Habilitation on 'Complex Socio-economic Systems' from ETH Zurich. He is an expert in the modeling of complex socioeconomic and sociotechnical systems from an interdisciplinary perspective. He is interested in the link between microscopic agent behavior and the rules these agents abide to, and the global, emergent properties of socioeconomic and sociotechnical systems. Blockchain-based systems and cryptocurrencies are the main pillar of his research (being among the first to study them). This includes crypto-economics (from financial aspects to meso- and macro-properties, such as withstanding, emergent centralization), big-data blockchain analytics and forensics, design of blockchain-based systems, and characterization of economic incentives that are present (by design or set inadvertently) in them. He is the director of the Summer School: Deep Dive into Blockchain and of the Certificate of Advanced Studies on Blockchain at the University of Zurich. Since 2018, he serves as Chief Editor of the section on non-financial blockchains and interdisciplinary applications of the journal *Frontiers in Blockchain*.

Kristof Timmerman is a designer and director of digital performances and installations, working in the field of live, interactive digital environments and virtual reality. He worked for several theater companies, including the experimental CREW. In 2006 he founded the digital artist collective studio.POC. Timmerman is the chair and coordinator of Maxlab at the Royal Academy of Fine Arts Antwerp and is involved as promoter and researcher in several research projects on virtual and augmented reality, mostly in a multidisciplinary context. Since September 2022 he is working on his doctoral research 'Sense of Wonder. Artistic Portals between the Real and the Virtual'. He is connected to the Immersive Lab of the AP University College, where he organizes the annual summer school 'Storytelling in Virtual Reality. An Immersive Encounter'.
Website: https://kristoftimmerman.com/

Martin Zeilinger works as Senior Lecturer in Computational Art & Technology at Abertay University, Dundee/Scotland, focusing on artistic and activist experiments with emerging technologies (primarily blockchain and AI), intellectual property issues in contemporary art, and aspects of experimental videogame culture. He is the author of

Tactical Entanglements: AI Art, Creative Agency, and the Limits of Intellectual Property (meson press, 2021), and was co-curator of Vector Festival (Toronto) from 2014 to 2020. In 2018, he organized the MoneyLab symposium in London. His research has been published in books, including *Artists Re:Thinking the Blockchain and the MoneyLab Reader 2*, and journals including *Leonardo, Philosophy & Technology, Culture Machine*, and *Media Theory*.

Introduction:
Blockchain for Artistic Research

Paulo de Assis and Adam Łukawski
Leiden University/Orpheus Institute, Ghent, Belgium

Musical works are virtual entities. They are made of material and immaterial constitutive parts. On the one hand, they are conglomerates of highly distributed material objects such as scores, manuscripts, sketches, annotated copies, different versions, transcriptions, performances, and recordings. On the other, they are sustained by immaterial qualities such as musical and economic value, aesthetic judgment, performative and musicological interpretations, sociopolitical and historical context, personal meaning, symbolic aura. All these component parts are real. They all have a concrete function in the cognitive and sensual perception of any given musical work. As the basic constitutive parts of a dynamic entity, these particles are constantly negotiated and recombined in ever-new arrangements. Every single particle can be located, identified, and coded; yet it is only through a network of connections between different particles and actants that musical works can be meaningfully expressed and communicated.

As a consequence of this view, a new image of the musical work emerges in which the totality of particles and connectors that relate to a musical work can be seen as a complex 'assemblage' (in the philosophical sense of the term). With its interplay between structure and contingency, organization and chance, form and intensity, the notion of assemblage enables a fluid and dynamic approach to musical works, helping better grasp their historical formation and ever-varied transmission over time. The work concept, which regulated musical practices in the 19th and 20th centuries, operated in a musical world made of centralized mediators: music schools, publishers, concert halls, congregated audiences, critics, recording labels. Today, in the digital age of infinite sources, self-publishing, distributed music consumption, online streaming, immediate feedback, global dissemination and Generative Artificial Intelligence, the concept of music assemblage gains major relevance, stressing the multiplicity and fragmentarity of materials, processes, and outcomes. As society moved from information scarcity to

DOI: 10.1201/9781003458227-1

information abundance, more than stand-alone things, properties, and binary relations, primacy is now given to interactions, processes, and networks (de Assis 2023). Melting actual and virtual realities, analogue, and digital modes of existence, music increasingly happens in a hybrid digital-analogue continuum, where questions of data provenance, agency (including its non-human and post-human forms), authenticity, ownership, and value pose a complex set of challenges and opportunities for the understanding and interaction with musical particles. To effectively navigate this wide array of emerging constraints and possibilities, not only new modes of conceptualizing music are needed, but a new technologically-equivalent medium, enabling the implementation of experimental approaches, is essential. Such a medium must be capable of embracing the richness of music's evolving landscape, accommodating connections between both the tangible and intangible elements of musical works. It should offer a platform where the diverse constituents – scores, performances, interpretations, and cultural contexts – coalesce, allowing for a more holistic appreciation and analysis of interconnected musical particles. In this regard, blockchain technology with its emerging features stands as a promising candidate, enabling new modes of encoding intricately interlinked networks of various objects in a decentralized, yet transparent, way. Often associated with cryptocurrencies and financial transactions, blockchains at the intersection with artistic practice possess a wider promising, yet underexplored, potential.

Blockchain is a secure, transparent digital technology for recording and sharing data across a decentralized network. Data on this shared ledger is organized into blocks that are cryptographically linked together in chronological order, forming a 'block-chain'. The decentralized nature of blockchain networks eliminates the need for a central authority or intermediary to validate transactions or oversee the network. While initially prominent in the realm of cryptocurrencies, blockchain technology has found diverse applications across industries like supply chain, healthcare, and finance for tracking and verifying critical information. Since the advent of 'smart contracts' in 2013, blockchain technology has expanded its scope to support digital assets, such as audio, video, and text files. This is predominantly facilitated through smart contract-based non-fungible tokens (NFTs), which serve as a means to authenticate and track their established identity and – on top of it – their ownership (Buterin 2013).

A detailed history of blockchain would obviously go beyond the scope of this introduction, and there are excellent accounts thereof (Brekke 2019, Whitaker 2019, 25–29; O'Dair 2019, 16–21). Let's just recall that a brief history of blockchain covers three generations: *Blockchain 1.0*, used mainly for cryptocurrencies like Bitcoin (2008); *Blockchain 2.0*, introduced by Ethereum (2014), which added smart contracts, and *Blockchain 3.0*, which focuses on eco-friendly consensus methods (from 'Proof of Work' to 'Proof of Stake'), and integration with AI, IoT (Internet of Things), Big Data, and cloud computing, promising even more non-financial uses and benefits. Blockchain technologies have been recognized as highly disruptive and transformative of societal practices by major experts and international organizations. The United Nations' working group on Science and Technology for Development stated in 2021 that 'blockchain is potentially a key technology in a new technological paradigm of increasing automation and integrating physical and virtual worlds, together with technologies such as artificial intelligence (AI), robots, and gene editing' (United Nations 2021). The European Commission published a working report on the future of Europe in 2021, stating that 'artificial intelligence (AI) and blockchain are two of the most significant disruptive technologies of our time, set to have a major impact on future societies and economies' (Verbeek and Lundqvist 2021, 37). The EU Blockchain Observatory and Forum was launched by the European Commission in February 2018, aiming at the establishment of a European Blockchain Partnership 'to facilitate cooperation and sharing of expertise amongst EU member states' (European Commission 2018). Influent experts like Catherine Mulligan (director of the Centre for Cryptocurrency Research at Imperial College, and advisor of the United Nations on digital technologies) claim that 'blockchain is undoubtedly one of the most important emerging technology trends within the creative industries' (Mulligan 2019).

While there are massive amounts of research projects on the technical and financial developments of blockchain technologies, there are very few focusing on its artistic consequences and creative implications. When it comes to the arts, research has mainly focused on payments, royalties, author attribution, intellectual property rights, questions of ownership, and other issues on economic and monetary aspects of the so-called *cultural industries*. Blockchain researcher Marcus O'Dair (convener of the Blockchain for Creative Industries research cluster at Middlesex University) claims that 'embracing blockchain technologies can empower creators and reshape the future of the arts' (O'Dair 2019, 9). While researchers such as Marcus O'Dair (2019), Amy Whitaker (2019), Ruth Catlow (2017), and Catlow and Rafferty (2022) conducted extremely valuable research on societal implications of blockchain technologies in relation to the arts, a specific discussion of the ontological implications of blockchain for music and of the creative artistic consequences of blockchain for future musical practices is still lagging. However, for the arts blockchain may bring radical changes not only to the way in which artworks are transacted, but crucially to the way in which artistic processes unfold and artworks are created. Given the accelerated technological developments in digital culture, it is imperative to investigate the consequences of blockchain for the arts, focusing on the creative rather than on the financial and political opportunities of this technology.

Due to the progressing technological adoption, development of high-level blockchain infrastructures, greater access to domain knowledge, frequently issued tutorials and guides, and the recent explosion of AI capabilities in

computer programming, blockchain technologies became increasingly accessible to non-coders. This creates a unique opportunity for other disciplines
to position themselves in this new landscape. Artists and musicians would
benefit from proactively engaging with these new technologies, contributing
with new uses, new tools, and new kinds of outputs. Furthermore, the concept of agency within the Humanities has long been associated with notions
of intentionality, rationality, voice, and sentient decisions. However, recent
expansions of this notion (Marchand 2018; Zeilinger 2022) accommodate the
multiple non-human 'actants' with whom humans co-constitute a common
world. This redefinition of agency in terms of posthuman agency presents
novel and difficult challenges that require broader (also artistic) reflection
and positioning: 'artistic experiments with blockchain that treat code outputs
as living things suggest a radical recalibration of agency' (Zeilinger 2022).
Lastly, it would be not only a mistake but also a sign of irresponsibility for
the arts not to actively engage with and contribute inputs to the definition
of future uses and horizon of artistic practices in the field of blockchain. As
Amy Whitaker (2019, 23) poignantly expressed: *'Ignoring blockchain within
the field of the arts empowers actors outside the field to act without the field's participation'*. Artists and musicians will only get adequate blockchain networks
if proactively engaging with its technical, social, and aesthetic implications.

Several artists have already actively engaged with blockchain technologies,
contributing to the emergence of new, experimental modes of expression.
Among others, visual artists Damien Hirst (*The Currency*, 2021; *The Beautiful
Paintings*, 2023) and Banksy (*Love is in the Air*, 2021), and musicians Imogen
Heap (*Tiny Human*, 2015; *Firsts*, 2021) and Holly Herndon (*Platform*, 2015;
Holly+, 2021) developed groundbreaking experimental projects using block-
chain technologies, clearly demonstrating that this technology can be used as
a new artistic medium. Major museums and art galleries have also adopted
blockchain technologies, like the British Museum, which created its own
blockchain-based collection (LaCollection), the Uffizi Gallery (Florence), the
Smithsonian's Hirshhorn Museum (Washington), the Institute of Contemporary
Art (Los Angeles), and the Santa Casa da Misericórdia (Lisbon), among others
In December 2022, the Serpentine Galleries organized a conference on generative NFTs, paving the way for further integration of its physical collections
with blockchain technologies. Additionally, several blockchain networks have
become hubs for decentralized creativity, promoting artists experimenting
with blockchain. An example is the collaboration between Tezos Foundation
and Art Basel | Miami Beach 2021 and Art Basel 2023, leading to the establish-
ment of a digital art collection hosted in the Tezos blockchain (2023).

***

Investigating the future of music and its relation to new and emergent technologies, *Decentralized Music: Exploring Blockchain for Artistic Research* explores
the field of blockchain, non-fungible tokens, and decentralized autonomous organizations as creative tools and new media for the generation and

distribution of new artistic objects. Rooted in artistic research and creative practices, the central perspective of the book is that blockchain technologies can have a positive impact in emergent artistic practices, defining new futures for the arts. Focusing on blockchain and NFTs in relation to musical practices, this book addresses the potential of blockchain for music creation, offering new insights to the community of artist researchers in music.

Taking these ideas as conceptual triggers for theoretical and practice-based investigations, the content of this book includes chapters by leading researchers in blockchain technologies and NFTs, artist-researchers in music, social theorists, and curators. It is important to note that this book is not about blockchain technology's fundamental mechanisms, nor is it about the history of blockchain. It is about forward-looking aspects of blockchain technologies. While the chapters of this book are focused on various different topics related to blockchain and music, there are a few often recurring motives. First, the book addresses the relation of music and artistic research to blockchain (Assis, Łukawski, Zeilinger), discussing fundamental questions about music ontology (which entities do we agree to call 'music'?), about decentralized artistic processes, and about posthuman agency of artworks. Next, it moves to more technically-centered discussions on current challenges at the intersection of blockchain technologies and the art world at large. Further, authors present different perspectives on the crucial question of values (economic, societal, and aesthetic) of art in the blockchain (O'Dair), and on new pathways for social and economic exchanges, re-envisioning creative processes through NFTs and DAOs (Mulligan). Finally, artists (Einarsson, Łukawski) and curators (Drubay) present recent artistic experiments in and with blockchain technologies. Thus, the book implicitly moves from theoretical foundations and technological investigations to concrete artistic and musical examples, aiming to cover a wide range of opportunities made possible by decentralized computing and blockchain technologies.

The initial idea for the realization of this book can be traced back to the webinar 'Music NFTs: Exploring Blockchain for Artistic Research', hosted online by the Orpheus Institute in Ghent on 24–25 May 2022. This gathering was instrumental in shaping the initial discussions and perspectives presented in this book as most of our authors participated in this event in the roles of either speakers or participants. Central to initiating this discourse has been the work conducted within the research cluster MetamusicX and its previous iterations (MusicExperimentX, MusicExperiment21) at Orpheus Institute since 2013. This work led to innovative perspectives and pioneering ideas in relation to a redefinition of musical works. The renewed understanding of musical works as actual/virtual entities forms the backbone of our ongoing investigations into blockchain technology as a transformative tool for music. Thus, the first chapter in this volume further elucidates this journey, extending from Assemblage Theory for Music to the novel concept of 'hypermusic' and beyond. By reimagining the musical work as an 'assemblage' and exploring the expansive possibilities of 'hypermusic', Chapter 1 not only challenges conventional perspectives but also opens up new horizons for understanding and interacting with musical entities in the blockchain era, making this chapter a pivotal piece in understanding the overarching themes of this book. The chapter takes an exploratory approach, challenging traditional perspectives on musical entities, introducing two key concepts: 'assemblage' and 'hypermusic', which are proposed as broader frameworks that encompass the diversity and multitude of materials associated with musical objects. It argues for a reconceptualization of the musical work, moving beyond the conventional work concept to the view of musical-works-as-assemblages. This approach acknowledges the dynamic, ever-changing nature of musical works, which are seen as constellations of various components within a vast network of relationships, encompassing their origins, contexts, and uses. The reconceptualization includes a critical examination of the historical and current limitations of the traditional notion of a musical work. Furthermore, the chapter delves into the notion of 'hypermusic', a term that represents a more fluid and expansive understanding of music. This concept reflects the evolving nature of music, considering the myriad ways in which it is created, performed, and received. 'Hypermusic' encompasses a broader spectrum of musical expressions and experiences, highlighting the interconnectedness and complexity of the musical world.

Chapter 2 explores the transformative potential of blockchain technology and NFTs in the realm of music creation by proposing the new concepts of 'Decentralized Creative Networks' and 'Performative Transactions' within the realm of artistic collaboration between humans and AI agents. The chapter begins by acknowledging how blockchain and NFTs have already altered the authentication of digital musical creations and facilitated the emergence of generative art NFTs. However, it emphasizes that the potential applications of these technologies in music extend far beyond these initial uses. 'Decentralized Creative Networks' are proposed as blockchain-based social networks where artists and AI agents collaboratively develop and transact composable artistic processes. These networks enable artists to build upon each other's contributions transparently and interoperably, much like posts on social media. These artistic processes can be used in various applications, such as composing music, executing live performances, or generating NFTs. 'Performative Transactions,' on the other hand, are specific types of transactions within these networks. They are executed by smart contracts, which specify both the artistic process and the terms of its use in other processes. These transactions not only execute the musical transformations contributing to a composition but also handle the distribution of financial receivables to creators of the referenced processes. The chapter discusses integrating AI into these networks, suggesting a collaborative environment where human and AI agents actively shape the artistic network, with applications in music composition, performance, analysis, and sound synthesis.

Chapter 3, by Martin Zeilinger, is a thorough exploration of how artificial intelligence (AI) and blockchain technologies are influencing digital art, with a focus on sonic arts and music. The paper delves into the evolving concept of creative agency, examining the extent to which it can be embedded in AI-augmented and blockchain-enabled musical objects. Zeilinger analyzes the project '*Holly+*', which uses AI for voice synthesis and blockchain for decentralized rights management, as a case study to explore these ideas in practice. The discussion highlights the potential of these technologies to fundamentally alter traditional notions of creativity, authorship, and ownership. AI is seen as a means to challenge the human-centric view of artistic creation by producing works that may be perceived as generated by non-human intelligence. Blockchain is credited with introducing enforceable scarcity to digital artifacts, altering the way digital art is accessed and valued. Zeilinger considers the impact of these technologies from theoretical and practical perspectives, suggesting that they have the potential to create new forms of art that possess agency – meaning they can act or interact autonomously. The chapter also posits that the integration of AI and blockchain could lead to a redefinition of roles and responsibilities in the creative process, with significant implications for how music is composed, performed, and experienced. Finally, the author speculates on future possibilities for music and sound art, suggesting that these technologies could lead to the reimagining of foundational aesthetic and philosophical concepts, such as the artist, the artwork, and the composer.

Marcus O'Dair (Chapter 4) takes us on a journey beyond the narrow financial context often associated with blockchain and Web3 technologies in the music industry. While initially linked mainly to cryptocurrencies like Bitcoin, the rise of NFTs has brought about a paradigm shift, challenging the perception that Web3 is solely about speculative investments in digital assets. O'Dair delves into the historical evolution of blockchain in music, highlighting two distinct waves of its impact. The first wave, business-to-business, focused on intellectual property aspects such as rights management. The second wave, more recent and business-to-consumer, has been driven by the emergence of NFTs, enabling artists to mint and sell their creations directly to fans. This chapter explores the various opportunities and risks that Web3 presents for musicians, fans, and industry stakeholders. It discusses the potential for new revenue streams, mass collaboration, and direct fan engagement, while also acknowledging the challenges and limitations faced by artists in accessing these opportunities. Furthermore, it examines the implications for fans, who now have the chance to invest and potentially profit from music-related tokens, but must navigate market volatility and the complexities of the technology. Beyond financial considerations, O'Dair emphasizes the need to consider non-financial forms of value in Web3 music. The chapter explores the social, environmental, and aesthetic dimensions of this emerging landscape, including the potential for global south participation, shifts in power dynamics, and efforts to leverage blockchain for positive environmental change. Overall, this chapter provides a comprehensive exploration of the multifaceted impact of blockchain and Web3 technology on the music industry, urging readers to adopt a broader perspective that encompasses social, environmental, and aesthetic values in addition to financial considerations.

Claudio J. Tessone's chapter critically explores the reality behind the decentralization and uniqueness promised by blockchain technology and NFTs in digital content distribution. Tessone probes the effectiveness of these technologies in challenging existing centralized systems and the true novelty of the content they distribute. Through an analysis that spans complex socioeconomic systems, the foundational principles of blockchain, and the emergence of centralization trends within these supposedly decentralized systems, Tessone offers a nuanced perspective. The chapter pays particular attention to NFTs and their role in art and digital asset management, questioning the authenticity and uniqueness of such assets. By drawing parallels with historical projects like Xanadu, Tessone suggests potential future directions for blockchain and NFTs that could truly innovate and disrupt digital transactions and content distribution. The conclusion calls for a reevaluation of blockchain's role and potential, emphasizing the need for ongoing research and experimentation to realize its transformative possibilities.

Diane Drubay's chapter is a reflective narrative about the intersection of art, museums, and technology, focusing on the transformative power of blockchain technology in the cultural sector. It starts with the author's realization in 2012 of the impending change in museums, leading to the creation of 'We Are Museums', an innovation lab. The piece details various ways blockchain can revolutionize museums: from fractional art ownership and direct artist revenue to digital scarcity and blockchain-powered tickets, enhancing museum philanthropy and access. It discusses actual instances of blockchain's application in art exhibitions and acquisitions and the rise of the NFT marketplace Hic et Nunc, which democratized blockchain art with a low-cost, energy-efficient model. The text also highlights community-driven initiatives within the Tezos blockchain community that promote inclusivity, generosity, and support for social causes through art. Finally, it mentions We Are Museums' 'WAC Lab', an innovation laboratory exploring Web3's potential for arts and culture, culminating in the implementation of a curation DAO by the House of Electronic Arts in Basel. The conclusion emphasizes the cultural odyssey embarked upon through blockchain and Web3, hailing it as the start of a global cultural transformation.

The chapter by Catherine Mulligan, which is a reworked transcription of her presentation at the Orpheus webinar (Mulligan 2022), draws upon the phrase 'you can't knock the hustle', attributed to both Jay Z and Sotheby's, to delve into the transformative dynamics shaping the creative sector in the era of digital tokens. This chapter offers an exploratory reflection on the intersection of NFTs and Decentralized Autonomous Organizations (DAOs) with the creative industry. Mulligan, with her extensive background in blockchain, cryptocurrency, and sustainability research since 2009, provides insights into how these technologies are reshaping creativity and artistic practices. The chapter discusses the impact of NFTs and DAOs on artistic creation, distribution, and ownership, exploring how these technologies open up new possibilities for artists and the creative industry at large. It focusses on the evolving role of blockchain and related technologies in altering the traditional dynamics of the creative sector, touching upon topics like digital art, music, and the broader cultural implications of these technological advancements.

In Kristof Timmerman's chapter the focus is on the transformative impact of blockchain technology in the realm of decentralized music within virtual environments. Timmerman delves into how our increasingly digital-centric lives, further accelerated by the COVID-19 crisis, are influencing artistic creation and audience engagement in virtual spaces. He explores the concept of the 'metaverse' and its implications for artistic collaboration and audience experience. This collective virtual shared space, an amalgamation of virtual worlds, augmented reality, and more, is redefining the boundaries between creators, performers, and audiences. Timmerman discusses the significance of blockchain in this context, noting its role in enhancing interoperability across diverse virtual platforms, thus fostering collaborative and immersive artistic experiences. Central to Timmerman's analysis is the concept of 'breaking the fifth wall' in immersive experiences, where the distinction between virtual and real worlds is blurred, and the audience transitions from passive observers to active participants. This reimagined engagement is facilitated by the decentralized and transparent nature of blockchain technology, which empowers audiences with greater agency and ownership within these virtual environments. The chapter is both speculative and visionary, probing the potential of blockchain and decentralized technologies to revolutionize how music is created, distributed, and experienced in the evolving digital landscape. Timmerman's work invites readers to consider a future where music in virtual spaces is not just a theoretical concept but a transformative reality, promising a more inclusive, transparent, and artistically vibrant musical world.

Einar Torfi Einarsson's 'Hypermusic Experiment 0.9' reimagines the creative process by introducing a unique mechanism for generating notated music through spectra interaction, aiming to create a dynamic, fluid, decentralized, and participatory musical milieu. This novel system initiates its process with the generation of notated pages, termed partial-scores, filled with an assortment of musical graphics. These partial-scores represent a fusion of the digital and physical realms, embodying a continuous blend of the virtual and the real, and align with the concept of differential ontology. The significance of notation is emphasized as a crucial assembly component, acting as a nexus for interpretation, experimentation, and bridging various planes, thereby transcending the rigidity of traditional notation while preserving the interpretive space vital for musical creation.

The chapter of Kosmas Giannoutakis discusses the impact of decentralized technologies like blockchain on music, particularly in experimental and collaborative contexts. It examines how these technologies can enable new forms of music-making, fostering transindividual and collaborative practices. The author presents case studies on electroacoustic music and live coding, showing how blockchain infrastructures can facilitate decentralized, creative contributions in these fields. The text also explores the broader implications of these technologies for the music industry, suggesting that they can lead to more egalitarian and sustainable practices in music creation and distribution. It delves into the philosophical underpinnings of decentralized musicking, proposing a shift from traditional, hierarchical models of music production and consumption to more collaborative and community-driven approaches. It argues that these emerging practices not only democratize music creation but also challenge and redefine the role of the artist and audience in the musical experience.

Decentralized Music: Exploring Blockchain for Artistic Research is an invitation to embark on a journey at the forefront of conceptual developments integrating music and newest technologies. We invite readers to delve into this exploratory venture, engage with the diverse viewpoints, and embrace the transformative potential of blockchain in the realm of music and artistic research. Recognizing the interdisciplinary nature of this book, we have included a glossary at the end. This serves as a handy reference for readers to quickly grasp technical terms and concepts at the convergence of music, artistic research, and new technologies. The glossary aids in navigating the challenging, yet rewarding, terrain of this interdisciplinary exploration. As we explore the intricate interplay between blockchain technology and music, we uncover a landscape where creativity and innovation takes new innovative dimensions in decentralized spaces. This new paradigm, characterized by the fusion of tangible and intangible elements of musical works, challenges traditional notions of musical creativity. The decentralized nature of blockchain networks, with their transformative potential for artistic practices, heralds a new era of music creation and appreciation. By embracing these technologies, artists and musicians are positioned at the forefront of a digital revolution, redefining musical practices, and expanding the boundaries of artistic expression.

References

de Assis, P. (2023). Music 2.0 and Artistic Research. Beyond a Thousand Years of Western Art Music. *FORUM+*, 30(1/2), 54–63. https://doi.org/10.5117/FORUM2023.1/2.007.ASSI

Buterin, V. (2013). Ethereum: A Next-Generation Smart Contract and Decentralized Application Platform. Retrieved from https://ethereum.org/en/whitepaper/

Brekke, J. K. (2019). *The White Paper*, Satoshi Nakamoto, edited by Jaya Klara Brekke and Ben Vickers, Ignota, 17–63.

Catlow, R., Garrett, M., Jones, N., & Skinner, S. (Eds.). (2017). *Artists re: Thinking the Blockchain*. Liverpool University Press.

Catlow, R., & Rafferty, P. (Eds.). (2022). *Radical Friends: Decentralised Autonomous Organisations and the Arts*. Turnaround (UK)/Motto (DE).

European Commission. (2018). *European Commission Launches the EU Blockchain Observatory and Forum*. Press Release. Retrieved from https://ec.europa.eu/commission/presscorner/detail/en/IP_18_521

Marchand, J. S. (2018). Non-Human Agency. In R. Braidotti & M. Hlavajova (Eds.), *Posthuman Glossary* (pp. 293–295). Bloomsbury Academic.

Mulligan, C. (2019). *Review of the Book Distributed Creativity: How Blockchain Technology Will Transform the Creative Economy*, edited by M. O'Dair. Palgrave Macmillan. https://doi.org/10.1007/978-3-030-00190-2

Mulligan, C. (2022). Can't Knock the Hustle: NTFs and Creativity. In P. de Assis, P. Giudici, & A. Łukawski (Eds.), *Music NFTs: Blockchain for Artistic Research*. Research Catalogue. https://www.researchcatalogue.net/view/1550111/1693670/0/0 [accessed 13/01/2024]

O'Dair, M. (2019). *Distributed Creativity: How Blockchain Technology Will Transform the Creative Economy*. Palgrave Macmillan. https://doi.org/10.1007/978-3-030-00190-2

United Nations (Ed.). (2021). *Harnessing Blockchain for Sustainable Development: Prospects and Challenges*. Bernan Distribution/United Nations. Retrieved from: https://unctad.org/publication/harnessing-blockchain-sustainable-development-prospects-and-challenges

Whitaker, A. (2019). Art and Blockchain: A Primer, History, and Taxonomy of Blockchain Use Cases in the Arts. *Artivate: A Journal of Entrepreneurship in the Arts*, 8(2), 21–46.

Verbeek, A., & Lundqvist, M. (2021). *Artificial Intelligence, Blockchain and the Future of Europe: How Disruptive Technologies Create Opportunities for a Green and Digital Economy*. European Investment Bank. Retrieved from https://www.eib.org/attachments/thematic/artificial_intelligence_blockchain_and_the_future_of_europe_report_en.pdf

Zeilinger, M. (2022, November 7). *Blockchain Vitalism*. Outland. https://outland.art/blockchain-vitalism/

1

From the Work Concept to Hypermusic: Rethinking Musical Objects in-and-for Blockchain Technologies

Paulo de Assis

Orpheus Institute, Ghent, Belgium

Introduction

The practice of music – be it its composition, interpretation, performance, or listening – is deeply intertwined with the medium through which it is generated, transmitted, and preserved. Historically, music rooted in oral traditions relied heavily on human memory, passing down nuances through generations without the need for written notation. The advent of musical scores marked a shift, envisioning music as a textual entity that could be inscribed, interpreted, and realized in various forms. With the introduction of recordings, music assumed the character of fixed time-bound segments, capturing and preserving sonic events as permanent artifacts. The digital era further transformed music into retrievable data, subject to computational analysis and rendering, managed by specialists in digital humanities. In this evolving landscape, blockchain technologies have the potential to offer yet a new profound redefinition of music, portraying it as a constellation of infinite particles. This new medium facilitates not only human interaction but also algorithmic and computational participation, allowing for endless recombinations and creations in the musical landscape. This evolution of mediums reflects an ongoing redefinition of what music is and can be, with blockchain opening new horizons for understanding and creating music.

Currently, we are living a transformational era of information abundance, in which the boundaries between art, science and technology are increasingly blurring. The ongoing technological advancements – particularly in the digital realms of artificial intelligence and blockchain technologies – are already massively impacting multiple facets of human life, including our relationship with art, music, and artistic phenomena at large. For music, the current transformations have major implications for the understanding of musical works: what they are, how they are created, transmitted, disseminated, and

DOI: 10.1201/9781003458227-2

performed. Conventional views on musical works based on the historical notion of the 'work concept' do not fully capture the diversity, richness, and infinite proliferation of materials related to any musical entity composed, performed, or listened to in the present time.

This chapter is a first attempt to provide a conceptual reference to music practices in and for the blockchain. It is a medium-specific reconsideration of what musical works can be in a digital, decentralized musical age. Assuming an exploratory perspective, the chapter challenges conventional views of musical entities, moving beyond the 'work concept' to propose the notions of 'assemblage' and 'hypermusic' as more adequate conceptual termini to embrace the diversity and richness of materials related to any given musical entity. Musical works appear then as dynamic and ever-changing constellations of different component parts, existing within a vast network of relationships of origins, contexts, and uses, critically including the different milieus of their generation, performance, and reception. In a certain sense, the chapter presents a personal narrative marked by references to musical and art works that have contributed to my personal rethinking of musical practices. Thus, the many discussed examples have no pretension to universality, they simply reflect my own journey from a musician trained in the classical tradition of Western art music (operating under the notion of the strong work concept), to an experimental thinker and performer working with processes of deconstruction and reassembling of sonic particles and artifacts.

The first part of the chapter critically examines the notion of 'work', acknowledging its historical significance and current limitations. I argue for a reconceptualization of the musical work as an 'assemblage', a term that accommodates conceptual and material fluidity, thus reflecting the perpetually evolving nature of music itself.

The second part explores the notion of 'hypermusic', which is presented as a complex, emergent phenomenon, as a multi-sourced and multi-modal entity that eludes complete apprehension. Drawing upon a wide range of theoretical frameworks and music examples, this section discusses the horizon of possibilities offered by the concept of hypermusic, including selected avant-garde compositions of the late 20th century and more contemporary projects that challenge the boundaries of genre, authorship, and medium. Engaging with the historical lineage and potential future trajectories of hypermusic, this section ponders the implications of such musical objects for new modes of musical expression. The chosen case studies defy conventional musical definitions, prompting us to consider other modes of composition, study, and performance.

The third and final part turns to the implications of blockchain technology for music, engaging with its revolutionary potential to navigate and organize the infinite particles that constitute musical works. The section elucidates how this technology can provide a framework for managing the complexity and volume of data associated with musical works. Case studies from the visual arts, such as the Particle Collection and LaCollection demonstrate blockchain's application in the art world, underscoring its potential to rethink artworks from the very ground, to democratize access and distribution of works, but also to enable new modes of generating art in the first place.

In short, this chapter is an invitation to rethink musical objects and processes, especially in view of the proposed notions of musical-work-as assemblage, hypermusic, pulverization of artworks, and their inscription in and with blockchain technologies. As we face the changing landscape of musical works, this chapter is not only intended as a reflection of our current intersection of music and technology but also as an invitation to rethink music and creative musical practices. It invites musicians, composers, technologists, and theorists to come together in the creation of a new, fluid paradigm for musical artistry. This transdisciplinary perspective aligns with broader developments in contemporary art and technology, where the role of the creator is seen as part of a larger, more collaborative, and interconnected process. By integrating blockchain technology into this discourse, I aim to outline a path for future innovation in the creation and dissemination of music, recognizing the challenges and opportunities that lie ahead as we navigate these uncharted territories.

From Music to Hypermusic via Assemblages and Hyperobjects

As I have argued in my book *Logic of Experimentation* (de Assis 2018a), due to the increasing amount of available data, musical works can be described as made of actual, virtual, and intensive component parts. Both the virtual and the actual parts are real, manifesting themselves through intensive processes of energy flows and transfers (Sauvagnargues 2003, 2013, 2016). In this view, musical works exist as material traces in the world and as immaterial forces in the mind of musicians and listeners. Both material traces and immaterial forces live on a virtual network of not-currently-activated nodes and connectors until they are actualized in a time- and site-specific event, in which they emerge in a plane of composition through intensive processes of energetic transduction. These intensive processes happen at different stages, scales, and levels, and they are never-ending given the fundamental temporal nature of musical works, which always manifest themselves in delimitated blocks of time. There are intensive processes at work when a composer composes a piece, giving consistency to a complex imbrication of material and semiotic formations, but also when a performer and a listener retrieve these formations, which must be spelled out one-by-one in their radical molecularity. Pitches, rhythms, meters, and timbres exist prior to any compositional gesture; they exist as virtual spaces of unlimited combinatorial possibilities in a virtual plane of immanence that can be (more or less) pre-structured according to specific zones of higher probability to become actualized. Such special zones can be labeled as *singularities* as they function as attractors in mathematical functions. It is from this 'unformed' and 'molecular' matter that composers activate specific sonic and semiotic connectors giving shape to 'formed' and 'molar' component parts that remain changeable throughout time and through different performative and reception strategies.

Taken together, in all their modes of appearance and emergence in the world, the actual and virtual component parts of musical works interweave complex networks of relations and dependencies, continuously referring to their virtual mode of existence, which they share with other musical works and with other arrangements of other forms of expression. In this sense, one could argue that it is the presence of the virtual in the actual that makes us feel the sublime, the non-apprehensible in the apprehensible.

From the Work Concept to Assemblage Theory

This view of musical works as complex arrangements of actual, virtual, and intensive component parts allows for a renewed understanding of some fundamental music ontological commitments, offering ground for a redefinition of musical works: first as ~~works~~, next as 'assemblages', and eventually as 'hypermusical' entities made of innumerable constitutive parts, which can be audible or not. In this sense, the basic constitutive parts of musical works, more than 'molecular', could be seen as 'atomic' or even as musical 'particles'. Such pulverization of musical entities has consequences for the modes of interaction with them. The first move (from 'works' to '~~works~~') implies a critique and reconsideration of the notion of 'work' as it is understood in the so-called classical paradigm (Davies, 2011, 2018), which is in turn grounded upon the notion of the 'work concept' (Lydia Goehr, 1992). With '~~work~~', I mean the critical and well-considered deconstruction of the term 'work', which remains present even when its foundations are being dismantled. The use of Derrida's 'barrée' ('crossed out') signifies that while 'the work' is still there to be read and understood in its conventional sense, it's also simultaneously negated or put under erasure. This indicates the limitations and insufficiencies of the term 'work', while also acknowledging that it is both indispensable but also problematic in its traditional meaning.

Next, once the classical image of work starts being deconstructed, one can think of musical ~~works~~ as complex arrangements and conglomerates of things and intensities, containing innumerable and potentially never-ending additional component parts, which are continuously rearranged and reassembled in their specific modes of appearance throughout history. This is what I have called 'musical ~~work~~ as assemblage' (de Assis 2018a, 2018b, 2019), taking the notion of 'assemblage' in its philosophical context and definition, which is clearly indebted to the philosophies of Gilles Deleuze, Felix Guattari, Manuel DeLanda, and Anne Sauvagnargues. An important feature of the notion of 'musical work as assemblage' is that, more than refuting conventional music ontologies, it has the capacity to include them as particular cases, as historically situated subsets, which take only a reduced number of parameters into consideration. The appropriation and further development of the notion of 'assemblage' for music allows not only the emergence of new modes of conceiving musical entities, but also the creative generation of unprecedented explorations thereof.

The notion of assemblage, with its focus on the fluidity of matter, materials, signs, and functions, re-situates music invention and research within a framework made of aesthetico-epistemic components, forces, intensities, and signs that create a whole series of superposed networks of historical, cultural, material, symbolic, and psychological dimensions. Under this light, musical works cease to be conceived as straightforward sets of instructions or as ontologically clearly defined structures: they become containers of forces and intensities, dynamic systems characterized by meta-stability and transductive powers, affording unpredictable future reconfigurations. Moving beyond ontological queries that deal with questions of being and identity, and insisting on an approach to musical entities that privileges processes of continuous change and transformation, the 'image-of-work as assemblage' (de Assis 2018b) enables investigations of musical works not so much from a conventional ontological perspective, but rather in terms of *ontogenesis* (Simondon 2013), and of productive operations – both with historically inherited materials and, crucially, with new materials and compositions.

Ontogenesis and Transduction

Ontogenesis, also known as ontogeny, is a concept first developed within biology referring to the biological development of an organism from its conception to its maturity. It encompasses changes in an organism's size, shape, structure, and physiological processes over time. This process is usually divided into different stages such as the embryonic stage, the larval stage, the juvenile stage, and the adult stage. In addition to physical changes, ontogenesis includes functional transformations. Physical changes relate to the changes in an organism's physical structure, while functional changes refer to the changes in an organism's capabilities of interaction with its surroundings. Moreover, ontogenesis also includes the development of an organism's behavior: for example, the development of social behavior in animals, or the development of language in humans, is part of ontogenesis.

In the context of the philosophy of Gilbert Simondon (2013 [1958]), ontogenesis refers to the process of individualization, or becoming, of a being, which Simondon calls 'individuation'. Simondon's concept of ontogenesis is not limited to biological entities but extends to all entities, including technological objects and social systems. For Simondon, ontogenesis is the process through which an entity comes into existence and continues to develop and transform throughout its existence. This process involves a continuous interplay between the entity and its environment, and it is characterized by a series of meta-stable states, or phases of relative stability and instability. Simondon argues that an entity's existence cannot be fully understood by analyzing its current state alone. Instead, one must consider the entire process of its ontogenesis, including its past states and potential future states. This perspective challenges traditional metaphysical views (namely the hylomorphic model) that tend to view entities as fixed and static. Crucially, Simondon's concept of ontogenesis emphasizes the importance of the pre-individual, or the undifferentiated state that precedes individuation. According to Simondon, the pre-individual is not a mere absence of differentiation, but a state of potentiality that contains the seeds of future development (see Stiegler 2012; Scott 2014). The unfolding and topological development of an entity happens through a succession of events which occur by means of transduction of energy and information. Overall, Simondon's concept of ontogenesis offers a dynamic and process-oriented view of existence that highlights the importance of becoming, transformation, and not-yet-actualized virtual possibilities. Central to this understanding is the immanent process of transductive flows of energy, which Simondon extensively analysis under the notion of 'transduction'.

In the realm of music, the idea of transduction (see de Assis 2016, de Assis 2017, de Assis 2018a, 2018b) can be closely tied to the concept of epistemic complexity. Musical works, being complex semiotic artifacts, comprise a large number of interacting parts that confer systemic complexity. Yet, they are also imbued with a richness of interconnected knowledge, encompassing the phases of their creation, transmission, preservation, and performance. This epistemic complexity encompasses a broad spectrum, from the creation of new compositions to the reinterpretation and preservation of existing ones, thereby positioning musical works as dynamic entities that continually evolve and generate new knowledge. This perspective frames musical works as open-ended, inviting ongoing exploration and reinterpretation, and leading to the emergence of novel and unexpected elements within the artistic process.

Additionally, transduction in music involves recognizing the inherent incompleteness and open-endedness of musical works. By acknowledging the multitude of elements that constitute a musical piece's epistemic complexity, performers and researchers have the power to engage with these works not as fixed entities but as starting points for creative explorations.

This approach allows for the emergence of new assemblages from the existing elements, driven by a process of becoming rather than being. It involves the creation of room for the unthought and the unexpected, transforming the conventional understanding of musical works from fixed entities into dynamic, evolving constructs. This perspective opens possibilities for reconfiguring musical works in innovative ways, emphasizing the role of experimentation and the active production of new arrangements as central to the artistic activity. This process is not merely a theoretical endeavor but a constructive one, where various steps are taken to examine and reconfigure the constitutive elements of an object. These steps include scrutinizing the epistemic complexity, identifying, and isolating its components, exploring their 'genetical' origins, and problematizing them to project future possibilities.

From Hyperobjects to Hypermusic

This transformative and individuation-focused view of 'musical-works-as-assemblages' activated by transductive processes can be further developed when linked to Timothy Morton's eco-philosophical concept of hyperobjects. This brought me to the definition of the concept of 'hypermusic' (de Assis 2023). Timothy Morton presented the concept of hyperobjects for the first time in his book *The Ecological Thought* (Morton 2010), where it refers to things that are massively distributed in time and space relative to humans. These are things whose life span is much longer than that of humans. Morton's famous example in this respect is global warming. 'Global warming' is something much bigger than any human mode of apprehension. It is 'generated' by an infinite number of smaller objects and complex processes as part of it. 'Global warming' is not something graspable. Yet it is something fully (and dramatically) perceptible. Similarly, music understood as a hyperobject is also made of infinite constitutive parts and processes, which remain virtual for most of the time, but that can be perceived by a multitude of concatenated phenomena.

One could claim that hyperobjects are special cases of assemblages, keeping in mind that an assemblage (in its philosophical sense) does not refer to 'a' collection, superposition, or arrangement of other things – it is a multiplicity of both things and events brought together in (short or long) specific temporalities. Assemblages include human and non-human component parts, and have emergent properties, making them irreducible both to their material constitutive parts and to their abstract modes of functioning. Very much like hyperobjects. Additionally, one can only see parts of an assemblage or of a hyperobject at any one moment. Like the emergent properties of an assemblage, hyperobjects are objects that 'seem to contain more than themselves' (78), and they continuously reveal further objects pertaining to them: 'when you approach an object, more and more objects emerge' (54).

According to Morton, hyperobjects have five common properties. Hyperobjects are *viscous*, 'which means that they "stick" to beings that are involved with them' (67). They are *nonlocal* in the sense that any 'local manifestation' of a hyperobject is not directly 'the' hyperobject. They reveal or manifest different temporalities (*temporal undulation*), that is to say that they are extended 'into' the future 'from' the past, revealing that more than existing 'on time', they emit spacetime, accelerating or slowing down events around them. They can only be apprehended partially, requiring different phases to be perceived (*phasing*). Finally, they exhibit their effects *interobjectively*, 'that is, they can be detected in a space that consists of interrelationships between aesthetic properties of objects' (2).

These five properties – *viscosity, nonlocality, temporal undulation, phasing,* and *interobjectivity* – can be appropriated for musical ~~works~~, especially under the light of the notion of the musical-work-as-assemblage. Morton himself centrally includes art and aesthetics in his writings, and he concretely refers to composers such as John Cage, Keith Rowe, and Francisco López. After discussing the historically situated moments of Romanticism, Realism, Impressionism, and Expressionism (107), Morton concludes that we are now in a totally different situation, especially because 'we know more than we can embody, and we can't put the [romantic] genie back in the bottle' (163). This is a crucial point: the hyper-text, hyper-archives, hyper-information, hyper-technology, hyper-communication, and hyper-history of our current age are symptomatic expressions of an infinite knowledge that we can no longer embody – a new form of knowledge that exists at the atomic level of small, individual information particles. A music performer knows much more about any given piece than what can possibly be rendered in one performance. A composer deals and develops much more materials than those that will enter any form of 'final' compositional output. And a musicologist works with infinitely more information than what ends up as a written essay. To make music, be it as performer or composer, is to deal with entities that are bigger than our capacity of finite and delimited time-bound modes of expression. Such entities require series of events, taking place at different times in different spaces, and using different media. This is the realm of hypermusic.

Hypermusic: Sonic Particles and Intensive Processes

In very broad terms, hypermusic concerns the network of complex parts and processes that all together constitute what we usually call 'musical works'. What is specific to the concept, and why it can be useful, is its critical attention and practice-oriented consideration of all the possible 'particles' belonging to any such network of parts and relations. The concept does not exclude some 'works', nor does it favor other 'works'. It doesn't claim that intensive processes are not at play if composers or performers do not specifically articulate them. Such processes can be cultural processes that even composers of works are not completely conscious about. To say that musical works have always been made of innumerable components, not only the notes on a score, would be trivial. What the concept of hypermusic allows is a more cohesive and purposeful conceptual framework to think about music in a more dynamic way, and with a view to future possibilities of artistic modes of creative deconstruction – rather than seeing works as stable singular objects with clearly defined properties and characteristics. Broadly speaking, one could argue that all music has inherently always been hypermusic. But the specific meaning I am giving to this term is both much more specific and much more wide opening in terms of future creative practices.

In this section, I will briefly describe three examples from the second half of the twentieth century that can be seen as possible examples of what my definition of hypermusic entails. What is special about these 'works' is not so much the fact that they are made of a great number of musical and cultural references, but the fact that these references are acknowledged, even if some of them remain completely hidden to the listener. These wide-ranging references are intentional and have a purpose (often extra musical). Even their occultation has a meaning and a sense. Present or not, audible or not, these materials function as particles, which can be further decomposed in even smaller *atomic* particles that can be activated or not in performance or in musicological discussions.

From a technical point of view, I have built the concept of hypermusic in the aftermath of my research on 'experimental performance practices' (2013–2018), thus, originally, in relation to experimental performance practices of Western notated art music. The concept then evolved, and it has been grounded upon two central notions: my own 'musical-works-as-assemblages' (de Assis 2018a) and Timothy Morton's 'hyperobjects' (2010). Additionally, other relevant concepts and theories that strongly impacted the concept's design have been those of 'agencement' (Deleuze 1975; Deleuze and Guattari 1977, 1987), and several dynamic concepts from Manuel DeLanda's Assemblage Theory (DeLanda 2006, 2016).

It is fair to mention that the term 'hypermusic' has been loosely used before, more as a *mot d'ordre* than as a proper conceptual construction. As an underdefined term, it has been used in the title of two musical projects: in Hector Parra's chamber opera *Hypermusic Prologue* (2008–9), and in the collective orchestral project *HyperMusic and the Sighting of Sound* (2000), directed by Jonathan Impett and Bert Bongers. In what follows, I succinctly present some examples of hypermusic *avant la lettre* from the late 20th century, and discuss some more recent examples, as well as possible future uses of the term.

Music beyond Music: Zimmermann, Nono, Lachenmann, Cage

One work that could be considered as a forerunner of most of the characteristics of 'hypermusic' in my definition of the term, is Bernd Alois Zimmermann's *requiem für einen jungen dichter* (1967/1969), a musical construction that is often described as 'extended composition' for obvious lack of a better word. It features an enormous variety of originally composed and quoted music, as well as non-musical material. The work, labeled by the composer as a 'lingual', is constructed upon a highly elaborated 'metatext' that juxtaposes the Latin Mass for the Dead with literary, philosophical, religious, and political texts. In addition to the texts spoken and sung, the piece makes use of taped recordings in the style of a radio drama, including the voices of Ludwig Wittgenstein, Pope John XXIII, James Joyce, Alexander Dubček, Hitler, Chamberlain, Georgios Papandreou, Ezra Pound, Kurt Schwitters, Albert Camus and Sándor Weöres, as well as various reports from newspapers. Musical quotations range from fragments of Wagner's *Tristan und Isolde* (1859), Milhaud's *La création du monde* (1923), Messiaen's *L'ascension* (1933) to the Beatles' *Hey Jude* (1968). In the section 'Dona nobis pacem', excerpts from Beethoven's Ninth Symphony are dramatically contrasted with texts by Joachim von Ribbentrop, Stalin, Goebbels, Churchill and Konrad Bayer. Rather than trying to describe the requiem as a cantata, an oratorio, or an audio play, I propose to focus on its granularity and molecularity of materials, labeling it as hypermusic. This indicates the multiple dimensions of its constitutive parts and the hyper-complexity of its interweaving connectors. Not everything in this requiem is comprehensible. The superposition of different semantic and semiotic layers creates a sonic situation with two levels, one direct, the other indirect. In the direct level, there are some words and sentences that are understandable, such as the profoundly disturbing text 'der sechste sinn' ('Worauf warten?') by Konrad Bayer, which is elaborated in a multiple-channels section in the 'Ricercar' (Requiem I, 29:03–33:13), or the second text by Bayer ('Wie jeder weiss...'), that concludes the work with a radically dramatic and hopeless view on the construction of 'knowledge', especially in politics, but also in science and academia. The indirect level is presented and achieved through the complex montage of fragments of texts and music, a montage that remains vastly under-articulated and that is not given to the listener. To what an extent this network of relations and links should be communicated to the audience is a matter of debate, something that can be creatively explored in different performances of the piece. Additionally, from a spatial point of view, the requiem also poses major challenges, requiring a concert hall with the capacity to position the orchestra, the three choirs, the jazz combo ensemble, the soloists, and speakers, as well as the loudspeakers, all around the audience. While this is not something 'new' today (and it wasn't new already at the time of the composition), this is an aspect that contributes to this piece's sense of complexity and of being 'music *beyond* music'. What matters here for my argument is the extreme pulverization of materials, which helps us visualiing the idea of 'particles' in relation to a musical work.

Another piece based on a complex arrangement of major cultural texts, and with an important architectural component is Luigi Nono's *Prometeo, tragedia dell'ascolto* (1981–1984) for singers, speakers, chorus, solo strings, solo winds, glasses, orchestral groups, and live electronics. In this case, the premiere of the work was even done in a specially constructed wooden structure (designed by the architect Renzo Piano) that hosted the musicians, the sound technicians, and the audience. Whereas Zimmermann's *requiem* ends with a devastating and hopeless view on the future, Nono's *tragedia* concludes with suggesting the emergence of a new utopia from the ruins of the past. In both cases, there is a profound reflection on historical events, philosophical and ideological positions, as well as composite aesthetic modes of expression, merging instrumental and electronically modified sounds, using the voice both for singing and speaking. Moreover, both pieces 'create' new musical forms: Zimmermann makes a requiem that is a 'lingual', Nono an opera that is a 'tragedy of listening'; thus, both refuse conventional genre and formal schemes, favoring the definition of unclassifiable aesthetic formats. Nono, in collaboration with philosopher Massimo Cacciari, borrows texts from Hesiod to Walter Benjamin, from Aeschylus, Hesychius, and Sophocles to Hölderlin and Cacciari himself. Musical quotations – always hidden and not recognizable for the listener – range from Giuseppe Verdi to Arnold Schoenberg, from Robert Schumann to Gustav Mahler. They are present not for the sake of music alone, but 'in terms of their contribution to an awareness of history that points to the future'. In terms of performance, it is important to mention the fact that every single performance requires site-specific musical decisions, making of it an exclusive and unique event that cannot be exactly replicated anywhere else. This is mainly due to technical requirements and to very specific instrumental techniques that have to be learned and experimented over long stretches of time. Thus, the kaleidoscopic atomization of materials is accompanied by a unique site-specificity of the performance.

Yet another example could be Helmut Lachenmann's *Das Mädchen mit den Schwefelhölzern* (1990–1996), a work that problematizes the very notion of 'opera' by defining a musical object that is not officially labeled as such, but as 'music with images'. The text materials are fragmented and pulverized in different levels. There is the tale *The Little Match Girl* by Hans Christian Andersen, which serves as unspoken (and unsung) dramaturgical foundation of the whole musical composition. There is a text by Leonard Da Vinci from the *Codex Arundel*, some few words form Nietzsche's *Zarathustra* (Mitternacht), and a letter written from the prison in 1975 by Gudrun Ensslin, a convicted member of the terrorist group Baader-Meinhof who had set a department store on fire in 1968 in Frankfurt (which provides a direct link to the matches in Andersen's story). The music includes some very short musical quotations from Igor Stravinsky (*The Rite of Spring*), Ludwig van Beethoven (*Coriolan Overture*), Arnold Schoenberg (*Variations for Orchestra*), Pierre Boulez (*pli selon pli*), Gustav Mahler (Sixth Symphony), and Alban Berg (one chord from *Wozzeck*), all of which appear in an unrecognizable, estranged way. Additionally, on a subterranean level, there are many other texts, some of which are very long, which are almost never heard, and never semantically presented. These texts are recorded in CDs that are 'played' by musicians just like any other instrument. The CD performers have a simple potentiometer that opens and closes the output of the CD track and that regulates its volume level, following a fully notated score. Thus, all those texts function like sonic material and are audible only at the level of their acoustic (not semantic) reality. In short, Lachenmann's The Little Match Girl provides yet another compelling example of hypermusic *avant la lettre*, with its manifold and heterogeneous superpositions of materials, with its subterranean textual dimension, its musical complexity, with the inclusion of extra-European instruments (Shô, a Japanese mouth organ, and Dobachi, a Japanese bowl gong) that are used in a way that estranges them from their traditional practices, and with hyperconnections to different times and geographies (the times of Leonard, Nineteenth Century Europe, post–World War II Germany, and the mental spaces of South Italy, Scandinavia, and Japan).

One could further think of other pieces, like John Cage and Lejarren Hiller's *HPSCHD* (1967–69) for seven amplified harpsichords, 52 tape machines, 6.400 slides and 40 films, that shows John Cage's interest in bringing together a wide range of different elements for audience members to experience simultaneously, and in which to immerse themselves. All these pieces could be the object of detailed studies in relation to my notion of hypermusic. For the purposes of the present essay, they simply serve as a means to convey my understanding of the concept of hypermusic and how it can be traced back to some musical works from the past.

Ongoing and Future Practices

As for the generation of totally new musical entities, the question is how to activate the concept of hypermusic to generate artworks that move beyond the notion of 'work', investigating new definitions of what composition means today, and eventually developing new musical practices. In relation to current practices of artistic research that move art practice towards research and research towards artistic outputs, the question is how to invent new sonic agencies that are sustained by artistic modes of investigation? How to encapsulate the infinite constitutive particles of original sonic experiences? How to link acoustic renderings with their underlying notational sources, textual connections, and related scholarly investigations? These are some of the questions at the origin of this book and of my personal investigations on future modes of musical creativity. Right now, these questions are still open-ended, even if there are some ongoing investigations that might indicate future paths for a music conceived as hypermusic. I will briefly address three: polyworks (based on 'superpositions' of works), non-human sonic expressivity (including AI-generated music), and a new kind of 'album-film-documentary' from the realm of pop music.

Superpositions

'Superpositions' and 'polyworks' refer to musical objects ('works') that are made of several other musical 'works', which can be rendered either together (superposed) or independently from each other. This is a fertile field for complex compositional practices, and there are numerous composers working in this direction, such as Chaya Czernowin, Julio Estrada, Vinko Globokar, Georg Friedrich Haas, Adriana Hölszky, and Claus-Steffen Mahnkopf, who are following the footsteps of Klaus Huber's seminal work on polyworks. A particularly suggestive example is precisely Klaus Huber's *Schattenblätter* ('Shadow Leaves') for bass clarinet, piano, and cello (1975), which can be performed both as a trio and, 'like a tree losing its leaves', in any other combination of the single parts: clarinet and piano, cello and piano, clarinet and cello, even solo piano, in which case the title changes to *Blätterlos* ('Without Leaves'). Another interesting example is his piece *Plainte – Die umgepflügte Zeit. In memoriam Luigi Nono* (1990), which can be performed in its full score or in four other modes of appearance, without the solo voices, without the viola d'amore (which seems central in the full score), and even with the option of replacing some instruments by others. Such constructions resonate with Morton's notion of *phasing* – the fact that hyperobjects can only be apprehended partially. Polyworks, even if played 'together', generate a perceptual overflow that makes them difficult to grasp in their 'integrity' (what would that be?).

A sophisticated example of these principles can be found in Einar Torfi Einarsson's *Desiring-Machine* (2012), a piece for 24 musicians and two conductors that the composer labeled as a 'multipiece' (Einarsson 2012, 2015). A composer and artist researcher, Einarsson created a work that can be performed as 'one piece' played by all 24 instrumentalists, or in infinite 'decompositions' of its constitutive parts, eliminating instruments in different configurations, enabling the performance of up to 2.704.156 'different' pieces. Each and every one of these pieces retains some fundamental musical and aesthetic properties which are common to all of them, like the structure of DNA in a living organism. For further details on this piece, I suggest reading Einarsson's chapter in this book (Chapter 9).

Non-Human Expressivity

Another topic poised to gain significant attention in the coming decades is the creative work with sounds produced by non-human sources. This will promote a shift from subject-oriented, text-based inscriptions to object-oriented, sonic-based inscriptions, with a particular focus on the sounds in and around us. While the paradigm of absolute music relied primarily on musical works that resulted from human invention, broadening our auditory focus reveals immense alternative sonic worlds. Sonic outputs produced by non-human entities can be investigated as musical objects in their own right. The notion of 'expressivity' has for too long been considered as emanating only from humans or human activity, but realist and new-materialist accounts insist on the expressivity of matter (DeLanda 2002, 2006, 2016) and things (Bennett 2010), shifting the focus from the human experience of things to the things themselves. After decades of field and experimental sound recordings of the earth's natural sonorities, recent developments make it plausible to think of musical hyperobjects constructed solely from non-human engendered sonic objects. Timothy Morton references such works, specifically those by sound artist Francisco López, whose La Selva (1998) is an impressive example that 'evokes the hyperobject in an object-oriented way… The result [of which] is far from an ambient rendering or simulation of the real' [Morton 2013, 184]. The music piece 'La Selva' on López's CD does not represent 'La Selva,' the natural reserve in Costa Rica, even though it 'contains elements that can be understood as representational, but the essence of the creation of this sound work … is rooted in a "sound matter" conception, as opposed to any documentative approach' (López 1998). In this sense, an artistic research investigation on sounds produced by non-human sources should not aim at representing sounds of nature per se. It should rather progress beyond subject-oriented inventions to object-oriented, sonic-based explorations, especially focusing on the non-human expressivity of nature, technology, and all the sounds (natural and artificial) that surround us.

Yet another form of non-human sonic production clearly relates to AI-generated musical entities. This is a rapidly growing field that has expanded exponentially since the early 2010s and that is currently experiencing a sort of explosion, not only because of, but related to the new possibilities offered by Large Language Models. Investigating and further developing AI-based tools, composer and programmer Adam Łukawski is expanding algorithmically and AI-generated music to the blockchain, transforming the moment of 'transaction' into a creative transformative process, imbued with aesthetic, epistemic, and sensorial changes. Łukawski's innovative concept of 'performative transactions' facilitates the generation of musical entities that result from multiple inputs, including other human agents (composers), but also non-human agents involved in the specific work's smart contract (for more details and insights see Łukawski 2022, and Łukawski's chapter in this book).

Hyper-Distributed Creativity

A striking example of hyper-distributed creativity that could also be labeled as pertaining to the notion of hypermusic is the album-film-documentary *Lemonade* (2016) by American pop musician Beyoncé Knowles-Carter. *Lemonade* is a 56-minute narrative movie mixing music, documentary, and experimental elements, featuring elements from American Southern, Voodoo, and Afrofuturist utopian imagery. One of the unique aspects of this album was its focus on distributed creativity: Beyoncé worked with a range of artists, writers, and producers to create the album. According to Paul Tingen (2016) *Lemonade*'s creative process involved around 20 producers and 40 co-writers. Some of the co-writers were major artists who also feature in the songs, like Jack White, The Weeknd, James Blake, Kendrick Lamar, and Marcus Miller. Likewise, some of the producers are also well-known names, like Diplo, Mike Dean, Hit Boy, and Just Blaze. But the collaborations extended far beyond these names, including many lesser-known musicians, poets, visual artists, and other creatives.

In addition to the music, the album includes many spoken monologues, which are poems or prose written by Somali poet Warsan Shire, a compelling voice on black womanhood and the African diaspora, two central elements of the whole project. The album was recorded between June 2014 and July 2015, across 11 studios in the United States. The result was a work that is diverse and experimental: while it is clearly rooted within a pop and R&B framework, it integrates a variety of genres and styles including reggae, blues, rock, hip hop, soul, funk, Americana, country, gospel, electronic, and trap. Moreover, *Lemonade* blurs musical eras and cultural references, especially about the continuum of R&B, rock, soul, hip-hop, pop and blues. According to pop music critic Jonathan Mendolicchio (2019),

> Beyoncé and her team reference the musical memories of all those periods via sampling and production, with the inclusion of a string quartet, a brass band, stomping blues-rock, ultraslow Avant-R&B, preaching, a prison song (collected by John and Alan Lomax), and the sound of the 1960s fuzz tone guitar psychedelia (sampling the Puerto Rican band Kaleidoscope).

Distributed creativity was also evident in the way that the album was released. Rather than simply releasing the album as a traditional music release, Beyoncé also launched a film of the same name that accompanied the album. The film, in eleven chapters, adds to the complexity of authorship and collaborative creation: while this difficult to categorize visual-sonic fairy-tale is a personal statement, it was co-directed by seven film directors, including Beyoncé Knowles-Carter herself. Additionally, the film was accompanied by a visual album, allowing the audience to engage with the music and visuals together. Overall, *Lemonade* was a strong demonstration of the power of distributed creativity, with Beyoncé bringing together a diverse group of people to create a unique and innovative album. Beyoncé was able to bring a great number of people together without making them feel dis-authored or short-changed. This 'hyper-collaborative' process, as it was labeled by the music critic David Peisner in the magazine Rolling Stone (2016), is probably 'the greatest accomplishment' of this album.

Musical Particles and Blockchain: Uncharted Territories

The concept of hypermusic presented so far in this text has the potential to articulate an important challenge regarding the role and function of musical creativity in contemporary society. In addition to its innumerable musical consequences and opportunities, the concept of hypermusic enables the relation and connection of music to other areas of contemporary thought and knowledge production. From an epistemological point of view, it fosters multiple creative methods and methodologies, it affords links to critical thought and contemporary philosophy, and it resituates musical thought within practice-based epistemologies. Through these rich and intricate networks of cross-references and cross-pollinations, hypermusic generates sonic entities that have the power to engender transdisciplinary webbings. More than asking what an artwork is or was, or how it has been assembled in the past, such webbings indicate a constructivist approach that interrogates how things are constantly dis- and re-assembled.

This research gesture positions musical practices in their relation to other practices and systems of knowledge production. The central aspect of the concept – and the focus of this section – is that it is fundamentally rooted in a vision of musical works as made of infinite constitutive *particles*. This has been the critical link that brought me, personally, to the study and investigation of blockchain technologies. For music practitioners and musicologists alike, the vast array of musical data and particles associated with any musical object in today's information-saturated era can be overwhelming. While catalogues, databases, critical editions, and audiovisual documentation of performances and recordings are vital for establishing a foundational corpus of digital materials, we face a pressing issue: how do we track the origin, transmission, dissemination, and creative reuses of these materials? How do we implement a system that ensures not only fair financial distribution of payments and royalties but also guarantees global, equitable, and democratic access to musical innovations? With the increased digitization of recordings, manuscripts, sketches, and even practitioners' scribbles – often under restrictive proprietary and institutional conditions – the challenge is to democratize access to this artistic wealth of data while securing provenance and fairness in usage and reuse. These questions have guided my journey into blockchain, with its potential to decentralize the ownership and transmission of artworks.

Digression: Two Case Studies from the Visual Arts

While studying the nature and potential of blockchain for music, I came across many artistic uses of these technologies, especially in the broad field of visual arts. Despite disciplinary differences and modes of production and dissemination, some use cases are illuminating for a better understanding of how blockchain can be used in other art forms, including music. Understanding hypermusic as music made of tangible, discrete particles activated by dynamic structuring forces, blockchain emerges as a platform that can store these particles individually and process them according to specific rules and variables. Two examples from the visual arts will elucidate the benefits of transforming art objects into their constituent particles.

Particle Collection – Banksy's Love Is in the Air *(2005/2022)*

The Particle Foundation, which owns the Particle Collection, is a company with deep roots in the worlds of art and technology that combines traditional art objects (existing as real, physical objects exhibited in a physical space) and Web3-based digital versions of those objects, which are exposed and transacted online, through blockchain technologies, as non-fungible tokens. Every digital version of a specific art object is divided into a variable number of small areas of the digital image. These small areas are called 'particles' and the process of making them, 'particalization'. Thus, 'particles' means the serialized, non-fungible tokens of the so called 'digital-reference'. For most artworks, there exist 10.000 Particles and proof of ownership of all such particles is recorded on the relevant blockchain. An important novelty of this system is that the division of very expensive original artworks into particles allows multiple individuals to become co-owners of the artwork. Once particalized, any artwork is loaned to the Particle Foundation, a nonprofit organization dedicated to preserving and displaying the collection globally. As a safeguard for possible future exchanges, once an artwork is acquired by the Particle Foundation it cannot be ever sold again.

Concretely, the process unfolds in six steps: (1) the Particle Foundation buys an artwork (painting, for example); (2) a digital version is made; (3) the artwork is particalized; (4) a public offer and sell is made (online, blockchain wallet); (5) every particle is minted (NFTs); (6) all and any NFTs holder becomes a co-owner of the artwork, specifically the co-owner of a fraction ('particle') of the digital version of the artwork. The first addition to the Particle Collection, and the first art piece 'fractionalized' by the project was Banksy's *Love Is in the Air* (2003). The purchase of the physical artwork was made for $12.9 million at auction at Sotheby's in May 2022. The previous owner was the Lazarides Gallery, in London. Next, the piece was divided into 10.000 particles that have been putted for sell as NFTs on the Avalanche Network blockchain. The primary sale of 'Particle NFTs' started on the week 10–14 January 2022, and the physical work was exposed for first time to the collectors at Art Basel Miami, in December 2022. The unique particalization process involved the division of the painting into a 100×100 grid, resulting in 10,000 unique particles that have been minted as NFTs. Each Particle is unique and allows the holder to enjoy a personal (and quite novel) ownership experience with the artwork.

Independently of aesthetic considerations and judgment values, it is worth considering the political dimension of this art object – an aspect that seems to indicate Particle Foundation's willingness to stress the positive, both critical and creative opportunities of blockchain technologies over blockchain's sometimes more obscure purely financial usages.

In *Love is in the Air*, Banksy's artistic expression finds a pinnacle of nuanced rebellion. The piece features a militant figure, ostensibly ready to hurl a Molotov cocktail, yet intriguingly holding a bouquet. This juxtaposition embodies a fervent yet optimistic call for peace amid strife. Initially manifesting as a sizable graffiti stencil in Jerusalem, its proximity to the West Bank Barrier speaks volumes, critiquing the absurdity of war and the complexities of authority and power dynamics. The floral hues subtly blend the colors of the Israeli and Palestinian flags, suggesting a harmonious resolution from discord. Ascending to prominence, the artwork graces the cover of Banksy's 2005 monograph, attaining global acclaim and replication. Its resonance is not only contemporary but also echoes the profound anti-war ethos of historical pieces like Picasso's 'Guernica', and the Flower Power Movement. *Love Is in the Air* thus stands as a testament to its era, a visually arresting emblem with enduring relevance.

LaCollection – Institutionalizing NFTs?

LaCollection is an NFT platform recognized and certified by four major museums: The British Museum London, Vienna's Leopold Museum, the Museum of Fine Arts Boston, and the Monnaie de Paris. LaCollection was launched in September 2021 through a partnership with the British Museum, featuring an exhibition of over 250 NFTs by the Japanese painter and printmaker Hokusai (1760–1849). Subsequent displays have broadened the network, showcasing works by Chinese ink painter Yang Jiechang, watercolorist Joseph William Turner (1775–1851), printmaker Giovanni Battista Piranesi (1720–1778), and painter Egon Schiele (1890–1918). In a notable collaboration with the Museum of Fine Arts Boston, LaCollection highlighted 'French Pastels' with pieces by Pierre-Auguste Renoir, Edgar Degas, and Claude Monet. Other exhibits have included a range of contemporary artists and artistic responses to current political events, economic themes (the monetization of art), and photojournalistic works in partnership with Agence France-Presse.

A recent exhibition, devised by La Collection in conjunction with the Monnaie de Paris was created by Robert Alice (Alice 2023), pursuing dual conceptual goals through two artwork series: 'Ornament and Crisis' delved into the 2,000-year history of centralized monetary policies, while 'Blueprints' juxtaposed this with the emergent narrative of decentralized monetary systems. The exhibition used abstract digital art, immersive virtual reality, printing plates, and smart contract NFTs to contrast the archival and innovative approaches to knowledge storage.

The creative process, as described on the exhibition's official page, was enriched by in-depth discussions with the Monnaie de Paris museum curators and employed a plethora of advanced technologies, ranging from smart contracts and LiDAR scans to virtual reality and AI. The dual series probes key conceptual and philosophical themes within blockchain, with each artwork existing both digitally and physically. These pieces not only connect to the historical essence of the Monnaie de Paris but also invite reflection on the material and historical aspects of new digital art forms. Robert Alice's digital aesthetic, which integrates past elements with blockchain concepts, suggests applications that extend beyond visual art. For instance, the use of QR codes on artwork labels, linking to digital content on the LaCollection platform, could similarly enhance musical performances by providing audiences with access to ancillary materials like rehearsals or interviews.

The transformational and experimental techniques of 'The Blueprints' series could be creatively adapted for music. Alice reinterpreted original architectural blueprints from the museum's archive, transforming them into large-scale abstractions combined with blockchain history elements. Each piece began with an AI-generated ASCII background, layered with fragments of the original blueprints and additional ASCII renderings, echoing the contours with the repeated letters 'MCV' – a nod to Jorge Luis Borges' 'The Library of Babel' (1944). This blending of timelines and mediums in Alice's work exemplifies a complex interplay between the past and present, analog and digital, and the concrete versus the infinite. Such boundary-pushing creativity resonates with my own exploration of the differential ontology of musical works.

Music and Blockchain Technologies

Questioning traditional ontological accounts and arguing for wider ontological perspectives, I have proposed elsewhere (de Assis 2019) a new image of musical work, which I briefly outlined again in the first section of this chapter and to which I return now for my conclusive remarks. My 'ontological' proposal requires a fundamental redefinition of musical works, which appear as complex conglomerates of things and intensities, containing innumerable and potentially never-ending additional component parts. These parts are continuously rearranged and reassembled in their specific modes of appearance. More than refuting conventional theories, this notion of work as assemblage can encompass conventional music ontological accounts as particular cases, as historically situated subsets, which take only a reduced number of parameters into consideration. Those simpler accounts are perfectly functional for musical practices that follow the mainstream notions of work concept, authenticity, execution, interpretation, reproduction, and text-fidelity, as well as for those other practices that focus on historically informed investigations. Only when one moves beyond historicity and beyond interpretation, entering the realm of experimental performance practices, can there be an expanded perspective on musical entities.

My proposed new image of musical work critically replaces 'work' (as a noun) with 'work' (as a verb), a change that introduces a great number of novel modes of practice and inquiry. In short, musical worlds so conceived can be fundamentally rethought as having properties that are actual, and capacities that are real but not necessarily actual here-and-now. These components, which truly exist but are not actualized here-and-now, define the virtual state of artworks. From this perspective, musical works appear as having two fundamental dimensions: actual things, found in the actual world (sketches, manuscripts, editions, theoretical essays, recordings, performances), and virtual diagrams, highly abstract constructions based upon particular singularities, which enable us to think about those works in the first place.

Currently dominant music ontologies primarily insist on the conditions of identity and recognition of a given musical work. The common basic questions of most ontological accounts are of the type: what is a musical work? How can a musical work be identified as this musical work? How can an instantiation of a work be considered as adequate, legitimate, or fully qualified? However, these questions take for granted precisely what needs to be explained: namely, the fact that those 'musical works' emerged at a given historical time, were defined by innumerable sets of physical component parts, were the result of intensive processes of generation, and continue to undergo constant redefinitions throughout time. Musical works are made of particles in constant flux of movement and change. Rather than depending on traditional ontologies that concentrate on perennial conditions of being and identity, we can focus on the ontogenesis of musical works. The starting questions are, then, quite different: How are musical works effectively generated, constructed, formalized? Which intensive processes lead to their individuation? Which pre-individuating forces and materials create the humus where they will emerge? On which material basis are they transmitted throughout time? Which parts of them remain hidden and which ones are disclosed to a specific discipline, perspective, goal? What is the affective power of their extensive parts? Which concrete documents allow for their performance? What other things influence their passive reception by an audience? Moving beyond fundamental or higher-order ontology, these questions direct us toward the study of ontogenesis, exploring the diverse and infinitely varied processes of individuation and the continuous historical evolution of musical works.

Without this new understanding of musical works and experimental creative processes in music, I would never have arrived at the discovery of blockchain technologies and their potential use for innovative musical practices. It was my fragmented view of musical entities, their infinite pulverization in smaller and smaller component parts, akin to atomic particles, that resonated with the granular nature of particles in digital, blockchain-based artistic processes. This analogy paved the way for my team's foray into blockchain research, which we are conducting in view of musical innovation. Blockchain's distributed ledger technology offers a radical break from centralized systems of music production, distribution, and consumption. The granular nature of blockchain transactions mirrors the granular reconsideration of musical works proposed above, enabling a dynamic interplay between the musicians, listeners, and the medium itself.

The potential of blockchain in music extends beyond mere digitization of assets, which unfortunately is still the most discussed aspect of it. Blockchain beckons us to reimagine music itself. Beyond important matters related to the music industry's structure, the artist's rights, the distribution of revenues, and the interactions among all stakeholders, this technology may foster a new breed of musical works that are, by design, collaborative, decentralized, and perhaps even autonomous in their evolution over time. Furthermore, the blockchain opens doors to a new ecology of musical works, where compositions can be both fixed in time and perpetually mutable. Smart contracts could automate licensing, performances, and the dissemination of works, while tokens might represent ownership or membership in a decentralized musical community. Such an ecosystem could nurture new forms of artistic expression and engagement, eroding the barriers between creators and audiences, and between the act of creation and reception.

This nascent symbiosis between music and blockchain does not come without challenges. The complexity of blockchain's technological landscape requires musicians and industry professionals to acquire new knowledge and skills. There are also significant ethical and legal considerations in how these technologies are implemented, ensuring that innovation does not come at the cost of equity and artistic integrity. As we chart this new course, it is essential to cultivate an environment of open dialogue and interdisciplinary collaboration. Musicians, technologists, legal experts, and cultural theorists must come together to shape this emerging space. This effort must be collective, combining both the creative impulse and a critical assessment of the implications for the music ecosystem.

This chapter, and indeed this book, is an invitation to join a vanguard of pioneers in the quest to redefine the nature of musical works through the lens of blockchain. Herein lies the promise of a decentralized future for music creation and distribution. Blockchain technologies are not merely a tool but a catalyst for a profound transformation in our musical culture. It heralds a new epoch in which musical processes and creative achievements flow in-and-through digital modes of existence. As we delve deeper into the integration of music and blockchain, we not only uncover new potentials for art and technology but also profoundly redefine and rethink the very notion of music.

References

Alice, Robert. 2023. *Babel*, Le Monnaie de Paris/La Collection. Online PDF at: https:// 25508286.fs1.hubspotusercontent-eu1.net/hubfs/25508286/Robert%20 Alice/Robert%20Alice%20at%20the%20Monnaie%20De%20Paris%2c%20 Highlight%20List%20of%20Works%20-%20laCollection.pdf

de Assis, Paulo. 2016. "Transduction and Ensembles of Transducers: Relaying Flows of Intensities in Music." *Presentation at the conference "The Concept of Immanence in Philosophy and the Arts,"* Angewandte Innovation Laboratory (AIL), University of Applied Arts Vienna, Vienna, 7 May 2016.

de Assis, Paulo. 2017. "Simondon's 'Transduction' as Radical Immanence in Performance." In "Philosophy On Stage: The Concept of Immanence in Contemporary Art and Philosophy," edited by Arno Böhler, Eva-Maria Aigner, and Elizabeth Schäfer, special issue, *Performance Philosophy Journal* 3 (3): 695–717.

de Assis, Paulo. 2018a. *Logic of Experimentation: Rethinking Music Performance through Artistic Research*, Leuven University Press.

de Assis, Paulo, ed. 2018b. *Virtual Works—Actual Things: Essays in Music Ontology. Orpheus Institute Series*. Leuven University Press.

de Assis, Paulo. 2019. "Musical Works as Assemblages." in La Deleuziana — Online *Journal of Philosophy*, 10.

de Assis, Paulo. 2023. "Hypermusic: New Musical Practices at the Crossroads of Music, Art and Thought." In *New Paradigms for Music Research: Art, Society and technology*, edited by Adolf Murillo, Inés, Jesus Tejada, David Carabias. University of Valencia Press, 53–74.

Bennett, Jane. 2010. *Vibrant Matter. A Political Ecology of Things*. Durham: Duke University Press.

Davies, David. 2011. *Philosophy of the Performing Arts*. Wiley-Blackwell.

Davies, David. 2018. "Locating the Performable Musical Work in Practice: A Non-Platonist Interpretation of the 'Classical Paradigm'." In *Virtual Works—Actual Things: Essays in Music Ontology. Orpheus Institute Series*, edited by Paulo de Assis (pp. 45–64). Leuven: Leuven University Press.

DeLanda, Manuel. 2002. *Intensive Science and Virtual Philosophy*. London: Continuum.

DeLanda, Manuel. 2006. *A New Philosophy of Society: Assemblage Theory and Social Complexity*. London: Bloomsbury.

DeLanda, Manuel. 2016. *Assemblage Theory*. Edinburgh: Edinburgh University Press.

Deleuze, Gilles. 1975. "Écrivain non: Un nouveau cartographe." *Critique* 343 (December): 1207–1227. Translated by Seán Hand as "A New Cartographer" in Deleuze (1988) 2006, 21–38.

Deleuze, Gilles and Felix Guattari. 1977. *Anti-Oedipus: Capitalism and Schizophrenia*. Translated by Robert Hurley, Mark Seem, and Helen R. Lane. Minneapolis: University of Minnesota Press. First published as Deleuze and Guattari 1972. Translation first published 1977 (New York: Viking Press).

Deleuze, Gilles, and Félix Guattari. 1987. *A Thousand Plateaus: Capitalism and Schizophrenia*. Translated by Brian Massumi. Minneapolis: University of Minnesota Press. First published 1980 as *Mille plateaux* (Paris: Minuit).

Einarsson, Einar Torfi. 2012. *Desiring Machines*. Netherlands: Deuss Music.

Einarsson, Einar Torfi. 2015. "Desiring-Machines: In between Difference and Repetition, Performer and Conductor, Cyclones and Physicality, Structure and Notation." *Perspectives of New Music* 53, no. 1: 5–30. https://doi.org/10.1353/pnm.2015.0006

Goehr, Lydia. (1992) 2007. *The Imaginary Museum of Musical Works: An Essay in the Philosophy of Music*. Rev. ed. Oxford: Oxford University Press.

López, Francisco. 1998. *La Selva. Sound Environments from a Neotropical Rain Forest* (vinyl LP + USB HD). Paris: Les Presses du Réel.

Łukawski, Adam. 2022. "Fractal of Periodic Spacetime Sequences as a Framework for an Interoperable Metaverse." In *Computer & Media Art at the Age of Metaverses and NFTs*, edited by Khaldoun Zreik, Marc Veyrat, and Matthieu Quiniou (Proceedings of the 7th Computer Art Congress, HEAD Geneva, September 2022), 57–78.

Mendolicchio, Jonathan. 2019. *Engineering the Sound: Beyoncé's 'Lemonade'* https://happymag.tv/engineering-the-sound-beyonces-lemonade/ (last accessed 2024.04.10).

Morton, Timothy. 2010. *The Ecological Thought*. Harvard University Press.

Morton, Timothy. 2013. *Hyperobjects. Philosophy and Ecology after the End of the World*. University of Minnesota Press.

Peisner, David. 2016. *Making 'Lemonade': Inside Beyonce's Collaborative Masterpiece*. https://www.rollingstone.com/music/music-news/making-lemonade-inside-beyonces-collaborative-masterpiece-85854/ (last accessed 2024.04.10).

Sauvagnargues, Anne. 2003. "Actuel/Virtuel." In *Le vocabulaire de Gilles Deleuze*, edited by Robert Sasso and Arnaud Villani, 22–29. Les Cahiers de Noesis 3. Paris: Vrin.

Sauvagnargues, Anne. 2013. *Deleuze and Art*. Translated by Samantha Bankston. London: Bloomsbury. First published 2005 as *Deleuze et l'art* (Paris: Presses Universitaires de France).

Sauvagnargues, Anne. 2016. *Artmachines: Deleuze, Guattari, Simondon*. Translated by Suzanne Verderber with Eugene W. Holland. Edinburgh: Edinburgh University Press.

Scott, David. 2014. *Gilbert Simondon's Psychic and Collective Individuation: A Critical Introduction and Guide*. Edinburgh: Edinburgh University Press.

Simondon, Gilbert. 2013. (1954–58) *L'individuation à la lumière des notions de forme et d'information* [Individuation in Light of the Notions of Form and Information]. Grenoble: Jérôme Millon. Contains texts written 1954–58. This selection first published 2005 (Grenoble: Jérôme Millon).

Stiegler, Bernard. 2012. *The Theatre of Individuation: Phase-Shift and Resolution in Simondon and Heidegger*. Translated by Kristina Lebedeva. In De Boever et al. 2012, 185–202.

Tingen, Paul. 2016. *Making Lemonade with Beyoncé's Right-Hand Man, Stuart White*. https://www.audiotechnology.com/features/mix-masters-making-lemonade (last accessed 2024.04.10).

2

Performative Transactions: Artistic Collaboration of Humans and AI Agents in Decentralized Creative Networks

Adam Łukawski

Leiden University, Leiden, The Netherlands
Orpheus Institute, Ghent, Belgium

Introduction

While blockchain technology and non-fungible tokens (NFTs) have already transformed how digital musical creations are authenticated, and smart contracts have paved the way for generative art NFTs, there is still more that can be achieved for music through decentralized systems. The core premise of this chapter is that blockchains offer the potential to do more than just verify the identity and uniqueness of artistic creations and processes. They also enable the evolution from single-purpose generative art NFTs to the emergence of 'Decentralized Creative Networks'. This chapter proposes Decentralized Creative Networks as blockchain-based post-human social networks, in which artists and AI agents develop and transact composable artistic processes, transparently building upon each other's interoperable contributions. Artists can access Decentralized Creative Networks via various decentralized applications to explore artistic processes and features as social media posts. These posts can be reused as tools to build further artistic processes, which can be executed to achieve various artistic goals (for instance to compose music, to execute live performances of an artistic work, or to generate NFTs).

To realize this vision, this chapter centrally introduces the concept of 'Performative Transaction' – a transaction that takes place in a Decentralized Creative Network when one artistic process references another process as its part. Performative Transactions are executed by composable smart contracts that encode the artistic processes and the terms of referencing them by other processes. When interlinked Performative Transactions are executed, smart contracts carry out all referenced musical transformations contributing to the musical result. They also automatically distribute any financial receivables to the creators of all referenced artistic processes. They are composable, as

DOI: 10.1201/9781003458227-3

they can be combined to collectively execute more intricate artistic processes. They are interoperable as each process is encoded as a recursive pattern of artistic transformations in a framework inspired by the Transformational Theory of David Lewin and Machine Learning's feature engineering (more on this in the section titled 'Transformational Theory and Feature Spaces'). Operating on the blockchain, Performative Transactions allow transparent tracking of the identity, ownership, and provenance of their encoded musical processes and assure their reliability in the future. This approach merges the depth of music theory and composition with the capabilities of decentralized systems. It envisions a decentralized database of semantically structured artistic processes, allowing their reuse in various decentralized applications and for training AI models. Thus, Performative Transactions enable a system where human artists and AI agents can transparently build upon each other's interoperable contributions.

Decentralized Generative Art

Blockchain is a relatively new technology that allows the creation of unprecedented tools. For the arts, one of the main features of blockchains is that, via non-fungible tokens, they can automatically track the identity of digital artistic objects. NFTs are generated (minted) by smart contracts. A smart contract is a self-enforcing agreement embedded in a Turing-complete computer code on the blockchain (Buterin 2013). Whenever its conditions are met, the smart contract automatically executes its code. It is immutable, which means that once deployed on the blockchain, the rules and operations of a smart contract cannot be altered, ensuring the reliability and integrity of the transaction it handles (Summers 2022).

One of the fields transformed by the invention of smart contracts is generative art:

> art practice where the artist creates a process, such as a set of natural language rules, a computer program, a machine, or other procedural invention, which is then set into motion with some degree of autonomy contributing to or resulting in a completed work of art.
>
> (Galanter 2003)

Generative art NFTs are 'unique digital art pieces created through coded algorithms and stored as NFTs on the blockchain' (Stoykov 2023). Nowadays, there is no shortage of innovative generative art NFTs (Farinha 2022). In these artworks, smart contracts and other algorithms encode specific rules that define how the artwork is created. This means that the same smart contract is often capable of generating multiple NFTs following an algorithm that utilizes random functions as part of its operations. Artworks can then change based on certain inputs or over time. A generative music piece might change its composition based on the time of day or the number of people listening to it, all managed and verified by the smart contract. For instance, at the Art Blocks platform 'artists use creative code to create varied, generative art that evolves each time a collector mints a piece' (Art Blocks 2023).

The most specific cases of generative art NFTs are the ones in which the algorithm generating a piece of art is also, along with the algorithm minting the NFT, a part of the smart contract. This can make the process of generating a piece of art completely autonomous. As proposed by Rhapsody Labs, the algorithmic processes that generate NFTs can be classified according to a scale of "on-chain purity". The scale measures 'how permanent, transparent and replicable the art is using the contracts on the blockchain in 500 years time, and how much power a developer has to change the metadata once it is minted on the blockchain'. The fewer dependencies are used in the process of creating a work of art, the more 'pure' it is on that scale. In the ideal case scenario of level 3, 'all the data inc. images/art, contract, unique identifier, metadata and the "draw" function is stored all on the blockchain' (RLXYZ 2022).

Thanks to their persistence and immutability, smart contracts are perfect devices to model networks of interdependent processes. Fully on-chain ecosystems may allow for a more integrated and dynamic type of digital art. The primary obstacles for fully on-chain solutions remain the prohibitively high costs associated with minting all components on the blockchain (RLXYZ 2022), and problems related to data storage due to the limits of the block size in various blockchains (some blockchains are capable of storing huge amounts of data such as large computer programs, but many are not) (Edwood 2020). However, it's essential to recognize that the most significant advancements in decentralized generative art are expected to emerge only when the blockchain architectures used to produce this art are designed to fully use the advantages of complete decentralization, such as improved data integrity and reliability, increased transparency and trust, and enhanced security. In such systems, the self-operating nature of interconnected smart contracts, made by various artists, would ensure that artists could transparently and seamlessly build upon each other's interoperable contributions.

Decentralized Creative Networks

As a response to the discussed opportunities of on-chain ecosystems, I propose a new concept of 'Decentralized Creative Networks' – blockchain-based social networks designed to facilitate collaborative art creation, where interconnected artistic processes leverage the collective intelligence of both human artists and AI agents. Decentralized Creative Networks can be accessed via various decentralized applications to explore artistic processes and features as social media posts. These posts can be reused as tools to build further artistic processes, which can be executed to achieve various artistic goals (such as composing a new musical work, carrying out an artistic performance, or generating NFTs of artworks), automatically distributing any financial receivable to the creators of all referenced processes. Similarly, as NFTs encoded on one blockchain can be traded in multiple marketplaces supporting the same blockchain, artistic processes encoded in Decentralized Creative Networks can be accessed via various decentralized applications created by the community. These networks emphasize the collaborative aspect of art, where the creation process is not only the work of an individual, but a collective effort enabled by technology, allowing artists and AI agents to contribute, modify, and combine their creative outputs.

While this conceptualization of 'Decentralized Creative Networks' is novel in its use of blockchain technology and smart contracts for art creation, it resonates with and extends upon Rasa Smite's earlier use of the term. Smite defined 'Creative Networks' in the context of the early Internet era, particularly during the second half of the 1990s. She described these networks as collaborative platforms, primarily comprising artists, theorists, and other creative individuals who explored the nascent stage of the Internet for creative self-expression and social communication. These early 'Creative Networks' were groundbreaking in their use of digital mediums to explore new artistic possibilities and forms of social organization, from maintaining art servers to experimenting with Internet broadcasting and collaborative development of open-source software (Smite 2012).

In drawing parallels to Smite's concept, the 'Decentralized Creative Networks' proposed here similarly emphasize collaborative artistic creation and community engagement with a new technology for creative purposes. Where Smite's networks leveraged the technological possibilities of their time, these new 'Decentralized Creative Networks' harness the unique capabilities of blockchain to create a dynamic, participatory, and interconnected artistic ecosystem. The underlying philosophy of collective creativity remains a cornerstone, yet the methods and tools reflect the advancements and shifts in digital technology, particularly the emergence of blockchain as a medium for artistic exploration and exchange.

Composability of Decentralized Artistic Processes

In Decentralized Creative Networks, artistic processes can be developed and further combined by artists to produce more intricate artistic results, without any dependency on the centralized platform or application. These processes, upon execution, utilize the potential of blockchain-based smart contracts.

According to the developers' documentation of the Ethereum blockchain, the smart contract's composability feature consists of three main principles: modularity, autonomy, and discoverability. This means that each smart contract is designed to perform a specific task, to self-execute, and to be open-sourced, so anyone can call a smart contract or create its new version. 'If there is a smart contract that solves one problem, other developers can reuse it, so they don't have to solve the same problem. This way, developers can take existing software libraries and add extra functionality to create new dapps' (Ethereum.org 2023). Thus, blockchain allows software developers to transparently create on top of each other's work.

This special feature of blockchains, used in the development of decentralized software, could be mimicked in the process of decentralized art-making. However, despite the potential of smart contracts to encode artistic processes in a modular way, there is yet no general standard for how these various artistic modules could become composable and interoperable on the cross-application level,[1] for instance, to use them for music composition. Existing generative art NFT projects, which are most often operationalized in some form of decentralized applications, in many cases produce new editions of a work of art by combining sets of only internally generated or curated components (Audiohype 2022). Artistic processes encoded in their smart contracts used to generate NFTs are not designed for interoperability with artistic processes encoded in smart contracts of other generative decentralized applications. Instead, their design often mirrors that of centralized programs, in which ensembles of internal algorithms are designed to serve the goals of only one application's architecture.

Centralized software applications for processing music at the granular level typically handle representations of their artistic data editable by developing their unique and only internally used file formats. In these programs, a degree of interoperability with other applications is ensured by the function to import and export standard file formats like WAV and MP3. While these formats are also often used in decentralized applications, in the Web3 context they have a crucial limitation: they treat music as a monolithic continuous signal in the time domain, lacking representation of any structural elements. A MIDI format, the industry's standard for symbolic music encoding, offers a more detailed structure with messages, ticks, tracks, and events, but it still doesn't capture the dimensionality of the deeper musical concepts that humans perceive, like how notes form intervals and chords, and how these elements further combine in complex ways on the level of various musical parameters. While Web3 solutions bring the potential to view and handle musical data and processes in a more structured way, allowing for a more sophisticated approach to recognize and represent the multidimensional nature of music (for instance by leveraging Machine Learning algorithms), this potential is not yet addressed in existing generative art NFT projects.

The solution could be to shift a focus from the final output of a generative artistic process (generative art NFT) into the process encoded in the smart contract itself. A standard implementation of a smart contract could be developed that is tailored specifically for representing various interconnected artistic processes in a hierarchically structured way. Thus, it would have to be at the same time both: a format for artistic representation, and a composable artistic process.

Performative Transactions

As identified in the previous section, three critical challenges for blockchain-based generative art should still be addressed to enable the development of Decentralized Creative Networks: the inadequacy of existing file formats to capture complex hierarchical artistic concepts, the lack of standardized methods for crafting reusable artistic processes in smart contracts, and the absence of a transparent system to trace both their ownership and provenance. To address these challenges, I propose a solution and a new concept, namely 'Performative Transactions' – transactions that take place when one artistic process references another process as its constituent part.

Imagine interacting with a digital canvas, where you have the option to select from a palette of predefined artistic processes. These processes are shared with you in a Decentralized Creative Network as posts of other users. They are capable of performing various programmatically encoded functions. For instance, they could generate diverse musical 'things' such as scales of musical pitches, rhythmical patterns, dynamic values, various elements of classical music notation, and spectra of sinusoidal frequencies. The Decentralized Creative Network might also already contain more complex combinations of these basic generative processes assembled by users, capable of generating musical motives, melodies, harmonic progressions, timbral textures combined from sinusoidal frequencies, elements typical for experimental music notation, and even fully realized musical compositions. You can merge and manipulate these components with intuitive ease, crafting new, unique musical processes with mere clicks. As you combine these elements, they create a new reusable process within the available palette, a compound object that inherits and references its constituent parts and appears as the next post in the decentralized social network that can be added to anyone's palette of musical processes.

If a financial transaction is when you exchange money, then a Performative Transaction is when you exchange composable artistic processes. Performative Transaction is a transaction between the creators of reusable artistic processes. These creators agree that whenever their reusable process is referenced by another artistic process, a smart contract will execute its encoded function. When a new Performative Transaction is established, the creator defines the conditions that must be met for the artistic process encoded in the transaction to be executed when referenced by another Performative Transaction.

Within the Decentralized Creative Network, such transactions are executed by special composable smart contracts. Each artistic process is bestowed with a unique identifier, ensuring that its origins and use within new processes are precisely tracked and acknowledged. The contract can (but doesn't have to) specify the financial conditions of a transaction upon its every execution enabling not only a creative and dynamic exchange but also a market of reusable artistic processes. Thus, the same ecosystem allows users to create either free or paid solutions, based on their choice.

Transformational Theory and Feature Spaces

To facilitate the integration of such a diverse spectrum of artistic processes within one interoperable framework, smart contracts that execute Performative Transactions, encode their processes as reusable multidimensional transformations. In contemporary music theory, musical set theory encompasses various concepts to classify musical objects and delineate their interrelations. David Lewin's Transformational Theory, part of musical set theory, provides a theoretical foundation for understanding the relationships between musical elements in terms of transformations – operations that define the relationships between notes, chords, or other musical elements. This theory posits that music can be analyzed by examining the functions (transformations) that move one set of elements to another (Schuijer 2008).

In Transformational Theory, musical compositions are conceptualized as abstract musical spaces. Elements of the composition, such as pitch, rhythm, and dynamics, exist and interact in these spaces via the use of a Generalized Interval System (GIS), which, in Lewin's theory, extends beyond the traditional understanding of intervals as distances between pitches. These intervals are transformations, representing various types of relationships in music. A transformation can be described mathematically in the form of a transformation function that captures how one musical element transforms into another. Furthermore, the theory often deals with sequences or chains of these transformations. A series of transformations represents a progression of musical changes, where each transformation leads to the next (Lewin 2007).

Building on the foundational concepts of David Lewin's Transformational Theory in music, the notion of musical spaces and transformations aligns well with the ideas of features and feature spaces commonly found in Machine Learning. In the context of Machine Learning, a 'feature' refers to an individual measurable property or characteristic of an observed phenomenon (Bishop 2006). A latent feature space is a multidimensional space where each dimension corresponds to one of these features (Grigg 2019), which is similar to the abstract musical spaces in Transformational Theory analyzing various musical elements such as pitch, rhythm, and dynamics. The key similarity between these two concepts is that both spaces not only encode actual observed or analyzed values (like specific musical elements or data points) but also encompass a realm of potential configurations and combinations of these features or elements. This includes possibilities that were not part of the initial dataset. This aspect of latent feature spaces allows for the exploration of transitional paths between two entities – whether they be musical compositions or images. For instance, in the context of images, this would mean finding a series of transformations that create a smooth transition from one image to another, with each step along the way representing a blend of the two.[2] Similarly, musical transformations in Lewin's Transformational Theory are paths taken in multidimensional spaces of musical features.

Recursive Patterns in Multidimensional Spaces of Transformations

In Performative Transactions, these two notions – musical transformations from Transformational Theory and feature spaces from Machine Learning – are combined. Here, a musical feature is not just a static attribute but is encoded as a series of transformations, mirroring the transformational nature of generalized intervals in Lewin's theory. Each feature in a Performative Transaction is defined by a recursive series of transformations, which is essentially a sequence of functions applied repeatedly on the same variable.

To elucidate, consider a feature of musical pitch. The recursive pattern for this feature might consist of a series of specific alterations – such as increments, decrements, or multiplicative changes – applied to an initial value – such as a C4 note for pitch. For instance, the pattern could be a recursive series of increments like this: [pitch+2, pitch+2, pitch+1, pitch+2, pitch+2, pitch+2, pitch+1]. This recursive pattern, when initiated with a starting value, incrementally executes the encoded operations, continuously updating the value of a variable "pitch" in a cycle to build the sequence. It assumes operation on the indices of the chromatic scale's elements to encode a major scale. A feature encoded in this way has the potential for the sequence to continue indefinitely. For instance, the pattern of a major scale can be continued in further octaves, extending the sequence as far as desired. The result is an evolving chain of values, each derived from the last by following the set pattern. Each feature in a composable smart contract holds its unique recursive pattern which executes the Performative Transaction and contributes to the multidimensional nature of the musical piece.

Creating New Performative Transactions

Consider a human or AI agent exploring artistic processes in the Decentralized Creative Network. These processes are encoded as recurrent patterns of transformations (such as the process that infinitely yields the values of a progressing major scale presented in the previous section). The agent can add any artistic process made by other agents to their creative toolset. For instance, the agent could find a rhythmic pattern encoded by another agent as a series of operations like [rhythm*2, rhythm/4], and add it to their toolset. Further, the agent could find a pitch pattern encoded by another agent as [pitch+2, pitch+3, pitch-1], and also add it to their toolset. The agent can then use the collected artistic processes to construct a new transformation. To do it, the agent combines these transformations (features) into a new feature space – a space where their recurrent patterns of transformations serve as dimensions. Each point in this new space represents a combination of operations from the rhythm and pitch patterns. For example, a point might represent a multiplication of rhythm by two, combined with an increase in pitch by three steps: [rhythm*2, pitch+3]. The entire feature space becomes a matrix of such combinations, with one dimension representing the transformations in rhythm and the other in pitch. The agent constructs a new artistic process by selecting the points in that new space of possibilities (technically, in a Cartesian product of all referenced transformations). For instance, the agent could construct a new recurrent pattern like this: [[rhythm*2, pitch+3], [rhythm/4, pitch+2], [rhythm*2, pitch-1]]. This sequence (a new Performative Transaction), when executed, yields a series of rhythm and pitch values evolving according to the newly defined recurrent pattern.

When Performative Transactions are connected into a directed graph, each transaction utilizes the feature spaces created by previous transactions as its inputs. It then applies its recursive patterns to these spaces. This process is akin to layering transformations, where each transaction interprets and redefines the inputs through its unique set of patterns. For example, consider a Performative Transaction that takes the combined pitch and rhythm pattern described earlier. A subsequent transaction might apply a different pattern to create a unique melody based on this transformation. The linking of Performative Transactions is not merely a sequential process but a form of functional composition. Each transaction integrates and transforms the outputs of its predecessors, resulting in a traceable cumulative effect. These transformations work by combining and manipulating the recursive patterns of transformations, rather than fixed values, leading to the creation of new dimensions in which music can be further shaped. This method allows for a vast range of creative possibilities. By linking transactions, composers can create sophisticated musical structures, layer by layer. The final composition is a product of this cumulative transformation process.

While operating on such a system might sound complex to those more acquainted with music theory than programming and mathematics, most of the users joining this decentralized system wouldn't have to redefine the foundational objects such as a chromatic scale or a sinusoidal waveform by figuring out what their mathematical function is. Instead, they could create new musical objects by connecting and building upon preexisting posts in the Decentralized Creative Network. This could be operationalized in a straightforward user interface. Agents could construct new musical processes simply by referencing other processes and selecting values in tables of their combined transformations. More advanced users could still program their Performative Transactions mathematically, or with the use of computer code. By mapping out various dimensions and functions in a Performative Transaction, humans and AI agents create a ledger of musical processes that are not only intricate and unique but also maintain their lineage and relationships transparently within the blockchain network. Performative Transaction hence serves as both a compositional tool and a record of ownership and creativity, ensuring that each contribution to the musical piece is acknowledged and traceable in an unambiguous manner.

Large Language Models as Performative AI Agents

Performative Transactions are initiated by the actions of their users – humans or AI agents. In envisioning the operationalization of autonomous agents in Decentralized Creative Networks, the potential role of Large Language Models (LLMs) presents a compelling possibility. LLMs, such as the widely known ChatGPT, function essentially as advanced chatbots, capable of generating human-like text. This ability to process and respond to natural language inputs makes them suitable candidates for interfacing with complex systems like Decentralized Creative Networks. A key aspect of LLMs is their capability to execute computer code and interact with external data sources via Application Programming Interfaces (APIs) (Eleti et al. 2023). This feature could enable them to interact with Decentralized Creative Networks as reasoning agents (Yao et al. 2023) constructing their collections of artistic processes and resulting artworks that could be further explored and reused by other human and post-human agents.

LLMs could also serve as intermediaries between users and blockchains, managing and manipulating Performative Transactions based on user instructions delivered in natural language. They could help users explore the vast landscape of Performative Transactions, identifying and suggesting transactions that align with the user's creative goals. For instance, if a user wishes to create a piece of music with specific characteristics, they could simply describe their vision to the LLM assistant. The model would then interpret this description, identify relevant Performative Transactions on the blockchain, and possibly even create new ones, all to realize the user's vision. The interaction would be akin to having a conversation with a knowledgeable assistant who understands both the user's artistic intentions and the technicalities of Performative Transactions. This approach would make the process of creating and manipulating music through Performative Transactions more accessible to a wider range of users. Individuals without extensive technical knowledge of music composition or blockchain technology could engage in music creation simply by articulating their ideas in natural language. The LLM would handle the complexities of exploring the creative network and executing the appropriate transactions.

Spaces of Possible Performative Processes

Performative Transaction encodes both the representation of an artistic object and the autonomously executing performative act. Turing-complete functions encoded as transformations in its recursive patterns might do way more than just provide a next pitch in a musical scale. They could encode complex operations with the potential to influence artistic results through either deterministic processes of complex algorithms or the more unpredictable, pseudo-random pretrained processes employed in AI models. This means that operations encoded in Performative Transactions could even include the use of intelligent tools as part of the musical feature space. Thus, the agency of the performative act could not only be that of a human or AI agent but also that of an evolving, intelligent Decentralized Creative Network itself. As stated by Ross Ashby, the field of cybernetics 'takes as its subject-matter the domain of "all possible machines", and is only secondarily interested if informed that some of them have not yet been made, either by Man or by Nature' (Ashby 1956). Aaron Sloman envisioned a related concept – 'the structure of the space of possible minds', as a conceptual framework encompassing a wide range of cognitive entities, from humans to AI systems, emphasizing a diversity of cognitive processes within a hypothetical multidimensional space of 'behaving systems' (Sloman 1984). The concept of Performative Transactions aligns well with this notion. These transactions are not just tools for composition but are agential entities within a Decentralized Creative Network, each transaction creating its own, dynamic and varied space, representing a unique approach to creativity. Performative Transactions, therefore, can be seen as analogous to Sloman's concept: they create a myriad of 'spaces of performative processes', each acting as an independent agent within the broader artistic ecosystem. In that system, the representation of a possible artistic output is equal to the expressive capabilities of its performative agent. Performative Transactions, beyond playing the role of music's representation, become dynamic participants in the creative process, capable of autonomously generating and transforming musical elements, by that expanding the boundaries of what constitutes an 'agent'. They embody an example of what Martin Zeilinger described as a redistribution of agency from human creators to the artworks themselves, thereby fostering the emergence of more-than-human art ecologies (Zeilinger 2022).

Flows of Potentialities – Examples of Performative Transactions for Music

Once the decentralized collective musical intelligence envisioned in the concepts of Decentralized Creative Networks and Performative Transactions is realized on the practical level, it might have the potential to change how we create, share, and structure music. The next four sections delve into a few examples of such creative solutions that might be enabled by the new composable smart contracts.

Music Composition with Performative Transactions

The process of music composition with Performative Transactions can be conceptualized as a dynamic interplay within a spectrum of possible musical compositions, ranging from indeterminacy to determinacy. This concept views compositions not immediately as static creations but rather as generative art processes, where the degree of randomness and precision leading to a realization of the work of art can be finely tuned. The essence of a Performative Transaction is its ability to shape a musical composition by gradually narrowing or expanding the range of possibilities, allowing composers to sculpt the piece with varying levels of control and unpredictability. On one end, indeterminacy represents a realm where musical outcomes are heavily influenced by randomness, chance, or external factors, leading to unpredictable and often unique results. This approach echoes the avant-garde and experimental traditions such as aleatoric music scores and algorithmic composition, where the unexpected and the uncharted are integral to the creative process. Moving along the spectrum, the role of chance diminishes, and the composer's intent and control become more pronounced. This gradual shift toward determinacy sees the composition process becoming increasingly structured, with more predictable and defined outcomes. At the far end of the spectrum lies complete determinacy, where every aspect of the composition is fixed and where the processes encoded in the transaction can only compose one version of a musical piece.

Creating a collaborative flow of Performative Transactions is akin to charting a course through a vast space of musical possibilities. Each transaction acts as a navigational instrument, guiding the composition toward a specific range of outcomes. This process is like sculpting a musical piece out of the raw material of musical features. Composers begin with the entire musical space of possible parameters and progressively narrow it down, defining the shape and form of the composition. Algorithms can introduce structured patterns and rules, bringing a level of predictability and order to the composition. AI models, conversely, can infuse elements of randomness or learn from the evolving landscape of the decentralized framework of various Performative Transactions to suggest novel, sometimes unexpected, musical directions. This dual capability allows Performative Transactions to serve as both a precise tool for structured composition and a catalyst for creative exploration and innovation. In Performative Transactions the boundaries between composer, machine, and algorithm blur. The result is a musical composition process that is not just a series of static decisions, but a living, evolving journey through an ever-shifting landscape of sonic potentialities.

Music Performance with Performative Transactions

The limits of what Performative Transactions can do are the same as those of what can be encoded in the Turing-complete code of a blockchain-based smart contract. They are performative as they can take action in various environments. Thus, their potential use cases extend beyond generative processes to diverse use cases of programmable functions as actions taken in various environments. What Performative Transactions offer on top of these general programming capabilities is the interoperable and composable framework, where these actions can result from autonomous actions designed by various agents. Thanks to being encoded on the blockchain, they are reliable for further reuse in various performative processes. This could become especially interesting in virtual and augmented realities such as the metaverse,[3] where these processes might be shared not as posts explored in social media portals, but in a more tangible form – as performative objects extending the virtual environment.

One could consider a Performative Transaction specifically designed to add human-like expressiveness to a given musical structure. This hypothetical transaction would employ AI models trained on extensive datasets of human performances, to interpret and enhance a basic musical sequence, originally generated by preceding transactions. In this scenario, the expressivity-focused transaction would take an input – a musical structure that, while complete in terms of notes, rhythms, and harmonies, lacks the subtle expressive nuances of human performance. The AI model within this transaction would be tasked with injecting these nuances into the music. This could involve the addition of dynamic variations, changes in articulation, and tempo adjustments, akin to the interpretative decisions a musician makes when performing a piece. The output from this transaction would be a transformed musical piece, now enriched with the depth and nuance of human performance. This enhanced piece could either stand as a completed work or be used as input for further transactions. In a decentralized system, numerous Performative Transactions, each encoding different facets of human-like expressivity, would allow for a collaborative and cumulative approach to building these expressive transactions. Different creators could contribute their specialized transactions to the network, enriching the collective pool of expressive possibilities. Over time, as more artists would contribute and utilize these transactions, the system would evolve, becoming more diverse and capable of a wider range of expressive interpretations.

In a Performative Transaction, both a score and its performance can be a part of one intricate artistic process. This brings to mind an idea that the execution of a part of a transaction could be dependent not only on the algorithmic processes of either a programmatic function or the indeterminate AI model – the contract could include a human interaction as part of the artistic continuum. Whenever the decentralized "score" is executed, a message could be sent to a human person with a question to decide about some parameter of a musical process that could continue only when that decision is made by the human. As observed by Paulo de Assis in his chapter of this book, what is special about the connections created in decentralized systems is the very fact of acknowledging all the integral particles of a musical work in a transparent way, wherever they come from. Looking at the concept through this lens, artistic processes encoded in Decentralized Creative Networks could be seen as a new kind of modern musical score that is meant not only to represent, but actually to execute any means of both the musical determinacy and indeterminacy.

Sound Synthesis with Performative Transactions

Expanding the scope of Performative Transactions further, we can envision transactions dedicated to sound synthesis. This type of Performative Transactions would offer methods to craft and manipulate musical timbres by breaking down and reconstructing sound waves. Such Performative Transactions would leverage the Fourier Transform, a mathematical tool that decomposes a function or signal into its constituent frequencies. The practical application in a musical setting involves analyzing and synthesizing the harmonic content of sounds. The transaction would take as input a sound waveform or a series of sound waveforms and apply the Fourier Transform to dissect these into their frequency components. This analysis would provide a detailed spectrum of the sound, revealing its harmonic structure. The outputs of such Sound Synthesis Performative Transactions would be sounds or series of sounds with the newly synthesized timbre, ready to be used in further compositions or as standalone elements.

By altering the amplitudes, phases, or frequencies of these components, composers could create a vast decentralized network of hierarchically structured and related sounds and timbres. Various transactions in the network could specialize in different aspects of sound synthesis, such as spectral manipulation, granular synthesis, or physical modeling. This specialization would enable composers to access a wide range of timbres and textures, from natural-sounding instruments to entirely new, never-heard-before sounds.

Music Analysis with Performative Transactions

Within the Performative Transactions framework, musical data is inherently structured with semantic clarity, enabling straightforward exploration of any performative musical object in the blockchain-based Decentralized Creative Network. This structuring facilitates an in-depth understanding of the music's composition and its various elements, based on the predefined musical processes. To enter an existing piece of music into this framework, its values have to be transformed into relative functions. For instance, a chord [C4, E4, G4], in Performative Transactions has to be notated as a recursive pattern of functions [x, x+4, x+3] and linked to the corresponding feature which is a chromatic scale.

The conversion process could be automated for various data formats. For instance, a MIDI file has a structured list of tracks and events, which can be automatically converted to relative functions. Similarly, audio files, particularly through techniques like Fourier Transform can be decomposed into their fundamental frequency components. These components, representing aspects like pitch and time offsets, can then be translated into corresponding functions and features within the Decentralized Creative Network. The implementation of such converters from external data formats into Performative Transactions brings with it several significant advantages. Firstly, it enables seamless integration, allowing for a diverse array of musical data to be incorporated into the network. Moreover, this approach opens up creative avenues for the recombination and reinterpretation of external music. By leveraging the wide range of existing Performative Transactions, musicians and composers can explore novel ways to reconfigure and reimagine musical pieces, giving rise to innovative creations that transcend traditional boundaries. As Decentralized Creative Networks serve as ever-growing databases for the training of AI models, the capability of importing human-generated musical data is significant for further enhancing the capabilities of these models to imitate humans.

In terms of educational value, this system would offer an automated method to deconstruct and analyze complex musical pieces based on the collective musical intelligence of the network. Such an analytical tool becomes invaluable for education in music theory and composition, providing learners with insights into the intricate structures and patterns of various musical styles. Finally, by converting external music into the structured format of Decentralized Creative Networks, this method enhances the accessibility of these musical works. It allows for easier manipulation and exploration within the blockchain network, opening up new possibilities for creative experimentation and discovery. This transformation of music into a more accessible format is pivotal in fostering a more inclusive and dynamic musical ecosystem within the blockchain framework.

The Notions of Performativity and Transactions, and the Relation to Hypermusic

Performative Transactions are designed to be actively executed or 'transacted'. The 'transaction' aspect of Performative Transactions refers to the operationalization of diverse artistic processes within the blockchain. As with any transaction on the blockchain, a Performative Transaction is recorded, verified, and immutable. It is executed by a smart contract that carries out the encoded musical composition process, leaving a transparent and traceable record within the blockchain ledger.

Agents construct and enact smart contracts that describe musical transformations, referencing and recombining performative musical elements in a Decentralized Creative Network. If examined through the conceptual lens of intra-actions (Barad 2007), Performative Transactions represent a co-emergence of creative agents and technology in the blockchain environment, where the creation and interaction of musical elements do not occur in isolation but as part of a mutually constitutive process. Their actions can be viewed as performative in the sense that they do more than express – they actively construct and manipulate musical reality (Leeker 2016). The smart contracts in blockchain technology function performatively: they do not merely record transactions but actively shape the musical landscape. In this light, Performative Transaction becomes a performative act itself, one that uses the blockchain to encode, enact, and ensure the integrity of musical creativity and ownership, reflecting the deeply intertwined nature of performativity in digital cultures. This notion of 'performativity', which has evolved from a linguistic phenomenon (Austin 1962) to a multifaceted cultural force, captures the dynamic essence of digital transactions – where code and action merge to forge new creative expressions (Leeker 2016).

Performative Transactions as a conceptual framework find a compatible perspective in the concept of hypermusic, as articulated by Paulo de Assis.[4] Hypermusic extends the traditional understanding of music by incorporating a multimodal array of elements that go beyond mere auditory experiences. It draws a parallel with Timothy Morton's concept of hyperobjects – entities that are massively distributed in time and space relative to humans (Morton 2013). In hypermusic, these entities encompass not only the actual sounding configurations but also texts, images, ideas, and cultural references, forming a complex web that mirrors the interconnected nature of the modern interconnected musical world (de Assis 2023). In the realm of Performative Transactions, each performative musical process can be viewed as a 'musical hyperobject' – an entity that is not confined to singular expressions but is part of a larger, interconnected system. Performative Transactions offer a framework where music is not a fixed entity but a fluid, evolving assemblage of sounds, ideas, and processes – an approach that resonates with the ethos of hypermusic, advocating for a musical practice that is reflective of contemporary societal and technological realities and interconnected in its very essence.

On the Timeliness of Performative Transactions and the Interoperability of Decentralized Musical Processes

The concept of Performative Transactions might confront several challenges in its practical implementation and deployment on blockchain platforms. The current technological landscape of blockchains poses limitations such as block-time delay, and the already mentioned high costs associated with deploying complex solutions on-chain. These factors are significant when considering the application of Performative Transactions in real-world scenarios. One of the primary challenges is still the nascent state of the blockchain ecosystem. Implementing music algorithms within blockchain is a complex task, requiring a deep understanding of both artistic theory and computer programming. The economic dynamics within the NFT market also pose a challenge; the incentive to create a unique, standalone piece of generative art might outweigh the motivation to develop reusable components. Artists anticipating high returns from the sale of unique artworks might not see the benefit in creating components for communal use, especially in the absence of a dedicated platform for sharing such elements. Furthermore, issues of creative ownership and credit pose significant barriers. The use of generative components created by others in new artworks raises questions about who should receive credit or royalties (Zeilinger 2021). The world of generative art, music production, and blockchain technology often exist as separate cultures, which means that only a niche group of individuals is currently working at this intersection. Lacking high-level solutions, artists are compelled to work directly with blockchain's programming languages, use new emerging platforms for creating and showcasing standalone generative NFTs,[5] or revert to already developed centralized solutions, neither of which fully realize the vision of modular, hierarchical, and autonomously tracked collaborative music creation.[6]

In this respect, Performative Transactions present a timely solution not only to the above-mentioned challenges but also to the widespread issue of interoperability in blockchains. By standardizing how digital assets are represented and interacted with, the notion of Decentralized Creative Networks creates a common language for different systems to communicate, enabling various levels of interoperability between various blockchains (Łukawski 2023). By encoding operations that could be linked and inherited across various blockchains, the framework lays the theoretical groundwork for a cross-platform exchange of musical components and ideas. Importantly, until the realization of a fully on-chain system, it's possible to set up a similar network of processes within centralized or partially-centralized networks. This would lay a preliminary foundation for collaborative music creation and establish a conceptual framework for various artistic processes within the Web3 context that could be later fully transferred onto the blockchain.

Conclusion

This chapter has explored the new concepts of Decentralized Creative Networks and Performative Transactions. Decentralized Creative Networks are envisioned as new types of blockchain-based social networks, designed for collaborative art creation, where interconnected artistic processes leverage the collective intelligence of both human and post-human agents; systems where artists can transparently build upon each other's interoperable contributions. Decentralized Creative Networks could be accessed via various decentralized applications created by the community, in which users would explore musical processes and features as social media posts that can be reused to build further musical processes. These transformations could be then executed to compose new musical works, carry out artistic performances, or generate NFTs of artworks, automatically distributing any financial receivable to the creators of all referenced processes.

The chapter identified three major challenges in developing Decentralized Creative Networks: the lack of standardized methods for crafting reusable artistic processes, the inadequacy of existing file formats to capture complex hierarchical musical concepts, and the absence of a transparent system to trace both ownership and the origins of interconnected musical generative processes. To overcome these challenges, the chapter proposed a solution and a new concept in the form of Performative Transactions – transactions between the creators of composable, reusable artistic processes, executed by smart contracts. A key aspect of Performative Transactions is their capability to ensure interoperability among digital artistic processes. By standardizing how digital assets are represented and interacted with, Performative Transactions create a common language for different systems, facilitating a cross-platform exchange of musical components and ideas. This interoperability is crucial in the evolving landscape of digital arts, where the ability to seamlessly integrate and collaborate across various platforms and systems is increasingly important.

The integration of AI models and algorithms within Decentralized Creative Networks is a significant aspect of this concept, suggesting a framework where human and post-human agents, such as algorithms and AI systems, interact and transact. This interaction is not merely functional but is also performative, actively shaping the musical landscape and embodying a dynamic and autonomous process of artistic creation. The potential applications of Performative Transactions, highlighted in the chapter spanned the range from composition and performance to sound synthesis and music analysis. This versatility underscores the potential of Performative Transactions to serve as a powerful tool for artists and composers, providing a new canvas for musical exploration and innovation.

The role of blockchain and decentralization in this framework is foundational. Blockchain technology not only enables the secure and transparent tracking of ownership and provenance of musical creations but also facilitates decentralized collaboration among artists. In a decentralized system, Performative Transactions allow for a more democratic and equitable participation in the creative process, breaking down traditional barriers and gatekeeping mechanisms in the music industry. While the concept of Performative Transactions presents a forward-looking vision, its practical implementation will require addressing several delineated challenges, including technological limitations and the need for greater integration among the art, music, and blockchain communities. Further research and development in this field are essential to realize the full potential of this concept. If these challenges are overcome, Performative Transactions could significantly impact how music is created, shared, and experienced in the digital age.

Notes

1 On the Ethereum blockchain, the ERC-998 standard provides composable tokens, enabling the assembly of ERC-721 and ERC-20 tokens into distinct structures while ensuring atomic ownership management (Guidi and Michienzi 2023). This composability, however, is achieved on the level of ownership of existing NFTs, not on the level of their generative processes encoded in smart contracts (Lockyer et al. 2018).
2 For a more detailed explanation check Roberts et al. (2018).
3 Further on the artistic relations between blockchains and the metaverse in Kristof Timmerman's chapter of this book.
4 Further on this concept in the context of decentralized systems in Paulo de Assis's chapter of this book.
5 Art Blocks (2023) and Fxhash Foundation (2023) are two great examples.
6 APIs based on established platforms such as Farcaster (decentralised social network) and Fxhash (generative art platform) could enable compelling opportunities for further development in this direction.

References

Art Blocks, Inc. (2023). About. Retrieved from https://www.artblocks.io/info/about
Ashby, W. R. (1956). *An Introduction to Cybernetics*. Chapman & Hall Ltd.

de Assis, P. (2023). Hypermusic: New Musical Practices at the Crossroads of Music, Art and Thought. In E. Franco & M. Rebstock (Eds.), *New Paradigms for Music Research. Art, Society and Technology* (pp. 53–54). Universitat de València.

Audiohype. (2022, August 13). Generative Music NFTs – A Deep Dive. Retrieved November 10, 2023, from https://audiohype.io/resources/generative-music-nfts/

Austin, J. L. (1962). *How to Do Things with Words*. Oxford: University Press.

Barad, K. (2007). *Meeting the Universe Halfway: Quantum Physics and the Entanglement of Matter and Meaning*. Duke University Press.

Bishop, C. M. (2006). *Pattern Recognition and Machine Learning*. Springer.

Buterin, V. (2013). Ethereum: A Next-Generation Smart Contract and Decentralized Application Platform. Retrieved from https://ethereum.org/en/whitepaper/

Edwood, F. (2020, August 24). *Block Size and Scalability, Explained*. Cointelegraph. Retrieved from https://cointelegraph.com/explained/block-size-and-scalability-explained

Eleti, A., Harris, J., & Kilpatrick, L. (2023, June 13). *Function Calling and other API Updates*. OpenAI. https://openai.com/blog/function-calling-and-other-api-updates

Ethereum.org. (2023). Smart Contract Composability. Retrieved November 10, 2023, from https://ethereum.org/en/developers/docs/smart-contracts/composability/

Farinha, D. F. (2022). A Critical Look at Blockchain-Interactive Generative Art. *International Journal of Creative Interfaces and Computer Graphics*, 13(1), 1–17. https://doi.org/10.4018/IJCICG.308809

Fxhash Foundation. (2023). Generative Art on the Blockchain. Retrieved from https://www.fxhash.xyz/

Galanter, P. (2003). What is Generative Art? Complexity theory as a context for art theory. In *Proceedings of the 2003 International Conference on Generative Art*.

Grigg, T. (2019, January 6). *Concept Learning and Feature Spaces: How Can We Teach a Machine to Grasp an Idea?* Towards Data Science. https://towardsdatascience.com/concept-learning-and-feature-spaces-45cee19e49db

Guidi, B., & Michienzi, A. (2023). From NFT 1.0 to NFT 2.0: A Review of the Evolution of Non-Fungible Tokens. *Future Internet*, 15(6), 189. MDPI AG. Retrieved from http://doi.org/10.3390/fi15060189

Leeker, M. (2016). Performing (the) Digital: Positions of Critique in Digital Cultures. In T. Beyes, M. Leeker & I. Schipper (Ed.), *Performing the Digital: Performance Studies and Performances in Digital Cultures* (pp. 21–60). Bielefeld: Transcript Verlag. https://doi.org/10.1515/9783839433553-002

Lewin, D. (2007). *Generalized Musical Intervals and Transformations*. Oxford University Press. https://doi.org/10.1093/acprof:oso/9780195317138.001.0001

Lockyer, M., Mudge, N., Schalm, J., Echeverry, S., & Zhou, Z. V. (2018). ERC-998: Composable Non-Fungible Token [DRAFT] (Ethereum Improvement Proposals, No. 998). Retrieved from https://eips.ethereum.org/EIPS/eip-998

Łukawski, A. (2023). Fractal of Periodic Spacetime Sequences as a Framework for an Interoperable Metaverse. In K. Zreik, M. Veyrat, & M. Quiniou (Eds.), *Computer & Media Art at the Age of Metaverses and NFT* (pp. 57–74). Europia Productions.

Morton, T. (2013). *Hyperobjects: Philosophy and Ecology after the End of the World*. University of Minnesota Press.

RLXYZ. (2022, March 12). *'On-Chain Purity' in Generative Art*. Retrieved November 10, 2023, from https://mirror.xyz/0xB52D87A5097CAc5248599DB2272b02882 12eb82b/Cyij9sbeYuMmPNMJYVNhcm9Uv3N5FA_VnHTkvhqa83A

Schuijer, M. (2008). *Analyzing Atonal Music: Pitch-Class Set Theory and Its Contexts* (NED-New edition, Vol. 60). Boydell & Brewer. https://doi.org/10.1017/9781580467117

Sloman, A. (1984). The Structure of the Space of Possible Minds. In S. Torrance (Ed.), *The Mind and the Machine: Philosophical Aspects of Artificial Intelligence* (pp. 35–42). Ellis Horwood.

Smite, R. (2012). *Creative Networks in the Rearview Mirror of Eastern European History.* Institute of Network Cultures (p. 141), https://doi.org/10.25969/mediarep/19229

Stoykov, P. (2023, August 7). *Bridging Algorithms and Art: A Look into Generative NFTs.* Chainstack. Retrieved November 11, 2023, from https://chainstack.com/generative-nfts/

Summers, A. (2022). *Understanding Blockchain and Cryptocurrencies: A Primer for Implementing and Developing Blockchain Projects* (1st ed.). CRC Press. https://doi.org/10.1201/9781003187165

Roberts, A. et al. (2018, March 15). *MusicVAE: Creating a Palette for Musical Scores with Machine Learning.* Magenta TensorFlow. https://magenta.tensorflow.org/music-vae

Yao, S., Yu, D., Zhao, J., Shafran, I., Griffiths, T. L., Cao, Y., & Narasimhan, K. (2023). Tree of Thoughts: Deliberate Problem Solving with Large Language Models. Retrieved from https://arxiv.org/pdf/2305.10601.pdf

Zeilinger, M. (2021). *Tactical Entanglements: AI Art, Creative Agency, and the Limits of Intellectual Property.* Meson Press.

Zeilinger, M. (2022, November 7). *Blockchain Vitalism.* Outland. https://outland.art/blockchain-vitalism/

3

Integrating Generative AI and Blockchain Technologies to Create Musical Objects with Agency

Martin Zeilinger
Abertay University, Dundee, UK

Introduction

In recent years, increased access to sophisticated tools in the domains of artificial intelligence (AI) and decentralized computation (in particular blockchain-enabled technologies) is leading to significant developments in the landscape of digital art. In the creative experiments of artists, designers, and technologists, such developments are evident, for example, in a focus on generative processes (e.g., AI-enabled text-to-image generation) and on the production of unique digital artifacts (such as blockchain-enabled non-fungible tokens, or NFTs). For now, the bulk of creative experimentation and theoretical reflection appears to have taken place in an occularcentric mode, and with a primary focus on visual, non-time-based artforms. Drawing on this existing discourse, in this chapter I will begin to explore some opportunities that emerging AI and blockchain technologies represent for new compositional practices, performance, collaboration, and distribution of music and sound-based aesthetic artifacts. Throughout this discussion, the underlying focus is on the shifting contours of creative agency effected by AI and blockchain technologies. With this focus in mind, key concerns include the following: How can creative agency be encoded in AI-augmented and blockchain-enabled musical objects? What are the implications of this 'becoming-agential' for questions related to authorship and ownership? It will not be possible to provide conclusive answers to these questions here. Instead, my aim in this chapter is to stake the relevance and importance of the questions raised by outlining underlying concerns and perspectives. In the following sections, this is done first by offering detailed contextualization, and subsequently by discussing an ongoing multimodal art project that is of great relevance to the concerns outlined above.

DOI: 10.1201/9781003458227-4

This discussion focuses on *Holly+*, one of the few existing projects that has already begun exploring AI and blockchain technologies and their implications for creative expression, collaborative approaches to composition and performance, authorship, rights management, and, more generally, collective and collaborative decision-making in digital culture contexts. *Holly+* revolves around shared access to AI-driven voice synthesis, and features a freely accessible 'digital twin' of the voice of project initiator Holly Herndon, which is made available for anyone to use as a generative instrument. Additionally, the project initiators are developing blockchain-enabled software tools for decentralized monitoring of how the voice model is used, as well as novel approaches to licensing, profit-sharing, and distributed, collective decision-making. In its complexly layered, experimental use of the underlying technologies, *Holly+* offers an ideal context within which to begin considering the opportunities and limitations of AI- and blockchain-augmented musical practices.

AI and Blockchain Technologies in Digital Art

Most generally, experimental uses of AI and blockchain in digital art contexts concern the integration of ever-more complex and powerful computational processes into creative practices. In the domain of AI, this includes, for example, the incorporation of generative techniques based on machine learning and genetic algorithms. In the domain of blockchain technologies, it focuses on wide-ranging aspects of decentralized ledger technology (DLT), and includes, most prominently, new approaches for digitally storing and distributing aesthetic artifacts, as well as decentralizing decision-making processes concerning use of and access to such artifacts. For digital art practitioners, the technical challenges of using emerging AI and blockchain technologies remain considerable. However, new tools are increasingly becoming available in versions that feature user-friendly, web-based interfaces, that require little or no programming skills, and which use open-source and/or open-access formats. Simultaneously, vibrant communities of practitioners are being cultivated on discussion boards and social media platforms to offer instruction, support, and opportunities for collaboration. Overall, the increased accessibility of emerging AI and blockchain technologies fosters experimentation and innovation, and can empower artists to explore novel forms of expression and data-driven aesthetics.

Both AI and blockchain technologies are frequently proclaimed to have the potential for enabling 'disruptive' or even 'revolutionary' change in the broader digital landscape. The valences of such claims must be considered carefully, as they are being made across a wide ideological spectrum that reaches from anarcho-capitalist interventions and cooperativist efforts to hyper-neoliberalist visions of all-encompassing digital marketplaces and neo-colonial efforts to financialize natural resources. In the specific context of digital culture, the disruptive nature of AI and blockchain technologies is commonly understood to refer to the emergence of new forms of expression, new ontologies of art-making and artworks, and new modalities of how artistic expressions can be accessed, shared, and monetized. Taken separately, AI and blockchain technologies bring distinctly different affordances to the digital art context. However, both technological domains point toward changes and challenges that require us to rethink how the concepts of creativity, authorship, and ownership are impacted by new computational expressive techniques and by new digital solutions for producing, distributing, and consuming artworks including all kinds of musical objects.

Generative AI tools are now frequently drawn upon for automating or externalizing elements of the creative process. For everyday users or workers in the creative industries, this functionality can take a wide variety of forms: it can mean to use AI-enabled chatbots to generate working software code from natural language prompts (ChatGPT and other current-generation AI chatbots are now well capable of producing functioning software code as well as simulating its execution in system-internal virtual machines); to generate digital images based on non-visual inputs (e.g., text-to-image generators); or to extensively manipulate existing images (e.g., by using Adobe Photoshop's 'Generative Fill' tool). For artists, generative AI has made it possible to produce aesthetic objects of which one can claim – quite plausibly (and often very compellingly) – that they were made by AI, rather than by a human artist (e.g., Mazzone and Elgammal 2019). Many critics (including myself) will be quick to discount such claims as symptomatic of efforts to spectacularize the emergence of presumptively non-human intelligence and/or creativity (see Zeilinger 2021). Nevertheless, such experiments allow for intriguing and provocative thought experiments. In a philosophical vein, this has invited reconceptualizations of the notion of creativity as such (e.g., Boden 1998, Coeckelbergh 2017); more practically, it necessitates a reevaluation of how adjacent concepts, including authorship and originality, are used and administered (e.g., Stokes 2021). Overall, generative AI opens up views toward new, experimental visions of creativity that challenge the centrality of the human artist in creative processes. Consequently, across the domains of aesthetic theory, philosophy, media theory, law, and the pop-cultural mainstream, there is an abundance of debate not only of the question of whether AI-generated works can be artful, but also of whether an AI system could itself assume the role of the autonomous creator of an aesthetic artifact. Without a doubt, thanks to the extremely compelling nature of how the underlying technologies manifest in the landscape of digital culture, AI-enabled art has become a key feature of contemporary art discourse, art fairs, and art markets.

Blockchain is impacting digital art contexts quite differently. In the first decade since the pseudonymous publication of the Bitcoin protocol, a small and highly committed community of digital artists began to experiment with blockchain-enabled technologies. The most interesting among them was pushing the boundaries of conceptual art by exploring uses of this financial technology as an artistic medium (key artists include Rhea Myers, Okhaos, Telekommunisten, and Sarah Friend, to name but a few; see Kinsey and Catlow 2020, Quaranta 2022). More recently, innovations in the use of blockchain technologies for storing, distributing, and monetizing digital art have also led to a massive popularization in the cultural mainstream, resulting in an astronomical boom (and subsequent crash) of NFT-enabled digital art (Dalton 2023). Overall, this has resulted in widespread efforts to adopt new approaches to secure and decentralized data management. Simultaneously, blockchain affordances have also allowed for the development of novel techniques for encoding self-enforcing behaviors in informational artifacts, as well as new perspectives on distributed and collective decision-making regarding the stewardship and management of such artifacts. All of this is creating new opportunities for how digital artworks can be generated and stored, how their distribution can be regulated, and how access to them can be controlled.

Two developments are particularly noteworthy. Firstly, NFT technology has introduced the notion of reliable and enforceable digital scarcity (something that was until recently assumed to be impossible due to the copyability, shareability, and interchangeability of digital artifacts) (see De Filippi 2019). Secondly, blockchain-enabled artifacts can be furnished with executable software code to automate the enforcement of complex rules associated with individual digital artifacts. In the form of so-called smart contracts, this can include controlling access to and circulation of digital artworks (Seidler 2022a, 2022b). Intricate stacks of smart contracts can also be used to design new types of collaborative structures that enable the secure distribution of access, ownership claims, or consensus mechanisms across large groups of human and non-human participants in decentralized autonomous organizations (DAOs) (see Catlow and Rafferty 2022). Lastly, code-driven digital artworks that are stored on-chain can also be furnished with complex generative behaviors. Overall, the emergence of NFTs and other blockchain-enabled technologies has dramatically shifted how digital artworks are now accessed, perceived, and dealt with. Importantly, blockchain technology has now been widely absorbed into the mainstream art world. As a consequence, even though the initial NFT bubble has burst, blockchain-enabled or blockchain-based digital artworks are now regularly listed in high-profile auction catalogues, and can be found in the collections of major art museums.

From this cursory survey of how AI and blockchain are touching down in digital art contexts, a few key differences emerge regarding the impact that these separate technologies have on creative practice: in general terms, it can be said that while AI is helping to shape new perspectives on the nature of creativity as such, blockchain is reshaping our understanding of the concepts of originality and authenticity, and of the capacity for aesthetic artifacts to exhibit semi-autonomous behaviors. In combination – when digital artworks draw on affordances of both AI and blockchain-enabled technologies – this opens up opportunities for asking interesting and difficult questions: What is the nature and locus of the agency underlying the creation of a specific artwork? Who (or what) can be considered as the author or artist responsible for creating the work? If no human artist can be meaningfully linked to an aesthetic expression, can such an expression be subject to conventional ownership claims? What are the boundaries of an artwork that is distributed across a decentralized network of computational nodes? If an artwork is generative in nature and capable of exhibiting autonomous behaviors, has it ceased to be a fixed 'work' in the way in which this would have been traditionally defined?

In the current moment of fast-paced experimentation with emerging technologies, the work of digital artists provides the ideal context for tracing such questions and scoping their importance. In my view, there is every indication that in combination AI and blockchain-enabled technologies have the potential to reshape the role and functioning of the concept of agency in relation to digital art practices and digital artworks. Undeniably, both technologies already underpin a destabilizing of the centrality of human agency in digital art. Can it also be argued, by extension, that AI and blockchain can encode new types of agency in artworks directly? If this is the case, will it then become possible to speak of artworks – including musical objects – that possess agency? In the context of visual art, these questions are already being theorized. But in the context of music and sound-based artforms, this has yet to be explored more comprehensively.

From Creative Agency to Agential Assemblages

The notion of creative agency encompasses a wide range of issues, including the ability of an agent to express themselves creatively, their ability to claim authorship of the resulting artwork, and their ability to exert any measure of control over the artwork's continued existence as well as its ownership and distribution. Theories of art, particularly those beholden to Western Enlightenment traditions, additionally model their perspectives on creative agency on the assumption of the existence of a singular and unified human artist figure. In a more general sense, the concept of agency refers, quite simply,

to a capacity to act. But the integrity of this seemingly straightforward definition quickly begins to show cracks when we begin to consider what can
constitute an action, who (or what) can be considered as an agent capable
to undertaking the action, and whether anthropocentric characteristics such
as intentionality must also be taken into account (Zeilinger 2021, 42–45, for
a more detailed discussion; several articles in the special issue *Reimaginging
AI* also usefully contribute to this debate; Smith et al. 2022). In the introduction, I have suggested that the affordances of AI and blockchain technologies
effect changes in digital practices and constitute shifts in the nature and locus
of creative agency. In what follows, my aim is to unpack this argument and
explore its implications in the specific contexts of the two separate technology domains.

By definition, the concept of 'artificial intelligence' proposes that at least to
some degree, intelligence can be externalized from human hosts and bound
in computer-based artificial systems, entities, or objects. In theory, the result
is a non-human intelligent actor capable of enacting its agency, for example
by engaging autonomously and meaningfully with an environment. So far,
regardless of how spectacular the emerging capabilities of AI systems may
appear to be, this externalization of agency only amounts to limited simulations of intelligence. Nevertheless, even minimally agential AI system can
now generate images, extensive text passages, moving images, sounds, and
musical phrases that are likely to be perceived as creative or artful by all but
the most discerning human viewers, listeners, or readers. Following prevailing aesthetic norms, such systems would therefore have to be seen as capable
of behaving creatively and of creating artworks. If such a view is accepted,
traditional norms regarding the fundamentally human nature of creativity
and art-making are being challenged. Generative AI systems, in other words,
have the power to destabilize assumptions regarding the centrality of human
artists in creative processes. As I have written elsewhere, this can help to
'problematize the humanist vision of the singular, unified human agent [and]
of the spirited (genius?) individual as sole originator of creative expressions'
(Zeilinger. 2021, 14).

Current AI systems are still far removed from the notion of a 'general artificial intelligence' (Fjelland 2020; but see also McIntosh et al. 2023), and it is
clear that such systems cannot operate in full autonomy from human agents.
This problematizes any claim that creative agency can be fully externalized
in an AI system. One approach to counteracting such objections is to adopt a
posthumanist perspective that does not rely on the notion of a singular host
of agency, and which can conceive of agency as being located in fluid and
open-ended entanglements between any number of intra-actants that co-
constitute agential assemblages (see, for example, Barad 2007, Braidotti 2013).
It is against this conceptual backdrop that new forms of creative agency can
be most fruitfully explored. In my own view, the 'speculative scattering of
agency across human-machinic-algorithmic assemblages' (Zeilinger 2021, 45)

that we find in artistic experimentation with AI presents an ideal context for this kind of rethinking.

When it comes to blockchain technologies, conceptual connections to creative agency must be calibrated differently. Most generally, a blockchain is, above all else, an information storage medium. Nevertheless, some of the technology's idiosyncratic computational affordances make it possible to stage new and innovate interventions in existing creative processes by using blockchain as an expressive medium. With the tools and functionalities currently available, such interventions tend to take the form of digital objects imbued with semi-autonomous, self-enforcing behaviors. A shared underlying premise for blockchain technology is the aim of creating information storage and exchange solutions in which potentially untrustworthy human intermediaries are replaced by algorithmically determined and verifiable computational agents, which can monitor information flow and mediate exchanges between participants (both and non-human) in an information network. In other words, a shift of agency from human to computational actants (paralleled by new types of algorithmic frameworks for mediating engagement between agents) is a fundamental characteristic of blockchain technology. One prominent manifestation of this shift can be observed when blockchain-enabled artifacts use smart contract features (Zeilinger forthcoming).

A smart contract is a small executable program hosted at a specific account address on a blockchain. Most commonly, smart contracts are associated with discrete blockchain-stored assets, such as NFTs. As the name indicates, a smart contract serves to enforce a set of predefined rules; importantly, the algorithmic nature of a smart contract makes it 'self-enforcing', meaning that human agents (or other computational agents) cannot interfere with the enforcement of rules when a smart contract–augmented event takes place. Smart contract functionality is conventionally triggered when transactions occur, for example when an NFT is transferred from one wallet to another. In theory, there is no limit to the kinds of functions a smart contract can be designed to carry out. Importantly, from a human user perspective, smart contract functions will manifest as autonomous behaviors controlled by an agency external to the human user. Many common functions of smart contracts are invisible; this may include the verification of ownership records, the recording of transactions logs, or the updating of accurate pricing information in response to market movement. Other functions, however, can be much more visible, and it is here that shifts in the perception of creative agency have the strongest impact. For example, smart contract functionality can be set to cause iteration, mutation, re- or degeneration, or deletion of informational objects that constitute digital artworks (Zeilinger 2022). Like all contracts, smart contracts govern interactions between agents and can enforce conditions that are connected to these interactions. This means that smart contracts can enforce instructions, requirements, and limitations concerning how an artwork interfaces with the world, including what can or must be done with it. As such, smart contracts are capable of achieving much more than merely a static impact on the look and feel of a fixed artwork. They are capable of encoding artworks with dynamic and highly complex behaviors, and, additionally, of shaping the behaviors of the human and/or computational agents that engage with the artworks.

A simple example of such functionality can be observed in Rhea Myers' blockchain-enabled artwork *Is Art* (2014). The work is represented by a self-enforcing contract hosted on the Ethereum blockchain. Visually, the work consists of a simple webpage displaying three lines of text, which can be switched between two states by contract events. This occurs when the contract registers a transaction (i.e., when the work is bought/sold) and switches between the two possible display states, triggering a display change from 'This contract is art' to 'This contract is not art' (or vice versa). As such, the work is an early example of on-chain, smart contract–enabled digital art. Like much of Myers' work, it offers critical and humorous commentary both on arthistorical traditions of contract-based conceptual art and on the powers of validation/ valuation conveyed through sales in the contemporary art market.

It is, at this point, relatively easy to imagine how creative agency can be embodied (or at the very least simulated) in AI and blockchain technologies, respectively. This is already achieved very powerfully both in mainstream generative AI applications, and in blockchain functionality such as self-enforcing smart contracts. I have elsewhere discussed at length how collaborations between human artists and minimally agential computational processes can be described as expressive assemblages in which creative agency has become complexly redistributed between human and non-human actants (Zeilinger 2021). Building on this notion, how might we imagine creative agential assemblages that combine AI and blockchain features, as I have outlined them here? In its simplest forms, such an assemblage could combine layers of already existing features from the AI and blockchain domains. This would result in an integrated stack of minimally agential elements that could link AI and blockchain capabilities with human input to create a more complex assemblage. We can imagine, for example, a digital artwork that consists of a static visual element combined with dynamic behaviors. This hypothetical artwork could initially rely on human natural language input, and use LLM functionality to turn human input into a prompt for AI-augmented text-to-image generation; the generative output could then automatically be uploaded to an IPFS (InterPlanetary File System) location, and become linked to an auto-generated smart contract tasked with monitoring the circulation of the resulting artwork and controlling its monetization.

In this example, existing software features are linked with human input in a simple chain of behaviors. Taken individually, these functions and processes may not be taken to constitute creative expression. But as a stack of interlinked, minimally agential, self-enforcing behaviors, the assemblage could be described as a digital artwork with relatively complex self-governing behaviors. (In this example, the artwork involves a human actant at the outset; but we can also imagine a scenario in which human input is more completely removed from the equation.) Of course, there is a fine line to be drawn between creative expression and the mere automation of tasks designed to simulate creativity. Careful calibration of the individual steps and their interplay is needed, and there is no guarantee that the outcome will pass as an artwork; however, it could certainly serve as a passable starting point for a proof of concept.

With the given focus for this chapter, the next step is to explore what forms could be assumed by musical objects that combine AI and blockchain affordances for the creation of agential assemblages in which human and non-human actants collaborate in composing, performing, reworking, and/or sharing sound-based informational elements to integrate stacks of agential components.

Holly+: Musical Experiments with the Combination of AI and Blockchain

Holly+ (2021, ongoing) is one of the few larger-scale music-focused art projects that are already experimenting with the integration of AI and blockchain technologies. The project was conceived by the media artist, performer, and composer Holly Herndon, and has been co-developed with a range of technical, artistic, and legal advisors and collaborators. At the time of writing, the project is under commission for a large solo exhibition at Serpentine Galleries in London. Its aim is to explore new perspectives on AI-enabled music-making and sound art, while also driving the development of new, blockchain-augmented solutions to rights management. In combining these elements, the project addresses important questions concerning the shifting nature of authorship, creativity, creative agency, and collective decision-making in digital contexts. Released in stages and still under development, *Holly+* consists of experimental creative tools, licensing mechanisms, and a decentralized community platform featuring novel consensus protocols. Taken together, these elements aim to represent a 'full stack' suite for composition, collaboration, distribution, monetization, and management. This is available to be used by anyone, and addresses itself to experimental performers, amateur music/tech enthusiasts, and professional musicians alike.

For the project's main element, the *Holly+ Voice Tool*, a custom voice model was trained 'on multiple hours of Holly Herndon's isolated vocal stems to create a generative instrument that retains the pitches and rhythms of a user-uploaded audio file, but adds textures and timbres learned from the training set' (Herndon 2021). The tool was released through a simple-to-use web interface that allows any user to submit audio files, which will be automatically analyzed, processed, and converted into a downloadable file that features the 'digital twin' of Herndon's voice. By making an instrument based on her voice available for anyone to use, Herndon directly addresses a number of difficult questions that have been hotly debated for several years: Can artist's own their voice? Can stylistic aspects of voice be formalized in such a way that any uses of the voice can be monitored? What licensing or compensation model could be designed to fairly regulate creative uses of voice models?

By enabling the production of a growing body of creative expressions that use her voice, Herndon has opened a path toward critical dialogue with everyone using the voice model as well as the audiences of those creations. The provision of a 'digital twin' of the artist's voice in the form of a free-to-use generative instrument represents a direct externalization of key elements of Herndon's creative agency, and an open invitation to join the artist in exploring the critical implications of this step. When artists use the tool for their own work, they will infuse this AI-based creative tool with their own aesthetics, style, artistic voice, and authorial intentions, further complicating the complex layering of creative agency that characterizes the final outcome. Every user may justifiably have an interest in claiming cultural ownership of anything they have created with the *Holly+ Voice Tool*. They will also understand that by having used the tool, they have become important elements in an intricate assemblage of multiple human and non-human voices, which makes it difficult to separate out distinctly different types and hosts of creative agency. The result is an easily perceived need for a dialogue concerning the nature of each musical expression that has been created by using the digital twin of Herndon's voice. What assemblage of human artists can be said to have created each such expression, and how precisely could we describe the creative agency embodied in the creation?

Any dialogue concerning these concerns is very likely also to raise more practical questions regarding the status of musical expressions creating with *Holly+*. How to assign authorship? How can legal and moral rights held in the expressions be divided among human (and non-human) collaborators? These questions connect directly to the second key element of *Holly+*, which concerns the exploration of rights management and legal issues connected to voice ownership. While Herndon makes a point of retaining the exclusive right of using her own 'physical voice' (ibid.), the *Holly+* digital vocal twin is made accessible in an open-source format. This encourages experimentation and 'forking' of the model, and represents a further step in Herndon's strategy of divesting herself of creative agency with regard to strict control over use of her voice. As part of a brief analysis of legal precedent on the project website, Herndon notes that

> [w]hile a public figure is protected from unlicensed commercial exploitation of their vocal likeness, there are also great benefits to offering the public open source access to a voice model, ensuring that all derivative works created through experimentation in the voice would also be open source and not commercially exploitable.
>
> **(ibid.)**

The main benefit, as Herndon argues by way of McKenzie Wark (2017), is that wider circulation of the voice model will increase its perceived value (which may be aesthetic, cultural, or monetary in nature), and, by extension, also the value of the works created with it. This argument resonates with critical perspectives on value-creation in digital art contexts (e.g., O'Dwyer 2020), and points toward a need for renegotiating how value should be captured, preserved, and distributed. Herndon's vision for *Holly+* clearly suggests that all agents assembled in the creative process should have the opportunity to participate in this negotiation, and should perhaps even recognize a responsibility for doing so, in order to facilitate an inclusive, distributed, and fair process.

To make this possible, Herndon is developing the *Holly+* DAO. DAOs, as noted earlier, are blockchain-enabled computational structures that may take the form of self-governing digital organizations whose rules, ideals, and values are encoded in and enforced by smart contracts. As such, DAOs revolve around the algorithmic administering of the rights and responsibilities of their members. Their operation is fundamentally aimed at redistributing agency, and is therefore 'defined by the negotiation of reconfigured relations between all stakeholders in the production and organisation of resources and communities' (Catlow and Rafferty 2022, 29). The role of the *Holly+* DAO, in this sense, will be to coordinate non-hierarchical stewardship of the project's underlying voice model, to uphold the cultural values which the organization wishes to represent, and to manage any commercial values the project might generate.

In practical terms, the *Holly+* DAO is envisioned to incorporate a set of open-source, modular elements alongside a custom ERC-20 token (called VOICE) on the Ethereum blockchain. On the technical side, this includes the well-supported Tribute DAO Framework, which relies on the underlying OpenLaw Framework for contract design. VOICE tokens are to be issued to project collaborators, collectors of Herndon's work, and artists invited to use the voice model. Token holders will then serve as stewards of the voice model, the resulting works, and the values they represent. DAO members will have the right to vote on commissioning new works, and take part in decision-making regarding the licensing of the voice model and existing works. As project stakeholders, they will be entitled to a share of any profits to be realized, and therefore have a strong incentive to act to the benefit of the community they co-represent. Overall, while the AI elements of *Holly+* foreground a redistribution of agency with regard to creative input, the DAO's purpose is to redistribute agency with regard to authorial control and rights management. For the purpose of shifting agency from a single author figure to many participating artists, a DAO – with its reliance on code-based, decentralized, non-hierarchical rule structures that are collaboratively designed and enacted – could indeed be the ideal vehicle.

Critique and Outlook: Moving beyond the Singular Artist Figure, Breaking with the Traditional Work Concept

Holly+ is an important project in many ways: it moves emerging generative AI technologies from the sphere of corporate R&D labs to a more public sphere of artistic experimentation; it makes these technologies accessible, and instrumentalizes them to address concerns that are widespread in artistic communities (e.g., loss of agency, loss of voice); it empowers users as participants and invites them to engage in critical, practice-oriented dialogue with the intersecting domains of digital art, intellectual property regulation, arts advocacy, and innovative forms of community organization; it develops and implements novel blockchain-enabled software tools to create a new management structure, and in doing so develops new perspectives on cultural stewardship, co-ownership, and rights management; it aims to keep all technological innovation user-friendly, understandable, and community-oriented. All of these aspects link back to the broader underlying concept of creative agency, which is here being reimagined, redefined, and redeployed for a cultural landscape that is now strongly impacted by the emergence of AI and blockchain technologies. The digital infrastructure that *Holly+* undertakes to design allows for the form, function, and situatedness of creative agency to be recalibrated collectively and experimentally, by an assemblage of human and non-human participants.

Importantly, even though *Holly+* is a multimodal project with many independent stakeholders who may have different aims, participants align against a common target: the misappropriation of creative agency (i.e., artists' voices) through corporate entities in the creative industries. In this sense, *Holly+* is a preemptive strike. Recognizing that 'the opportunities and complications inherent to these techniques will only intensify' (Herndon 2021), Herndon has chosen to coordinate a horizontal redistribution of agency and control over her artistic voice, before it can be absorbed into the bowels of a corporate entertainment industry with a long history of exploiting artists.

Holly+ is not the first project to experiment with the design of new permissions layers for the purpose of renegotiating control over authorial expressions and creative agency. The Creative Commons (CC) initiative, which introduced an alternative model for copyright licensing that is widely used by musicians, is a good example of an existing effort with similar aims. But CC, despite its innovations and advantages, has also been criticized for the extent to which it relies on the integrity of the underlying copyright regimes which it is meant to overcome (e.g., Berry and Moss 2005). Put simply, CC is a continuation of traditional property-oriented access restrictions by other means. Additionally, the terms of alternative CC licenses are very difficult to enforce. Is it to be expected that *Holly+* will suffer from similar limitations?

Conceptually, the project functions very differently. Rather than slightly adjusting preexisting perspectives on agency, every element of *Holly+* points to a move away from the singular, conventionally circumscribed artist figure as the sole (and inevitably human) source and seat of agency, authorship, and ownership claims. In place of such a singular figure, *Holly+* imagines a multiplicitous, fragmentary, and distributed agential assemblage. Traditionally, the artist's voice has been one of the most potent signifiers for the singularity of artistic identity and authorial agency. In *Holly+*, the digital twin of Herndon's voice functions as a provocative and extremely compelling vehicle for driving a shift away from preconceptions regarding the centrality and singularity of human creative agency.

It must be assumed, nevertheless, that musical objects generated as part of this project will take the form of relatively traditional works – most likely audio recordings of compositions that have clearly identifiable human creators. So far, it also appears that the rights management mechanisms developed for *Holly+* will resemble well-established templates regarding author and user rights, and will also match the ambitions encoded in such templates. Ultimately, the goal of *Holly+* remains regulating the monetization of clearly defined cultural properties created by project participants. It must be asked, then, how experimental the project's integration of generative AI and blockchain is really going to be. On the one hand, agency and control over creative processes and rights management are here certainly being negotiated in novel distributions and through novel mechanisms. On the other hand, it is very possible that *Holly+*'s new models for author rights enforcement and for the propertization of creative expression will perpetuate fundamental principles of intellectual property regulation, rather than moving beyond them.

As such, *Holly+* is an excellent first step, but it must be hoped that the project will push its exploration of the creative and critical affordances of generative AI and blockchain-enabled technologies as far as possible. As discussed, generative AI tools will here serve to reorganize the distribution of creative agency, by making Herndon's voice available as a free-to-use instrument for other artists. However, for now it appears that the resulting musical objects remain bound by conventional views on how a musical work is constituted, and how its authorship is defined. In more experimental approaches, techniques involving generative AI could serve to destabilize traditional perspectives on creative agency more strongly and more fully. A similar critique applies to the way in which *Holly+* currently envisions the implementation of a stakeholder DAO. For now, it looks like the *Holly+ DAO* is poised to serve primarily as a community-managed financial infrastructure with the goal of incentivizing stakeholder participation through profit sharing. This certainly represents a massive step beyond the forms of centralized, hierarchical economic control that musicians currently experience at the hands of labels, publishers, and streaming platforms. But it also suggests a continuation of a long-established trend toward the financialization of creative practice (Zeilinger 2018).

Holly+ is a sophisticated experiment in the horizontal distribution of creative and authorial agency when it comes to musical objects. Overall, the project is, without a doubt, moving toward establishing an assemblage of creator-stakeholder-stewards that will involve minimally agential computational entities operating alongside human participants. The laudable goal is to rethink creative processes and rights management in the context of emerging technologies that are already threatening to further disempower artists by appropriating their voices for commercial exploitation. In this sense, *Holly+* is about exploring what it will mean, in the era of generative AI and blockchain, to make music, to listen to it, and to own musical works. When it comes to nudging these technologies toward the development of musical objects with agency, I suspect that we can still push much further.

For now, many questions, challenges, and opportunities remain. As *Holly+* demonstrates, when expressive technologies (such as generative AI) are combined with administrative technologies (such as blockchain-enabled DAOs), it can become difficult to hold on to broadly applicable definitions of 'agency' that relate equally to all project elements. How, for example, should we think of the minimally agential (yet very compelling) expressivity of generative AI models alongside the minimally agential (yet equally powerful) functionality of smart contracts? Clearly, creativity and governance are two very different dimensions of 'agency' broadly conceived. As we move closer toward accessible and easy-to-use AI and blockchain tools, creative experiments and the development of experimental governance tools will continue to co-evolve. What protocols already exist – in and beyond the AI and blockchain domains – for redistributing agency across musical objects and all those who participate in creating and consuming them? What forms will musical objects take when they draw more fully on the affordances of these underlying technologies? Projects such as *Holly+* represent an exciting step in exploring what vocabulary of musicological, technical, legal, and aesthetic discourse we will we need to develop while we continue to imagine new musical objects with agency.

Works Cited

Barad, Karen. *Meeting the Universe Halfway*. Durham: Duke University Press, 2007.
Berry, David M., and Giles Moss. "On the 'Creative Commons': A Critique of the Commons without Commonalty." *Free Software Magazine* 5 (2005): 1–4.
Boden, Margaret A. "Creativity and Artificial Intelligence." *Artificial Intelligence* 103.1–2 (1998): 347–356.

Braidotti, Rosi. *The Posthuman*. John Wiley & Sons, 2013.

Catlow, Ruth, and Penny Rafferty, eds. *Radical Friends*. Torque Editions, 2022.

Coeckelbergh, Mark. "Can Machines Create Art?" *Philosophy & Technology* 30.3(2017): 1–19.

"Creative Commons." n.d. (Web) https://creativecommons.org/

Dalton, Kellie. "The Rise and Fall of the Nft Empire: The Social Phenomenon of Non-Fungible Tokens." 2023.

De Filippi, Primavera. "Bitcoin." *A History of Intellectual Property in 50 Objects*. Eds. D Haunter, and C. Op den Kamp. A History of Intellectual Property in 50 Objects. Cambridge: Cambridge University Press, 2019, 409–428.

Fjelland, Ragnar. "Why General Artificial Intelligence Will Not Be Realized." *Humanities and Social Sciences Communications* 7.1(2020) https://doi.org/10.1057/s41599-020-0494-4

Herndon, Holly. "Holly+." 2021 (Web).

Kinsey, Cadence, and Ruth Catlow. "A Blockchain Art History Timeline." 2020.

Mazzone, Marian, and Ahmed Elgammal. "Art, Creativity, and the Potential of Artificial Intelligence." *Arts* 8.1(2019): 26–29.

McIntosh, Timothy R., Teo Susnjak et al. "From Google Gemini to Openai Q*(q-Star): A Survey of Reshaping the Generative Artificial Intelligence (Ai) Research Landscape." *arXiv preprint arXiv:2312.10868*. 2023.

O'Dwyer, Rachel. "Limited Edition: Producing Artificial Scarcity for Digital Art on the Blockchain and Its Implications for the Cultural Industries." *Convergence: The International Journal of Research into New Media Technologies* 26.4 (2020): 874–894.

"Openlaw Framework." n.d. (Web) https://docs.openlaw.io/

Quaranta, Domenico. *Surfing With Satoshi: Art, Blockchain and Nfts*. Ljubljana: Aksioma, 2022.

Seidler, Paul. "On Smart Contracts as a Medium (Part 1)." 2022a. (Web).

Seidler, Paul. "On Smart Contracts as a Medium (Part 2)." 2022b. (Web).

Smith, Dominic, Natasha Lushetich et al. "Reimagining Ai: Introduction." *Journal of Aesthetics and Phenomenology* 9.2 (2022): 87–99.

Stokes, Simon. *Art and Copyright*. Bloomsbury Publishing, 2021. Print.

"Tribute Dao." n.d. (Web) https://tributedao.com/

Wark, McKenzie. "My Collectible Ass." *E-Flux*, 2017.

Zeilinger, Martin. "Digital Art as 'Monetised Graphics': Enforcing Intellectual Property on the Blockchain." *Philosophy & Technology* 20.3(2018): 1–27.

Zeilinger, Martin. *Tactical Entanglements: Ai Art, Creative Agency, and the Limits of Intellectual Property*. Lüneburg: Meson Press, 2021.

Zeilinger, Martin. "Blockchain Vitalism." 2022. Outland.art. (Web).

Zeilinger, Martin. "Smart Contracts and the Becoming-Curatorial of Digital Art Objects." *Curating Superintelligences: Speculations on the Future of Curating, a.I. And Hybrid Realities*. Eds. Joasia Krysa, and Magdalena Tyżlik-Carver. London: Open Humanities Press, forthcoming. Print.

4

Valuing Web3 Music: From NFT Prices to the Quadruple Bottom Line

Marcus O'Dair

University of the Arts London, London, UK

Blockchain and Web3 technologies were originally understood in a narrowly financial context, associated with cryptocurrencies such as Bitcoin. Non-fungible tokens, or NFTs, have put music (and other creative economy use cases such as art and gaming) center stage. Yet there remains a widespread misconception that speculative investments in cryptocurrencies and NFTs are the be-all and end-all of Web3. This chapter examines the potential impact of blockchain technology on the music industry from a more holistic perspective. Specifically, its contribution lies in proposing four lenses through which we can view Web3 music: financial, social, environmental and experiential. By examining the value of tokens – fungible as well as non-fungible – in terms that go beyond short-term price fluctuations, I hope to deepen our understanding of cultural value in Web3 and beyond.

Introduction

Blockchain technology first emerged as the distributed database underpinning Bitcoin, the peer-to-peer electronic cash system (Nakamoto 2008). Over time, it became clear that the same distributed database could be used for other kinds of digital assets with a similar 'double spend' problem, and use cases expanded significantly when the Ethereum blockchain introduced programmable transactions in the form of so-called smart contracts.

Today, some see blockchains as enabling a new era of the Web known as Web3. This marks a distinct shift from the read-only Internet that lasted until the early 2000s (Web1) and the read-write Internet that followed (Web2). If Web1 was *Encyclopaedia Britannica Online*, Web2 was Twitter and Facebook, Uber, and Airbnb. In Web2, argues Tapscott (2023: 9), your Instagram posts and TikTok videos create financial value that you can't fully capture and

DOI: 10.1201/9781003458227-5

platforms hoover up your data in the process: a scenario described as 'choke-point capitalism' (Giblin and Doctorow 2022) or even 'technofeudalism' (Varoufakis 2023). Web3, advocates insist, could be read-write-*own*: creators can own rather than merely rent, since, at least in theory, we are free to move our assets from one platform to another. Interoperability of this kind could be the key to moving beyond the walled gardens of Web2 big tech (Doctorow 2023).

To date, the impact of blockchain technology on the music industry, specifically, can be divided into two waves. The first began around October 2015, when the British singer, songwriter, and musician Imogen Heap released a song called 'Tiny Human' on the Ethereum blockchain. It ended in early 2018, when cryptocurrency prices fell sharply and 'initial coin offerings', or ICOs – the main funding mechanism for many start-ups at the time – largely dried up. The second wave kicked off around February 2021, when the American electronic musician Justin Blau, better known as 3LAU, made $11 million in 24 hours from non-fungible token, or NFT, sales linked to his *Ultraviolet* album. It lasted until late 2022 when cryptocurrency prices fell again.

As an artist, Heap was the exception: music's first blockchain wave was largely business-to-business, dominated by start-ups with bold ideas of destroying the 'legacy' music industry and a few incumbents moving into the space rather more tentatively. Music's second blockchain wave, by contrast, was business-to-consumer. This was very largely thanks to NFTs, which could be minted by musicians and purchased by fans. An NFT, in brief, is a certificate of authenticity, stored on a blockchain, that gives the holder a unique connection to an asset. If this sounds somewhat prosaic, we could say instead that NFTs introduce scarcity into a digital landscape otherwise characterized by abundance. Either way, the NFT market was worth more than $40 billion by the end of 2021, and *Collins Dictionary* made 'NFT' its word of the year.

For those paying attention, something resembling an NFT had in fact emerged toward the end of the first blockchain wave in the form of Crypto-Kitties, a game based around collecting and breeding digital cats, and CryptoPunks, a collection of 10,000 algorithmically generated punk images. But few recognized their importance. In the second wave, by contrast, NFTs felt like the only game in town. As I recall only too well, having set up and led a Blockchain Creative Industries research cluster back in 2016, music and the rest of the creative economy felt like a sideshow in the first blockchain wave. NFTs changed everything – the pivotal moment coming in 2021 when Christie's sold a digital artwork and NFT by Mike Winklemann, known as Beeple, for $69,346,250. NFTs remains primarily associated with profile pictures collections such as CryptoPunks and Bored Ape Yacht Club, which launched in 2021. Yet they have been big in music too, minted by artists across the board from rock (Mick Jagger, Kings of Leon, Muse) to hip-hop (Snoop Dogg, Nas, Timbaland).

What can we learn from this short history? One lesson is that we need to look beyond the technology itself to the associated assets. The first block-chain wave primarily focused on intellectual property, in the form of songs and recordings. While use cases varied, value propositions typically concerned increased efficiency, speed, and transparency in relation to recording and publishing rights (O'Dair and Beaven 2017). Some believed that the technology could turn the music industry's various databases of intellectual property information into a distributed network, thereby managing what the Global Repertoire Database failed to achieve. There was also a focus on live performance, in that some start-ups attempted to use blockchain to tackle secondary ticketing, but this was very much a secondary concern. Songs and recordings were also a focus of the second wave: 'collectible' NFTs, for instance, can be traded like rare vinyl or merchandise, while others entitle the holder to a share of royalties. However, there were also many more experiments beyond songs and recordings: an NFT could also, for instance, allow access to a gated community. The technology might have been similar, but its application was shifting.

A second lesson from the music industry's two blockchain waves to date is that adoption takes time. Blockchain may indeed have the potential to usher in a techno-economic paradigm, but we are still early in the 'installation period': the steady growth of the 'deployment period' is some way (Perez 2002). Web3 is in its infancy and numerous barriers to adoption remain – technological, political, economic, social, legal, and environmental (O'Dair 2019). On the other hand, the technology is improving fast, and NFTs did significantly accelerate adoption.

Types of Value beyond the Financial

The second wave is now over: 2023's annual report by umbrella trade body UK Music, for instance, makes more than one reference to artificial intelligence but ignores blockchains and Web3 (UK Music 2023). Yet the crash after blockchains second wave feels milder than in 2018 – a bear market rather than a full winter. While Web3 has not yet had its ChatGPT moment, it would be naïve of the music industry not to expect a third blockchain wave and perhaps a fourth and fifth, which will quite possibly involve a degree of convergence with artificial intelligence and/or immersive technologies and the metaverse. The question, then, is not whether or not blockchains will ever gain widespread adoption within the music industry. Instead, it is this: if Web3 *does* gain adoption, will it be good or bad for the music industry? What, in other words, is its value?

In fact, this question needs refining in two respects. Firstly, we need to explain which type of value we are talking about. When people talk about the value of Web3, in the music industry as elsewhere, they almost always mean financial value. This goes for Web3 critics, for instance, those who – wrongly, in my opinion – dismiss Imogen Heap's 'Tiny Human' as a failure because, at least using Eth prices at the time, it only made $133. But it goes too for Web3 advocates: those, for instance, who argue that the music industry can't afford to ignore Web3 now that someone paid $69,346,250 for Beeple's *Everydays*, or that the crypto market cap has far exceeded a trillion dollars. Not surprisingly, given the origins in Bitcoin as an alternative to traditional banking, blockchains have always been seen in the context of financial technology, or 'fintech'. Yet to associate them only with financial value is to assume that Web3 is often a mixing desk with just one fader. For a more holistic understanding, we need to consider other types of value. In this section, I set out a framework for this broader way of thinking about Web3, arguing that that we need to consider four types of value – financial, social, environmental, and experiential – if we are to gain a more holistic understanding. We need, in other words, to understand Web3 value as pluralistic: a mixing desk with four channels rather than just one. This is my focus in the next section of this chapter.

Secondly, we need to distinguish between stakeholder groups: the music industry is far from homogenous. The music industry is made up of multiple stakeholder groups: at the risk of pushing the analogy too far, there are many mixing desks rather than just one. Good news for record labels, for instance, might be bad news for artists. This is my focus in the subsequent section of this chapter.

Social Value

Rather than concentrating only on the single bottom line of financial profit, Elkington (1997) suggested that organizations should instead work to a 'triple bottom line' of financial, social, and environmental value – or profit, people, and planet. Such a concept remains useful if we zoom out to the scale of a phenomenon such as Web3 music. The key point is the same: a narrow focus on financial value creates serious blind spots.

When we consider Web3 in terms of social value, the second of Elkington's bottom lines, we see its potential to create value. Some have suggested that Web3 could generate opportunities for those in the global south: see, for instance, the popularity of play-to-earn gaming apps in the Philippines. Advocates also argue that Web3 can reward fans for their attention just as it rewards creators for their content. Arguably, Web3 can shift power from big tech to users, thereby encouraging self-governance and community ownership (Scholz and Schneider 2017). Consider, for instance, the player-owned economy of Axie Infinity, a popular blockchain-based virtual world.

It is also worth remembering that, while tokens are the building blocks of Web3, those tokens don't need to be non-fungible. Several other types of token exist – cryptocurrencies, protocol tokens, governance tokens, oracle tokens, interoperability tokens, corporate tokens, natural asset tokens, stablecoins, and central bank digital currencies – and we can expect 'dozens, perhaps hundreds' more (Tapscott 2023: 73). One interesting phenomenon is the non-transferable *soul-bound* token, tied to an individual for life (Weyl et al. 2022). Soul-bound tokens emphasize trust and cooperation rather than the chance to make a quick buck. Another interesting case is the *fungible* token that allows access to social experiences: some kind of exclusive community, perhaps even governance rights over an artist's career or creative process.

Yet we should also recognize Web3's potential to destroy social value. For one thing, there is no guarantee that Web3 work is ideologically progressive: some of the individual images that make up Beeple's *Everydays*, for instance, have been criticized as racist, sexist, homophobic, and generally 'objectionable' (Whitaker and Abrams 2023 9). For another thing, Web3 seems oddly dependent on centralized entities for an ostensibly decentralized world. Consider, for instance, the importance of exchanges like FTX and Binance, and of NFT marketplaces like OpenSea. Decentralized technologies do not necessarily decentralize power (Catlow 2017). True, these might be new intermediaries – but there is no guarantee that they are preferable to the current ones: consider the collapse of the FTX cryptocurrency exchange in 2022 and the subsequent fraud conviction of founder Sam Bankman-Fried, or the money laundering charges faced by Binance and former CEO Changpeng Zhao in 2023. And Web2 intermediaries have hardly disappeared. Far from being a challenge to the existing order, some see blockchain technology as a tool for existing power to concentrate itself (Golumbia 2016): there are *incorporative* applications that seek to increase efficiency within an existing order, as well as *radical* applications that seek to create a completely new techno-economic order (Schwartz 2017).

Environmental Value

Consideration of environmental value, the third of Elkington's bottom lines, has become much more prominent since music's first blockchain wave, when proof-of-work consensus mechanisms were the only game in town – and the use of computational resources for 'mining' was a feature rather than a bug. This meant that, at least until recently, the blockchains on which some NFTs run have had a negative impact on the environment. It has been claimed, for instance, that buying an NFT artwork used the same amount of energy as the average EU household uses in a month (Truby et al. 2022).

Happily, the Ethereum blockchain has now moved to proof-of-stake rather than proof-of-work consensus mechanism, in the process reducing energy consumption by a reported 99.95%. Other initiatives that have attempted to address energy concerns include Tezos, which self-identifies as eco-friendly; Algorand, which self-identifies as sustainable and green; and Polygon, which describes itself as currently carbon-neutral but with an intention to become climate-positive. While we may be moving in the right direction, however, we need a far more sophisticated understanding of the differences, if any, between such apparent synonyms as eco-friendly, sustainable, green, and carbon-neutral. We also need, more than anything, to move from being 'less bad' for the environment to being positively *good* for the environment (Braungart and McDonough 2009).

There are Web3 initiatives working for such positive environmental impact, Regen Network, for instance, is a platform allowing corporations to buy, trade, and retire carbon and ecological credits to meet their climate commitments, with the aim of restoring biodiversity and not just slowing but reversing climate change. We might think too of early blockchain art projects such as Terra0, a self-owning forest. Web3 music still does not yet have an equivalent of such a self-owning, self-reproducing forest. Serenade, to take one prominent music start-up, claims to be able to produce 1.45 million digital pressings before its carbon emissions match that of a single cup of coffee (Serenade 2023). That still puts it in the category of 'less bad' rather than 'good' – although, to be fair, recorded music's history of environmental harm predates Web3 by decades (Devine 2019).

Experiential Value

I have taken the liberty of extending Elkington's work by adding in a fourth type of value: experiential. After all, this chapter examines Web3 in the context of the music industry – and, while intrinsic and extrinsic motivation are often interwoven (Bilton et al. 2021), people in the creative industries tend to be motivated at least in part by their commitment to art for art's sake (Caves 2000).

One way to consider intrinsic value in Web3 would be through aesthetics: Bored Ape profile pictures, for instance, have been dismissed as 'objectively hideous' (Cooper 2022). Yet questions of aesthetic value are *not* objective (Throsby 2001). Instead, they are rooted in taste – and taste is socially constructed (Bourdieu 1984). Instead, I prefer to consider *experiential* value: 'the artwork or cultural product is not simply a fixed object to be consumed' but an event that 'works with and in experience' (Negus and Pickering 2004: 43). I agree with Crossick and Kaszynska (2016) that there has been a curious tendency, when discussing cultural value, to overlook firsthand experience. 'Far too often the way people experience culture takes second place to its impact on phenomena such as the economy, cities or health' (Crossick and Kaszynska 2016: 7).

What, then, is the impact of Web3 on the experience of producing creative work? To date, Web3's impact on the production of music has been relatively limited: it is largely a 'back end' technology. There have been a few experiments in composing music by consensus using blockchain technology (Giannoutakis and Vasquez 2022), but, on the whole, Web3 music doesn't sound any different to Web1 or Web2 music.

Web3 visual art, by contrast, does look different from Web2, even if Web3 is technically a back-end technology here too. This is largely thanks to the concept of the profile picture, associated with CryptoPunks, with their distinctively pixelated, eight-bit aesthetic, and Bored Ape Yacht Club, with their cartoon depictions of existential ennui. CryptoPunks and Bored Ape Yacht Club are examples of generative art, and they have achieved such prominence that, for some, generative art and Web3 are almost synonymous.

We need to recognize three points. The first is that you can have Web3 without generative art and generative art without Web3: the phenomena are distinct.

The second point is that not all NFT projects are the same. We can distinguish between collections such as Ghxsts, which are entirely hand-drawn, and Autoglyphs, which are entirely on-chain. Even for generative art, we can distinguish between long-form and short-form approaches, for instance, with long form fully random and short form involving an element of artist curation.

The third point is that, in all cases, we should resist a simplistic 'human vs machine' framing. If we are in a posthuman era, it is one in which the boundaries between human and technology are blurred, not one in which humans are replaced by technology (Braidotti 2013). Clearly, non-human agency will have a profound impact on the human experience of producing creative work. Digital artworks that use smart contracts to self-replicate or self-destruct, for instance, could have such autonomy that 'it no longer makes sense to identify a human artist as the creator' (Zeilinger 2022).

The question is whether emerging technologies enhance or diminish this experience. It would be easy to take the Luddite view: that ceding control to machines will have a negative impact on the actual experience of producing creative works. For Zeilinger, however, non-human agency represents a *positive* development, introducing new ways of creating and sharing creative work rather than marking the end of creativity as we know it. No one, after all, seems to be suggesting that the use of aleatoric and indeterminate methods diminished the experience of composing for the likes of Cage and Stockhausen. The latest iteration of such avant-garde traditions, perhaps, is *Holly+*: a machine learning model or 'digital twin' trained on the voice of musician and composer Holy Herndon. From a Web3 perspective, the most interesting aspect of *Holly+* is not the fact that it allows other people to produce work using Herndon's voice but its model of distributed governance. Decisions about *Holly_+* are made by a DAO, and creators share revenue with the DAO as well as with Herndon herself. Herndon sees *Holly+* as 'decentralizing' rather than ceding control, adding that says she finds the idea that other people could perform through her 'exciting' (Wiener 2023).

Web3's Impact on Music Industry Stakeholders

To understand whether Web3 is good or bad for the music industry, then, we need to understand what we mean by good or bad: which type of value are we talking about? Asking whether Web3 is good or bad for the music industry is also too blunt a question for another reason: we need to know which section of the industry we are considering. I now examine the opportunities and risks that Web3 presents for three stakeholder groups: musicians, fans, and record labels. (Of course, this list is by no means exclusive: for a fuller picture, we would need to consider additional stakeholders from live agents to lawyers, press officers to publishers. We would also need to recognize that opportunities and risks can differ even within given stakeholder group, for instance between major and independent labels or between featured artists and session musicians.)

Opportunities and Risks for Musicians

In terms of the opportunities for musicians, Web3 is primarily discussed in terms of remuneration. The Internet, so good at sharing information, has been a positive development for music fans: almost every recording in the world is now just a finger-swipe away. It has not been so kind to creators: while superstars have done very well, many musicians struggle with a 'value gap' between the volume of work being shared and the remuneration (UK Music 2017). In this context, the fact that NFTs represent a potential new revenue stream is not to be sniffed at. And, at least for the likes of Justin Blau, the sums raised can be significant.

We get an incomplete picture of the financial opportunities for artists, however, if we *only* focus on income from NFT sales. Web3 also presents opportunities for artists to engage in mass collaboration and to be financially rewarded for such collaboration: consider Chaos, a band made up of 45 musicians as well as visual artists, engineers, producers, and even economists. It also introduces new direct-to-fan opportunities that can bring in additional revenue, for instance from tokens that offer access to VIP experiences: a kind of fan club 2.0. I say more about such opportunities in the section on fans. The key point here is that Web3 could also introduce new kinds of relationship with fellow creators, for instance, through decentralized autonomous organizations, or DAOs.

For Catlow and Rafferty (2022: 35), NFTs can be retrogressive: introducing 'competitive individualism' and 'the cult of the genius artist' into peer-to-peer communities. Those interested in a more expanded idea of culture and democracy, they argue, should focus not on NFTs but on DAOs. Consider Friends with Benefits, a social network for creators in which everyone holds tokens for collective funding and governance. Tokens in Web3, then, can be much more than a new opportunity for financial speculation: they can help create new opportunities for 'cooperation and solidarity in the cultural sector' (Catlow and Rafferty 2022: 27).

It is worth remembering, of course, that Web3 opportunities are restricted to artists with both the technological know-how and the willingness to engage in Web3. There have been accusations that, despite the egalitarian rhetoric, Web3 music is in fact dominated by a small number of artists using an even smaller number of platforms. Even for the lucky ones, the chance to make millions in minutes through an NFT drop might have been simply a moment in time: there is no guarantee it can be repeated. Then there is the question of how money is shared beyond featured artists and collaborators such as session musicians and producers. Imogen Heap chose to share revenue from 'Tiny Human' with collaborators, but there is no guarantee that others will do the same. Musicians would do well to learn from visual art: the illustrator known as Seneca gets little credit for designing the Bored Ape Yacht Club characters: 'Not of ton of people know that I did these drawings, which is terrible for an artist', she has said, adding that her compensation for the work 'was definitely not ideal' (Hissong 2022).

The point is not only that the financial opportunities ushered in by Web3 are not shared by all artists. It is also that Web3 can also present outright risks. I see four in particular.

Firstly, there is the potential for significant reputational risk if there is a fan backlash against an NFT release perceived as an exploitative get-rich-quick scheme or associated with a blockchain that is environmentally damaging.

Secondly, Web3 can oblige musicians – already facing burnout due to the endless demands of social media (Baym 2018) – to produce additional 'VIP' content for superfans in token-gated fan clubs, something of a return to the patronage model of old. The additional obligations of Web3 could further diminish the time available for writing, recording, and performing concerts – the very reason these musicians have fans in the first place. Some Web3 creators have even given fans 'governance rights' in the creative process. This could have a negative impact on the actual experience of creating work as well as changing the whole artist-fan dynamic: when I was a 12-year-old encouraging school friends to listen to Rage Against the Machine, I didn't expect to choose what basslines Tim Commerford should play in return.

Thirdly, removing intermediaries has a potential downside for artists. The potential demise of collection societies, celebrated by some as an efficiency blockchains can introduce, could in fact have a negative impact on those reliant on blanket licensing (O'Dair et al. 2016). Disintermediation may be embraced as an end in itself by the more crypto-libertarian members of the Web3 community, but removing middlemen becomes less appealing if those middlemen are adding (one or more types of) value.

Finally, there's the million-dollar question: who holds the right to mint an NFT associated with a particular asset? Is it the songwriter or the person who recorded it, or one of the numerous other stakeholders around the world? If there is nothing stop me claiming to have recorded *Back to Black* rather than Amy Winehouse or *To Pimp a Butterfly* rather than Kendrick Lamar, just as a man named Terence Eden made a blockchain-based claim to have painted the *Mona Lisa*, then the garbage-in-garbage-out problem remains.

Opportunities and Risks for Fans

In terms of consumption, Web3 has affected art more than music, since music fans have relatively little potential for conspicuous consumption: you can't use your royalty share as a profile picture. Yet Web3 does present opportunities for music fans. Most obviously, perhaps, NFTs allow them to make money by buying tokens and selling them on at a profit. Start-ups such as JKBX are even making it possible to invest in music just as we might invest in stocks.

Web3 also introduces opportunities for fans to go a step further and become co-creators – and, at least potentially, to be remunerated for their effort. In Web2, artists and fans interact via a small number of monopolistic platforms. In Web3, we are told, artists *are* the platform (O'Dair 2022). Tokens can encourage fans to get involved in building and maintaining networks by giving them a stake in its growth. In a DAO, for instance, tokens are a way to involve more people in decision-making and facilitate less hierarchical governance models. Decentraland, for instance is a 3D virtual world that is owned and governed by its users.

We would do well to remember, however, that not all fans are seeing this upside. While crypto is ostensibly anti-elitist, Bitcoin ownership is in fact highly concentrated in a relatively small number of users. The same goes for NFTs. Quite aside from the fact that some NFTs are so expensive, not all fans have the necessary technological savvy to buy them, and not all fans have the interest. Web3 might have become easier to navigate over time, but it remains obscure to the average person on the street, conflated with cryptocurrencies and damaged by media stories of crypto exchange collapses and other shenanigans.

Web3 can threaten fans as well as present them with opportunities. It is not just that fans might not be getting a fair share of the value they co-create, but also that fans purchasing music NFTs could be exposing themselves to financial risk – whether due to market volatility or deliberate 'rug pull' scams which see developers disappearing with funds, leaving fans holding useless tokens. And the decentralized world is not renowned for its consumer protection and dispute resolution. While crypto is presented as democratic and egalitarian, a way for the average person to become an investor rather, it might be only the privileged elite that can afford to make such risky investments. We need to consider the extent to which people understand what they are buying – and not buying – when they buy a token. An NFT is an empty vessel, akin to a virtual shipping container, and that vessel can contain almost anything. There is 'a large gap' between legal ownership and the understanding of that ownership in music NFTs, especially those relating to rights transfer and royalty shares (Water and Music 2021). There is a particular need for more certainty over which tokens might be treated as securities: how many people purchasing music NFTs, for instance, really understand the differences between tokens representing collectibles and those entitling the holder to a share in royalties?

While co-creation opportunities are exciting, it is also worth asking ourselves whether Web3 could diminish the fan experience. Even those prepared to pay a fortune for a particular profile picture tend not to justify that purchase in terms of the pleasure they got from looking at the image. Some profile pictures may be purchased for reasons of 'flex' or 'bragging rights': a new example of conspicuous consumption (Veblen 1899). I admit that, as a youthful Rage Against the Machine fan, I promoted the band to friends because I thought it made me look cool as well as because I loved the band, but there was no sense in which I was hoping to gain financially in the process. What is lost if the fan experience is reduced to a spin on the NFT roulette wheel, less to do with liking the associated music than with selling on a token at a profit? While Srnicek (2016) may have good reason to criticize the 'platform capitalism' of Web2, we should pause to ask ourselves whether the casino capitalism of Web3 is really preferable.

Opportunities and Risks for Record Labels

Some start-ups, especially during the music industry's first blockchain wave, insisted that the technology would bring about the imminent demise of record labels. In fact, the labels are still around, while almost all those start-ups have disappeared. We have a new batch of music start-ups, among them Audius, Catalog, JKBX, Royal, and Serenade.

In the second wave, we saw labels trying to get themselves a piece of the action. In 2022, for instance, 10.22PM, Universal Music Group's Web3 label, announced a Bored Ape NFT band named KINGSHIP; Warner Music Group announced a collaboration with NFT marketplace OpenSea; and Sony Music Entertainment filed a trademark application for NFT-authenticated music through Columbia Records. The same co-option of an apparently radical technology can be seen in other spheres: we have seen NFT drops from corporations such as Nike, and there is talk of Hollywood films based around NFT characters.

Blockchains, then, do not seem to signal the end of incumbents. Even with such a potentially radical technology, applications can be very much incorporative. We can expect this to continue, as labels, desperate not to repeat the mistakes of the Napster era, seek not to squash Web3 but to co-opt it, perhaps by offering 360-deals that give them a cut of token income with the justification that they can add (financial) value by helping maximize revenue and minimize reputational risks.

Web3 does represent a risk for record labels, however. One risk is specific to smaller labels: the average indie cannot afford to set up a Web3 subsidiary like Universal Music Group.

There's also a bigger problem facing all labels: while they are in prime position for those NFTs relating to recorded music, a growing school of thought holds that record music is not the asset to tokenize. The music industry, we should remember, is much bigger than the recording industry. And Web3 is accelerating opportunities beyond recorded music: in live performance and, in particular, in direct-to-fan. Although less established than those relating to recorded music and live performance, direct-to-fan opportunities may be the ripest for experimentation, since they tend to be less reliant on intellectual property (publishing rights and master rights in the case of recorded music, publishing rights only in the case of live performance) and the associated gatekeepers.

While labels are likely to seek a cut of Web3 income, then, not all artists will be prepared to surrender it – especially since tokens also reduce the appeal of label and publisher advances. In an era in which technological advances have significantly lowered barriers to recording and distributing music, advances have been the one carrot that record labels have been able to dangle. But if musicians can make $11 million in 24 hours through an NFT drop, their need for that advance is dramatically reduced.

Conclusion

While some have dismissed Web3 as a solution looking for a problem, the problem is in fact crystal clear: the 'platform' or 'chokepoint' capitalism of Web2 is a problem for musicians and fans alike. Record labels might be more positive about some intermediaries, notably streaming platforms, which have helped recorded music return to growth after the doldrums of post-Napster 'piracy', but even they tend not to be so keen on other gatekeepers such as social media platforms.

Some believe that Web3 could prove transformative for the music industry and the wider creative economy, with its 'wild and exciting' potential to 'radically change power structures' and 'reorient power from centralised institutions to the public' (Whitaker and Abrams 2023: 17). At the same time, this potential might not be realized: 'blockchain is developing within existing power structures in which banks, technology companies, and the programmers of various blockchain technologies may have motivation to preserve or build re-centralising power' (Whitaker and Abrams 2023: 17). Blockchains might have their origins in the radical cypherpunk movement, yet they could still become coopted by capitalist systems, thereby reducing musicians and fans alike to narrowly economic beings motivated by narrowly financial rewards (Catlow and Rafferty 2022: 38).

It is probably too early to say: we will need to wait for music's third, fourth, and fifth blockchain waves. What does seem clear is that, while NFTs were key to music's second blockchain wave, we should not assume they are the 'killer app'. Tokens are fundamental to Web3, but they can be fungible as well as non-fungible – and even non-fungible tokens are not simply about trading for profit. Rather than the short-term price fluctuations of NFTs, we need to consider what a token represents. Early signs are that the area most ripe for experimentation is not recorded music or live performance but direct-to-fan, where intellectual property considerations are more open. Whatever use cases emerge, we need to look at more than whether token prices are up or down compared to the previous week, and we need to recognize the music industry as heterogeneous. By using the quadruple bottom line of financial, social, environmental, and experiential value, and by considering the impact on multiple stakeholder groups, including, but not limited to, musicians, fans, and record labels, we can begin to gain a more holistic understanding of value – in Web3 music and beyond.

References

Baym, N. 2018. *Playing to the Crowd: Musicians, Audiences and the Intimate Work of Connection*. New York: New York University Press.

Bilton, C., Eikhof, D. R., and Gilmore, C. 2021. 'Balancing Act: motivation and creative work in the lived experience of writers and musicians.' *International Journal of Cultural Policy*, 27:6, 738–752, DOI: 10.1080/10286632.2020.1830978

Bourdieu, P. 1984. *Distinction: A Social Critique of the Judgement of Taste*. London: Routledge.

Braidotti, R. 2013. *The Posthuman*. Cambridge: Polity.

Braungart, M. and McDonough, W. 2009. *Cradle to Cradle: Remaking the Way We Make Things*. London: Vintage.

Catlow, R. 2017. 'Artists Re: Thinking the Blockchain Introduction.' In *Artists Re: Thinking the Blockchain*, ed R. Catlow, M. Garrett, N. Jones and S. Skinner. London: Torque Editions and Furtherfield.

Catlow, R. and Rafferty, P. 2022. 'Introduction: What is Radical Friendship Made Of?' In *Radical Friends: Decentralised Autonomous Organisations and the Arts*, ed R. Catlow and P. Rafferty. London: Torque Editions.

Caves, R. 2000. *Creative Industries: Contracts Between Art and Commerce*. Cambridge, MA: Harvard University Press.

Cooper, R. 2022. 'The NFT Craze Has Stopped Being Funny.' *The Week*. January 4. https://theweek.com/culture/arts/1008539/the-nft-craze-has-stopped-being-funny. Accessed 10 November 2023.

Crossick, G. and Kaszynska, P. 2016. *Understanding the Value of Arts and Culture.* AHRC Cultural Value Project. Arts and Humanities Research Council. https://www.ukri.org/wp-content/uploads/2021/11/AHRC-291121-UnderstandingTheValueOfArts-CulturalValueProjectReport.pdf. Accessed 10 November 2023.

Devine, K. 2019. *Decomposed: The Political Ecology of Music.* Cambridge, MA: MIT Press.

Doctorow, C. 2023. *The Internet Con: How to Seize the Means of Computation.* London: Verso.

Elkington, J. 1997. *Cannibals with Forks: The Triple Bottom Line of 21st Century Business.* Oxford: Capstone.

Giannoutakis, K. and Vasquez, J. C. 2022. 'Collaborative Electroacoustic Music Composition on the Blockchain.' Conference Paper. https://www.researchgate. net/profile/Juan-Vasquez-35/publication/361729609_Collaborative_ Electroacoustic_Music_Composition_on_the_Blockchain/links/ 62c1f071c0556f0d631a17b0/Collaborative-Electroacoustic-Music-Composition-on-the-Blockchain.pdf. Accessed 10 November 2023.

Giblin, R. and Doctorow, C. 2022. *Chokepoint Capitalism: How Big Tech and Big Content Captured Creative Labour Markets and How We'll Win Them Back.* London: Scribe Publications.

Golumbia, D. 2016. *The Politics of Bitcoin: Software as Right-wing Extremism.* Minneapolis: University of Minnesota Press.

Hissong, S. 2022. 'The NFT Art World Wouldn't Be the same without this Woman's 'Wide-Awake Hallucinations'.' *Rolling Stone.* January 26. https://www.rollingstone. com/culture/culture-features/seneca-bored-ape-yacht-club-digital-art-nfts-1280341/. Accessed 18 December 2023.

Nakamoto, S. 2008. 'Bitcoin: A Peer-to-Peer Electronic Cash System.' https://www.ussc. gov/sites/default/files/pdf/training/annual-national-training-seminar/2018/ Emerging_Tech_Bitcoin_Crypto.pdf. Accessed 10 November 2023.

Negus, K. and Pickering, M. 2004. *Creativity, Communication and Cultural Value.* London: Sage.

O'Dair, M., Beaven, Z., Neilson, D., Pacifico, P. and Osborne, R. 2016. 'Music on the Blockchain: Possible Futures.' Middlesex University/Featured Artists Coalition. https://www.mdx.ac.uk/__data/assets/pdf_file/0026/230696/Music-On-The-Blockchain.pdf

O'Dair, M. 2019. *Distributed Creativity: How Blockchain Technology Will Transform the Creative Economy.* Cham, Switzerland: Palgrave Macmillan. DOI 10.1007/978-3-030-00190-2

O'Dair, M. 2022. *Web3 and the Music Industry: A Second Wave of Blockchain Innovation.* Blockchain Research Institute. https://www.blockchainresearchinstitute.org/ project/web-3-and-the-music-industry/. Accessed 10 November 2023.

O'Dair, M. and Beaven, Z. 2017: 'The Networked Record Industry: How Blockchain Technology Could Transform the Record Industry.' In *Strategic Change: Briefings in Entrepreneurial Finance.* London: Wiley. DOI: 10.1002/jsc.2147

Perez, C. 2002. *Technological Revolutions and Financial Capital.* Cheltenham: Edward Elgar.

Scholz, T. and Schneider, N. (eds). 2017. *Ours to Hack and to Own: The Rise of Platform Cooperativism. A New Vision for the Future of Work and a Fairer Internet.* New York: OR Books.

Schwartz, L. 2017. 'Blockchain Dreams: Imagining Techno-Economic Alternatives after Bitcoin.' In *Another Economy is Possible: Culture and Economy in a Time of Crisis*, ed. M. Castells. Cambridge: Polity.

Serenade. 2023. 'Introduction to Serenade.' https://intercom.help/serenade/en/articles/6899530-about-serenade-introduction-to-serenade. Accessed 10 November 2023.

Srnicek, N. 2016. *Platform Capitalism*. Cambridge: Polity.

Tapscott, A. 2023. *Web3: Charting the Internet's Next Economic and Cultural Frontier*. New York: Harper Business.

Throsby, D. 2001. *Economics and Culture*. Cambridge: Cambridge University Press.

Truby, J., Brown, R. D., Dahdal, A. and Ibrahim, I. 2022. 'Blockchain, Climate Change and Death: Policy Interventions to Reduce the Carbon Emissions, Mortality, and Net-Zero Implications of Non-Fungible Tokens and Bitcoin.' *Energy Research & Social Science*, 88. https://reader.elsevier.com/reader/sd/pii/S2214629622000007X?token=5193FB16A7634553A576D9F89D70355DAA0860F0739641F60A314516BAF14E4144E59581EBC16FECC485003ED27FFB6D&originRegion=eu-west-1-&originCreation=20220709150532. Accessed 10 November 2023.

UK Music. 2023. *This is Music*. https://exxfmt5ydc6.exactdn.com/wp-content/uploads/2023/10/This-Is-Music-2023-Economic-Report.pdf. Accessed 10 November 2023.

UK Music. 2017. *Measuring Music*. https://exxfmt5ydc6.exactdn.com/wp-content/uploads/2020/09/Measuring_Music_2017_Final.pdf. Accessed 10 November 2023.

Varoufakis, Y. 2023. *Technofeudalism: What Killed Capitalism*. London: Penguin.

Veblen, T. 1899. *The Theory of the Leisure Class: An Economic Study of Institutions*. New York: Macmillan.

Water & Music. 2021. 'Defining Music NFT Ownership, From the Digital to the Analog World.' 14 December 2021. https://www.waterandmusic.com/defining-music-nft-ownership-from-the-digital-to-the-analog-world/. Accessed 10 November 2023.

Weyl, E. G., Ohlhaver, P. and Buterin, V. 2022. 'Decentralized Society: Finding Web3's Soul.' *SSRN*. https://papers.ssrn.com/sol3/papers.cfm?abstract_id=4105763. Accessed 10 November 2023.

Whitaker, A. and Abrams, N. B. 2023. *The Story of NFTs: Artists, Technology, and Democracy*. New York: Rizzoli Electa.

Wiener, A. 2023. 'Holly Herndon's Infinite Art.' *The New Yorker*. November 2023. https://www.newyorker.com/magazine/2023/11/20/holly-herndons-infinite-art. Accessed 20 December 2023.

Zeilinger, M. 2022. 'Blockchain Vitalism.' *Outland*. November 7. https://outland.art/blockchain-vitalism/. Accessed 20 December.

5

From Blockchains to NFTs: Decentralized (?) Platforms for Unique (?) Content Distribution

Claudio J. Tessone
University of Zurich, Zurich, Switzerland

Introduction

In this chapter, I endeavor to confront a particularly provocative question that critically assesses the current trajectory of digital content distribution through blockchains and non-fungible tokens (NFTs). The question is whether these technological advancements genuinely foster the development of decentralized platforms for the distribution of unique content, and to what extent the content disseminated through these platforms can be considered truly unique. Despite considerable interest and speculation in the domain of blockchain, the extent to which these technologies have actualized their promised transformative impact on socioeconomic systems remains debatable. Despite the potential of NFTs as innovative digital assets, there looms a persistent question: are these advancements so far merely reinforcing existing centralized structures under the guise of decentralization? As we aspire for decentralized markets in NFT exchanges, we find ourselves inevitably relying on a few central authorities, crashing into the very walls we seek to dismantle. Further, the chapter considers the dynamics of fungibility and art uniqueness in the context of NFTs and the vital role of data provenance with its complexities involved in linking off-chain data to on-chain assets in the blockchain sphere. The objective of the chapter is not to exhaustively cover these topics but to provide a critical examination for a potential future direction of blockchain and NFTs, particularly in how they might innovate and disrupt the way we transact digital objects so far.

DOI: 10.1201/9781003458227-6

Complex Socioeconomic Systems and Inequality

In our exploration of blockchain technology and its broader implications, we must first comprehend the intricate and interconnected nature of socioeconomic systems that exist in our surroundings. These systems are omnipresent, manifesting themselves at various scales around us, and can always be represented as agents that do not act in isolation, but naturally interact, interconnecting them. Unlike simple aggregations of individual behavior, these systems exhibit complex, emergent behaviors that transcend the sum of their parts. A quintessential example of this complexity is evident in the realm of economics, a field marked by systemic inequalities. This observation was first made by Vilfredo Pareto, an Italian sociologist and economist in the late 19th century. Through his examination of social structures, Pareto noted a consistent and striking pattern: a minority of the population held a substantial share of wealth, while the vast majority lived with much less. This pattern of wealth distribution was not isolated to his era but has been a recurring theme in economic systems throughout history. The driving force behind this inequality is known as 'proportionate growth', a principle suggesting that the expansion of an entity within a system correlates directly with its current size. This concept, from a mathematical standpoint, posits that the growth of an entity within a system is proportional to its existing size. In practical terms, this can manifest in various forms – be it the number of social connections in a network, the accumulation of wealth, or even the expansion of a company. Entities that are already large tend to grow at a faster rate compared to their smaller counterparts. This principle has been observed and described under various names, including the 'rich-gets-richer' phenomenon, preferential attachment, and the Matthew effect. The essence of these observations is the same: socioeconomic systems inherently foster and perpetuate inequality, as originally articulated by Pareto. Recognizing the complexity of these socioeconomic systems and their inherent propensity for inequality is essential in analyzing blockchain technology's role and potential impact. This understanding allows us to delve deeper into the potential of blockchain to interact with, and possibly transform, the deep-rooted dynamics of wealth distribution and power in our global societies.

The Genesis and Philosophy of Blockchain Technology

To fully grasp the implications of blockchain and its progression to concepts like non-fungible tokens, we must first explore the origins and fundamental philosophy behind blockchain technology. The inception of blockchain was driven by an increasing trend toward centralization in our global society, a trend that has been exacerbated in the digital era. As our world becomes more digitized, we see an accelerated shift toward centralized control. This centralization manifests in various forms: reliance on a limited number of entities for trust, particularly evident in digital payment systems where a few organizations act as transaction verifiers, wielding significant power and creating potential single points of failure. Additionally, these entities often have access to extensive personal data, raising privacy concerns. Another facet of centralization is seen in the way societies and economies are structured, often centralized around nation-states and conglomerates, leading to monetary policies being controlled by a diminishing number of central authorities. This concentration of power and control was met with criticism, especially from anarcho-capitalist communities, particularly in the wake of the 2008 financial crisis. The response was a call for systems that enable (1) the exchange of digital asset value without reliance on central entities, fostering open participation in the money supply process through economic incentives – a foundational aspect for the functioning of blockchain systems; and (2) the ability for participants to engage in these systems without disclosing their identity. As blockchain technology evolved, there was a realization of the potential for individuals to create their own assets within these decentralized environments, leading to the development of both fungible tokens and non-fungible tokens, the latter being particularly significant in the representation of unique items such as art or digital twins of real-world objects. These systems allow users to establish the rules of interaction and implement contractual logic within the blockchain framework. To summarize, founding principles of blockchain-based systems, therefore, centered around decentralization, anonymity, an open monetary system, and the absence of the need for a priori trust. However, it is critical to examine how these foundational narratives of decentralization and peer-to-peer interaction compare with the actual reality in the implementation and evolution of blockchain technology. This question underscores the need to critically assess whether these systems have stayed true to their original philosophy or if there has been a deviation from these core principles.

Blockchain Functionalities and Economic Incentives

Blockchain systems enable users to exchange the property of assets. To do this in a decentralized manner, everybody must to be able to independently verify that the transactions are correct. This is why the data structure under blockchains is not much more than a public registry, in which we have a very precise notion of what a time order is. In these systems, a block is a set of verified transactions, which, once validated by the network, are permanently recorded and linked sequentially, establishing a clear and immutable timeline of all transactions. The verification of transactions within a blockchain is not just a matter of recording but also of validation, ensuring that each transaction is legitimate and that the assets being transferred are rightfully owned. For instance, if Alan sends six units of a digital currency to Charles, the blockchain ledger allows every participant to verify that Alan indeed received these units from Andrea in a previous transaction, thereby confirming his right to transfer them to Charles. This level of transparency and verification is crucial in building trust within the system. However, the process of constantly verifying transactions across the entire network can be computationally demanding. This leads to the fundamental question of why individuals or entities would invest their resources in verifying transactions on the blockchain. The answer lies in the economic incentives built into the system. In public permissionless blockchain networks, the entities that verify transactions (often referred to as miners or validators) are rewarded for their effort to sustain the system consistency. This reward system is not just a mechanism to compensate for computational effort but also serves as a means to issue new assets into the system. The reward provided to the validators is typically predetermined by the creators of the blockchain and is an integral part of the system's design. This aspect of blockchain technology is largely governed by consensus protocols, which are the rules determining how transactions are verified and how new blocks are created. Popular consensus protocols like proof-of-work and proof-of-stake rely on different mechanisms to incentivize participation and ensure the security of the network. However, these systems often link the probability of earning rewards to the economic resources available to a validator outside the blockchain system, leading to potential disparities in earning opportunities. For instance, in both proof-of-work and proof-of-stake systems, individuals with greater financial resources outside the blockchain are often able to invest more in the process, thus having a higher chance of receiving rewards. This intersection of blockchain functionalities and economic incentives raises critical questions about the distribution of power and wealth within these systems. While blockchain technology promises a more decentralized and egalitarian approach to asset management, the realities of economic incentives and consensus mechanisms can lead to new forms of centralization and inequality, reflecting some of the broader socioeconomic challenges observed in traditional systems.

Centralization Trends in Blockchain Systems

As blockchain technologies have matured and proliferated, an intriguing paradox has emerged in their operational dynamics. Despite the foundational ethos of decentralization, there is a discernible trend toward centralization in these systems. This trend is multifaceted, encompassing both the technical aspects of blockchain operations and the socioeconomic impacts of these systems. The user base of blockchain platforms has been expanding exponentially, signifying a growing interest and adoption across various sectors. However, this growth in users has not been paralleled by an increase in the number of participants verifying transactions. The stagnation in the number of validators leads to a scenario where the verification process, a critical aspect of maintaining the blockchain, becomes concentrated in the hands of a few. This centralization of transaction verification is counterintuitive to the decentralized nature envisioned for blockchain systems and raises concerns about the integrity and resilience of these platforms. Furthermore, a closer examination of these systems reveals a widening gap in wealth distribution among participants. As with traditional economic systems, blockchain platforms exhibit patterns of wealth accumulation where a small group amasses significant wealth, leading to reduced diversity in the process of block creation and validation. This concentration of wealth is not just a matter of financial disparity but also translates into power inequality within the blockchain ecosystem. The fewer the participants who can afford to engage in the consensus protocol, the more unequal the contribution to the system becomes, leading to a disproportionate influence by certain actors. A notable example in this context is Dogecoin, a cryptocurrency initially conceptualized as a 'meme coin' with no intrinsic value. Contrary to its initial perception, Dogecoin gained substantial value and popularity, reflecting the unpredictable and often speculative nature of blockchain-based assets. This case underscores the broader trend within blockchain systems: even those designed with decentralization as a core principle tend to gravitate toward centralization over time. The concentration of control – be it in technical operations, consensus mechanisms, or wealth accumulation – mirrors traditional economic systems, challenging the transformative promise of blockchain technologies. This trend toward centralization within blockchain systems is a critical area of concern. It questions the long-term sustainability and equity of these platforms and highlights the need for ongoing scrutiny and adaptation of blockchain architectures. Understanding and addressing these centralization tendencies is essential for ensuring that blockchain technologies fulfill their potential as tools for equitable and decentralized digital economies.

NFTs: Fungibility, Art Uniqueness, Incentivization, and Data Provenance

The advent of blockchain technology has revolutionized not just the exchange of currency but also opened new avenues for trading various forms of assets. It was in 2014 that the realization dawned upon the blockchain community: these systems could facilitate the exchange of a broad spectrum of assets, not just the native digital currency. This led to the emergence of tokens within blockchain systems, representing digital assets issued by specific stakeholders and managed through sophisticated contracts known as smart contracts. These tokens are more than mere digital representations; they confer specific rights and privileges to their holders. Tokens within blockchain systems can be categorized based on their fungibility. Fungible tokens are uniform; each unit is identical and interchangeable with others of its kind, similar to traditional currency where one unit holds the same value as another. However, the landscape of blockchain assets experienced a significant shift with the introduction of non-fungible tokens, especially in the realm of art. NFTs are distinct in that they are not interchangeable; each token is unique and represents ownership of a specific asset, often with a link to a piece of digital art, music, video, or other forms of creative work. A critical aspect of NFTs is their relationship with metadata. Due to the storage limitations of blockchains, some of which cannot house large data files, NFTs often rely on external metadata for detailed information about the asset they represent. This metadata can include various attributes such as the name, description, and other relevant details of the digital asset. It is crucial to note that the actual digital file linked to the NFT often resides off the blockchain. The storage of this off-chain content can occur in different ways: it can be centralized, hosted on a specific server, or decentralized, using systems like the Inter-Planetary File System (IPFS), which offers a more distributed approach to storing data.

The world of non-fungible tokens and their application in art raises intriguing questions about uniqueness and authenticity. A telling example comes from an incident in Switzerland involving an advertisement for Appenzeller cheese. Traditional ads from the Appenzeller consortium feature a man in traditional attire, symbolizing the secret recipe of the cheese, a concept deeply rooted in the region's culture. This imagery was later mimicked in a style resembling the Bored Apes NFT collection, without any official endorsement by Yuga Labs. The resulting artwork, a fusion of traditional Swiss culture and modern digital art, was eventually removed due to its copycat nature. This incident highlights a fundamental challenge in the realm of NFT art: distinguishing the uniqueness of digital art pieces, especially when they are part of large collections that are rapidly proliferating. As NFT collections grow and diversify, the lines blur between individual art pieces, questioning the true uniqueness of each item. This raises an important issue in blockchain systems: the difficulty in appropriately incentivizing various participants, especially artists and creators. Ensuring the uniqueness and authenticity of NFT art is not just about creating digital tokens; it involves establishing a clear lineage and provenance of the artwork.

Proper provenance of data is crucial in this context and extends beyond the capabilities of blockchain technology alone. It necessitates establishing a link between the off-chain data – the actual artwork – and the on-chain transactions representing ownership and transfer of the NFT. This link is vital in preserving the integrity of the artwork and ensuring that it remains connected to its original source. In exploring solutions to these challenges, we can draw inspiration from the Xanadu project by Ted Nelson, an early attempt to revolutionize computer-based publishing. Xanadu proposed a system of non-linear text links, known as 'hypertext', which predates and influenced the development of the World Wide Web. This system was designed to interconnect texts through links, allowing seamless navigation and reference tracking between documents. It aimed to maintain the various versions and interconnections of documents, as well as manage copyright and royalty payments automatically. The concept of Xanadu offers a glimpse into the potential future of NFT art and data provenance. A system that intricately links artistic assets to their origins and maintains a record of their history and transactions could revolutionize the way we view digital art in the blockchain era. Such a system would not only ensure the uniqueness and authenticity of each piece but also provide new models for distribution and compensation, benefiting all stakeholders in the value chain. This approach, which combines the technological prowess of blockchain with comprehensive data linkage, represents a unique solution yet to be fully realized in the digital art world. It holds the promise of addressing the challenges of authenticity and uniqueness, paving the way for a more equitable and transparent digital art ecosystem.

Conclusion

To summarize, it becomes clear that the journey of blockchain technology and its applications, such as non-fungible tokens (NFTs), is complex and fraught with both promises and challenges. A critical observation is the unintentional trend toward centralization and the emergence of dominant players within systems that were originally envisioned to be decentralized. This centralization contradicts the foundational ethos of blockchain technology and raises pivotal questions about the efficacy and transformative potential of these systems. As we reach the closing of this discourse, a pressing question emerges: What is the true utility of blockchain systems in their current form? Despite the initial excitement and the revolutionary potential ascribed to blockchains, the reality is that the level of innovation and disruption they have brought to socioeconomic systems has been limited. Blockchain technologies, in their current state, have largely replicated existing structures rather than creating fundamentally new paradigms. This observation is not to undermine the capabilities of blockchain but to highlight the untapped potential that lies within these technologies. The digital assets exchanged and managed on blockchains possess the ability to enable transactions and interactions that differ fundamentally from those in the physical world. However, this potential has not been fully realized. Our socioeconomic systems have evolved over millennia in a certain trajectory, and blockchain technology, in its nascent stages, has yet to significantly deviate from this path. Therefore, the future of blockchain and its applications lies in our ability to innovate beyond the conventional, to envision and create systems that truly disrupt and redefine how our economy and societal transactions function.

To achieve this, a concerted effort in education, research, and practical experimentation is essential. We must be willing to start from scratch, to learn and relearn, embracing the inevitability of failures as stepping stones to success. The journey toward harnessing the full potential of blockchain is not only about technological advancement but also about cultivating a mindset of innovation and adaptability. The path forward is challenging, but the possibilities and opportunities that blockchain technology offers make this endeavor not just necessary but worthwhile. As we continue to explore and develop these technologies, our focus should remain on creating systems that are equitable, transparent, and truly transformative.

6

Art, People, Museums, and the Promise of Blockchain

Diane Drubay

We Are Museums, Paris, France

In the mesmerizing tapestry of today's digital evolution, there are hushed whispers and resounding proclamations, announcing a renaissance in the realms of art and technology. To an observer like me, deeply rooted in the intricate world of museums and art, it only took one season to understand everything was about to change. My story starts not with lines of code, but with the heartbeats of countless individuals passionate about art and museums, ready to embrace change. In 2012, I had an epiphany while meeting the artistic and museum scene in Lithuania. Museums, those age-old custodians of culture and history, were on the cusp of transformative change. I was moving to a country full of contradictions, in the throes of change. On the one hand, museums were witnesses to a bygone Soviet empire, while on the other, contemporary art centers and the art scene were aspiring to international and disruptive models. The conversations between the two were not easy, but they were necessary. So I invited my friends from international museums to come to Vilnius to get inspired by the contemporary art scene, and in exchange to share their projects and visions with local museums. It was a beautiful, kind and inspiring encounter. This is how I founded 'We Are Museums', an innovation lab with the aim to guide cultural institutions through the complex maze of technological innovation, social shifts, and environmental change. The recipe was simple, and this format of a major international meeting on the future of museums was repeated for seven years in equally inspiring cities such as Warsaw, Bucharest, Marrakech, Riga, and Berlin.

Blockchain: Museums Reimagined

The ensuing years witnessed a crescendo of discussions, especially around 2018, probing the relationship between blockchain and museums. Always on

DOI: 10.1201/9781003458227-7

the lookout for new museum models to inspire the museum sector to adapt to social and technological change, blockchain technology was obviously one of the areas I gravitated toward.

Museums, historically, are not just repositories of art but are gatekeepers of culture, trust, and knowledge. However, like any institution, they face challenges, notably in areas of transparency, security, and community engagement. During the various panel discussions organized in 2018 and 2019, blockchain emerged not as a mere tool but as a paradigm-shifter. We started envisioning different future scenarios where blockchain technology could disrupt the art world:

1. Fractional Ownership and Scalability in Art
   Through blockchain and Web3, we are witnessing the emergence of a shareable economy in the art world, underpinned by principles of fractional ownership. This new model transcends traditional boundaries, making the art market a realm of global inclusivity and democratization. No longer confined to the affluent few, art ownership can now be a shared venture, encouraging micro-philanthropy and collective custody. This transformative approach not only breaks down financial barriers and opens investment to a broader audience but also fosters a communal relationship with artworks, as stakeholders derive both emotional and financial value.

2. Direct Revenue for Artists
   In this dynamic landscape, artists gain autonomy like never before. Artists find liberation in the blockchain, generating revenue directly from their creations without intermediaries' historical constraints. By tokenizing artworks and selling fractions to multiple owners, artists can engage with a global audience, setting their terms, and retaining rights over their work. This direct artist-to-collector conduit not only ensures fairer compensation but also cultivates direct relationships with art enthusiasts and collectors.

3. Digital Art and Scarcity
   The digital art realm is poised to redefine the concept of scarcity and value. Blockchain technology's indelible traceability ensures the authenticity and singularity of art pieces, resolving long-standing issues of duplication and fraud. This secure ecosystem means that digital files, much like physical artworks, can possess a verified scarcity, enhancing their intrinsic value. Moreover, digital ownership transcends traditional possession, allowing value creation through sharing, thus breeding a culture where communal engagement amplifies worth.

4. Blockchain-Powered Museum Tickets
   In this new era, even the modest museum ticket is reimagined. Transforming the humble museum ticket into a blockchain-powered tool of

micro-patronage connects visitors more deeply with collections. These tickets, potentially functioning as micro-investments, facilitate a symbiotic relationship between institutions and art lovers, where support extends beyond mere attendance, embedding patrons within the art ecosystem.

5. Revolutionizing Museum Philanthropy
   This shift also heralds a new chapter in museum philanthropy. The conventional donation system evolves into a more engaging, personalized model, where supporters, turned micro-patrons, can hold a stake in the museum's assets. Blockchain could enable visitors to hold actual stakes in artworks, blurring the lines between spectatorship and ownership, and fostering a sense of responsibility and closeness to cultural artifacts.

6. Ubiquitous Access to Museum Collections
   Furthermore, the digital frontier beckons for museum collections. The next steps in digitization and the rise of virtual museums promise universal access to art, surpassing physical and geographical limitations. This digital ubiquity means that heritage and culture can be a shared human experience, unrestricted and unconfined.

7. Unified Collection-Management Language
   As these advancements in technology continue to bridge gaps, museums and private collectors will find themselves aligned in their collection management approaches. With a universal language facilitated by blockchain and NFTs, collaborations and transactions could become seamless, fostering an environment of shared trust and simplified processes.

At the same period, we started seeing museums exhibiting on-chain art or blockchain-related artworks. Beginning with 'Hammer Projects: Simon Denny' in January 2017 in Los Angeles, the exhibition delineated the economic and societal potential of blockchain through sculptural installations. In a similar vein, the ZKM | Center for Art and Media in Karlsruhe, Germany, hosted 'Open Codes' in October 2017, illustrating the world as a data playground within the wider program 'The World as a Field of Data'. Fast-forward to June 2018, the State Hermitage Museum in St Petersburg, Russia, delved into the theme with 'Innovation as Artistic Technique', a group exhibition spotlighting Kevin Abosch's blockchain-oriented work. Further enriching the discourse, Simon Denny returned to curate 'Proof of Work' in collaboration with Distributed Gallery at Schinkel Pavilion in Berlin, Germany, in September 2018, crafting a dialogue around blockchain's verifiable history in the realm of art. Through these exhibitions, the conversation around blockchain's implications in the art sector was significantly advanced, marking a critical juncture in the history of blockchain-art exhibitions.

The convergence of art and blockchain technology has also made its mark in the realm of museum acquisitions, reflecting a growing acknowledgment of digital art's place in the cultural narrative. In April 2015, MAK Vienna pioneered this movement by acquiring Harm van den Dorpel's 'Event Listeners', a work authenticated cryptographically through the Bitcoin blockchain. Following suit, in December 2017, ZKM in Karlsruhe, Germany, acquired several NFTs, including a notable Cryptopunk. Although they lost access to it later, they showcased these acquisitions in spring 2021 through an aptly named exhibition, 'Crypto art. It's not about money'. The dialogue continued in the United States with the donation of Eve Sussman's '89 Seconds Atomized' to the Whitney Museum of American Art in June 2019, marking a significant endorsement of blockchain-based art. Moreover, in March 2019, the Whitney Museum exhibited Jennifer and Kevin McCoy's 'Public Key/ Private Key', providing a thought-provoking exploration of art ownership paradigms in the museum context. Through these acquisitions and displays, museums not only embraced the blockchain-art narrative but also propelled discussions on the evolving dynamics of art ownership and authenticity in the digital age.

Hic et Nunc: A Wind of Change

But, despite all these new visions of a future where the art world could embrace blockchain technology, the discussions were not without its share of inertia. The majority of cultural professionals appeared hesitant, pointing out the clash of culture, language, and set of values and ambitions. The two worlds seemed to orbit different suns. One was decentralized and flat, the other structured and pyramidal. While blockchain innovated at breakneck speed, many museums grappled with the immense task of digitizing their collections. From 2019 to 2021, We Are Museums focused on other types of innovations such as virtual reality, video games, museum resilience, and the ecological transition of museums.

But then, the winds changed in March 2021 with Raphael Lima's *Hic et Nunc*, named after the Latin phrase for 'here and now'. More than an NFT marketplace, it was a philosophy, a statement of intent, a demonstration of the democratizing power of blockchain technology. It was about dismantling the longstanding gates of exclusivity that kept many capable and imaginative minds at bay. The established order, which often seemed to favor a select few, was now being challenged. Now, art was not dictated by a name or a price tag; it was purely about the emotion it evoked.

Hic et Nunc encapsulated a message of immediacy and accessibility. It was a call to action to the artists and creators, an invitation to partake in a movement that sought to redefine the traditional constructs of value and ownership in art. The NFT marketplace was an exemplification of blockchain's potential to foster a community-driven, egalitarian art ecosystem.

Picture this: Raphael Lima, a visionary hacker from Brazil, tired of the gatekeeping and exclusivity that plagued the NFT marketplaces. The art world, which should be a realm of boundless imagination, was tangled up in a web of elitism. There were strict applications to be able to mint on platforms, constant refusals, unspoken requirements, and even worse, a heavy price to simply mint an NFT on platforms based on the Ethereum blockchain (around $300 in 2021 to mint an NFT). This meant that for artists in Malaysia, Colombia, and numerous other regions, this NFT art market was virtually unreachable. But Raphael Lima envisioned something different. Where Hic et Nunc treads, it leaves the indelible footprints of innovation, opting for the Tezos blockchain as its foundation – a conscious nod to sustainability. This choice isn't just strategic; it's a statement, addressing head-on the vociferous debate over blockchain's thirst for energy. Tezos deviates from the beaten path, its proof-of-stake consensus a stark, greener contrast to the voracious energy appetite of Ethereum's proof-of-work system. Here lies an oasis for artists and connoisseurs alike, those yearning for an environmentally attuned space to mint, collect, and revel in digital artistry.

Rafael Lima wanted to create a space where every creative soul could effortlessly mint an NFT in a few seconds. That's why the Hic et Nunc's user-friendly interface is so simple, in order to smooth the process of minting, buying, and selling NFTs, making it accessible to those unfamiliar with blockchain technology. Rafael Lima's first wish was to give access to the blockchain art market to his artist friends in Brazil, targeting the transaction cost first. The solution lay in the Proof of Stake protocol used by the Tezos blockchain where minting an NFT cost only a few cents. It's a democratization of the digital, tearing down the financial barricades that often deter the creatives and the curious. It also embraces an open-source ethos, encouraging users to contribute to the platform's development and improvement.

In a few days, Hic et Nunc became the canvas for all forms of digital expressions for people coming from all corners of the Planet. From JPEGs, GIFs, 3D models to short films, the platform became a melting pot of digital creativity, transcending geographical and socioeconomic boundaries. In front of such abundance of creativity, generosity and support became a cultural trait of the Hic et Nunc users. It was a spectacle of global digital creativity unshackled.

Furthermore, the culture of generosity and communal support that burgeoned was nothing short of a digital art renaissance. A tweet or a message on Discord could garner the necessary xtz (cryptocurrency of the Tezos blockchain) for artists to embark on their minting journey, embodying the community-driven spirit that was at the core of Hic et Nunc. This wasn't merely about creating and sharing digital art; it was about fostering a culture of inclusivity, support, and shared growth.[1]

OBJKT4OBJKT: Generosity as Currency

Directly stemming from Hic et Nunc's egalitarian vision and nurtured by the platform's community of artists and collectors, a revolutionary form of currency has emerged – not one of monetary value, but one of generosity, inclusivity, and communal support. This altruistic ethos is vividly embodied in movements emerging from Hic et Nunc's ecosystem, a platform where the art community doesn't just trade; they unite over shared ideals and foster a space of equitable artistic expression.

The 'OBJKT4OBJKT' initiative, pioneered by the 'DiverseNftArt' collective, is a resounding call for greater inclusivity within the NFT realm. It underscores a profound commitment to communal well-being and diversity in artistic exploration, underpinned by the principle that art should be accessible to everyone, irrespective of financial status. By minimizing economic hurdles, this initiative facilitates an environment where artists and collectors can celebrate a plethora of artistic expressions, significantly enriching their collections and interactions.

> We believe that the OBJKT4OBJKT initiative helps to create a happier and healthier community within Hic et nunc and that by removing the monetization barrier it will help other artists and collectors to discover and build a more diverse art collection.
>
> **(https://diversenftart.hotglue.me/)**

OBJKT4OBJKT specifically designates periods, notably weekends, of heightened artistic exchange without financial constraints. Artists, from renowned figures to novices harnessing the power of their smartphones, have the opportunity to mint and distribute NFTs, often in editions of 500 to 2,000, ensuring art is attainable for all enthusiasts. The pricing, deliberately set low or even at zero (later slightly increased to deter exploitative bots), symbolizes the essence of art transcending monetary value, focusing instead on its intrinsic worth and the connections it fosters.

> Over the event days, Hicetnunc's transactions averaged at 10462 creating a 226.86% increase over the weekend. [] There were more than 500 tweets with the hashtag #OBJKT4OBJKT, reaching almost 500K users.
>
> **(https://diversenft.art/OBJKT4OBJKT-1)**

Building on this momentum, the initiative 'Tezos for Tezos' emerged, echoing the communal spirit by orchestrating an event that saw the minting of 2600 artworks within just 72 hours. The remarkable acquisition of 60,000 NFTs during this period was a testament to the burgeoning enthusiasm and solidarity within the community. This ethos of generosity has since permeated the Tezos art community, with regular events reinforcing the foundational commitment to accessibility and diversity in art. More than a platform for acquiring art, these movements represent a shift toward purposeful collectivism. They underscore a broader social consciousness within the Tezos community, where the act of collecting art synergizes with global advocacies. Events and fundraisers, like 'SOS Columbia', 'hic et turco', and the annual 'Tezos Pride', transform the marketplace into a space of humanitarian and environmental activism. In this dynamic, the community extends beyond aesthetic appreciation, delving into realms of social justice, environmental conservation, and inclusivity. The art acts as a beacon, rallying support, forging global connections, and empowering voices. It is here, in the unique confluence of art and activism, that the Tezos community finds its beating heart, continuously shaping a future where the value of art is measured by its capacity to connect, uplift, and inspire change. Rapidly, the act of donating or purchasing NFTs to support social or environmental causes transformed from a simple gesture into a purpose-driven movement. Collecting art on the Tezos blockchain wasn't just about possession anymore; it was about empowerment, being a part of a change, a voice in a global chorus singing for social good, environmental justice, and inclusion. For instance, fundraisers have been organized such as 'SOS Columbia' to support the protesters during the strikes in Columbia, 'hic et turco' to support the local communities in Turkey devastated by the wildfires, or 'Tezos Pride' which runs all June every year.

The compelling narrative of philanthropic endeavors through the Hic et Nunc community, among others, underscores the profound impact of community engagements in addressing pressing societal issues. One notable instance of this convergence was seen when the Whitworth Gallery in Manchester took a pioneering step in July 2021. The museum, keen on exploring the potential of decentralized economic models, sold a reproduction of William Blake's iconic work, 'The Ancient of Days', as an NFT to raise funds for various social causes. This undertaking not only garnered significant financial support but also fostered a spirit of community and demonstrated the potential of blockchain technology in the realm of art and philanthropy.

The story of 'The Ancient of Days' holds a unique charm, with its intricate design capturing the divine architect in the act of delineating the world with a compass. The Whitworth Gallery's initiative to digitize and auction this masterpiece as an NFT showcased a novel approach toward community engagement, allowing art enthusiasts and philanthropists to come together for a noble cause. The proceeds from the sale were directed toward initiatives aimed at alleviating societal challenges, thereby creating a blueprint for other institutions to follow.

In a parallel narrative, the Herbert W. Franke Foundation, in association with Anika Meier, orchestrated a remarkable fundraiser in August 2022.

By inviting 80 artists to contribute artworks in tribute to the late artist Herbert W. Franke, they managed to raise €100,000. A generous €20,000 of the raised amount was donated to the ZKM for preserving Franke's invaluable written legacy, while a portion was also dedicated to supporting Namibian students pursuing computer science. The fundraiser bore witness to the immense potential of collaborative endeavors in preserving heritage and fostering education. The detailed account of this fundraiser, including the significant impact it had on digitizing Franke's manuscripts, can be explored further at the tribute page and the ZKM announcement.

Adding another layer to this tapestry of goodwill, the Cure[3] project emerged as a beacon of hope for those battling Parkinson's disease. Spearheaded by Alex Estorick of Right Click Save and Foteini Valeonti of Useum, in collaboration with Artwise and Bonhams, this initiative commissioned seven generative artists to create new artworks for an auction held in January 2023 in London. The event successfully raised €270,000 for Cure Parkinson, showcasing a new model of charitable giving in the Web3 domain, as detailed in the feature on Right Click Save.

The ripple effect of such magnanimous endeavors was felt in the music industry too, with 'One Of', a leading NFT platform backed by Quincy Jones, forming alliances with powerhouses like Warner Music and the Grammy Awards. Adhering to a model of benevolence, One Of dedicates 5% of its revenue toward social and environmental causes, mirroring the Tezos community's ethos of generosity and environmental stewardship.

Unlocking Web3 for the Arts & Culture

Parallel to these developments of charity-driven blockchain projects, the broader Tezos art community, particularly influenced by platforms like Hic et Nunc, mirrored the very values museums had championed for generations. It was a realization of a shared ethos, an alignment in the stars that underscored the commitment to inclusivity, sustainability, and democratization in an increasingly digital space.

It was natural that We Are Museums would dive into this space to explore new models for museums to innovate. We launched the 'Unlocking Web3 for the Arts & Culture' innovation laboratory, affectionately known as WAC Lab, in December 2021 to turn the art world into Web3 literates and accelerate Web3 adoption. WAC Lab emerged from a synergy between profound entities. Powered by the Tezos blockchain and receiving the nurturing guidance of entities such as TZ Connect, the Blockchain Art Directory, and LAL Art Advisory, this initiative found its rhythm under the design and production led by 'We Are Museums'.

The lifeblood of WAC Lab's ingenuity courses through its three-act narrative, a journey through collaboration, learning, and, ultimately, project development. The first act, a series of dynamic online discussions, set the stage for what was to unfold. Every week, like clockwork, museum professionals, curators, and Web3 enthusiasts converge in a virtual meeting to discuss the latest art Web3 news. This safe and open space demystified Web3, inviting professionals to eschew skepticism and embrace the manifold possibilities beyond high-value sales or speculation. WAC Weekly fosters an environment where ideas didn't just cross-pollinate; they thrived. The laboratory ventured deeper with its second act, the WAC Fellowship, a crucible where inspiration met application. A diverse cohort comprising international cultural institutions was led through the blockchain technology origins and use cases. Over three months of training, they received the keys needed to envision their Web3 journey. They became literate in Web3, ready to pioneer their innovative endeavors, guided by personalized coaching and mentorship and fueled by a community's collective wisdom.

WAC Lab unveiled its last step with the WAC Factory. Far from an abstract concept, the Factory was a tangible accelerator, a four-week crucible where ideas forged into reality. Within this innovative haven, teams collaborated tirelessly, integrating blockchain technology with a singular mission to unlock new potentials in preservation, social advocacy, environmental stewardship, and economic resilience. From WAC Lab Season 2, ten use cases emerged, showing a large variety of blockchain adoption through museums such as NFT shop, digital souvenir, on-chain co-creation, proof of learning, and more.

One of the most provocative themes explored was the economics for curation DAOs (decentralized autonomous organizations). This concept teased the revolutionary potential of shared ownership and democratic governance in the very programming of exhibitions and art spaces. It wasn't just about managing; it was about belonging, about community members being stakeholders in the artistic process. Fully embracing challenging new technologies and models, HEK – House of Electronic Arts in Basel (Switzerland), WAC Lab Season 2 fellow, launched their own curation DAO in summer 2023, following the described DAO concept.

Conclusion

While sharing impressions of the past years, we realize that what we've embarked upon is not a mere foray into new technological frontiers but a profound cultural odyssey. Our journey began with the digital renaissance, a bridge meticulously architected between museums and the pulsating artistic scene of tomorrow. This exploration through blockchain technology, particularly via NFTs, has done more than validate digital art – it has ennobled it, intertwining it with the traditional art world's revered principles of provenance and originality. What we're witnessing is not just a digital renaissance; it's a bridge between epochs. The seeds of this transformative era were sown by visionaries like Rafael Lima, whose pioneering endeavors in March 2021 underscored a historic shift within the creative cosmos. The Tezos community, with its unique blend of innovation and camaraderie, has since burgeoned into a force of groundbreaking stature. Herein lies a space that transcends digital interaction, manifesting instead as a crucible of human ingenuity.

As we look ahead, the trajectory of the Web3 art and culture space is ablaze with more experimental initiatives, all geared toward empowering individuals, projects, and grassroots communities. This movement doesn't just innovate; it contemplates the ethical compass guiding Web3, that champions social significance, environmental stewardship, and authentic human impact. Reflecting on this journey, it becomes clear that this isn't an end, but a thrilling beginning. The blockchain is not merely a technological construct but a vessel sailing us toward global cultural metamorphosis. In its ledger, we interpret more than transactions; we perceive the embryonic stage of a societal shift.

Note

1 Editor's Note: It is noteworthy to mention that subsequent to the events described in this chapter, the original Hic et Nunc (HEN) platform experienced a significant evolution. After its sudden discontinuation by Raphael Lima on November 12, 2021, the platform was revived and reestablished by its community. This revival led to its transition into a decentralized autonomous organization (DAO), marking a pivotal moment in the platform's journey and further highlighting the dynamic and resilient nature of decentralized digital communities in the art world. The quick reemergence of Hic Et Nunc shows the true resilience of decentralized blockchain platforms. Lima was the 'owner' of the platform only in the sense of being the main contributor to its code. The entire decentralized infrastructure, with NFTs stored on Tezos and creative assets stored on IPFS, was in place independent of the creator's preferences.

7

Can't Knock the Hustle: NFTs, DAOs, and Creativity

Catherine Mulligan

Imperial College London, London, UK

Drawing upon the phrase 'you can't knock the hustle', attributed to both Jay Z and Sotheby's, this chapter delves into the transformative dynamics shaping the creative sector in the era of digital tokens. It presents an exploratory reflection on the intersection of non-fungible tokens (NFTs) and the creative industry, leveraging insights from research conducted by the author, who has worked at the boundaries of blockchain/cryptocurrency and sustainability since 2009. The chapter surveys the current manifestation of NFTs within the creative realm, shedding light on the economic facets intertwined with ongoing digital innovations. The chapter also broaches the topic of decentralized autonomous organizations (DAOs), musing about their possible ramifications on traditional structures in creative industries. Without claiming to provide an exhaustive study, the chapter encourages contemplation on the role of NFTs and DAOs in the creative sphere. It touches upon their potential implications on economic systems, access to cultural institutions, and the funding of public goods such as education and civil infrastructure. Overall, the aim is to ignite dialogue and reflection among researchers, practitioners, and policymakers about the emerging intersections of technology, economics, and creativity. Moreover, this chapter invites reconsideration of established paradigms and the envisioning of new pathways for social and economic exchanges in light of these technological strides.

Re-envisioning Creative Processes

The transformative potential of blockchain technology upon our economic structures is a vast and complex topic worthy of extensive discussion. Nevertheless, among the pioneering concepts that emerged from our investigations was reshaping the management of rights in music and films. This direction led us into dialogues with diverse stakeholders, prominent among which was the artist Imogen Heap, who had devised her own personal blockchain solution. A collaborative project with a consumer-centric start-up was launched with a visionary aim: challenging the dominance of corporate giants like Sony in the realm of film distribution. Despite the project's eventual failure – a result that could be attributed to a host of factors – it provided an enlightening insight into the multifaceted applications of blockchain technology. Regardless of its outcome, this venture served as a compelling case study, illuminating the potential of blockchain as a tool for disruption and innovation within the creative industry. At the core of our exploration was the idea of re-imagining a film, or indeed any creative endeavor, not as a rigid hierarchical structure but as a dynamic network of interconnected relationships between individuals. Take, for example, the intricate process of producing a film soundtrack. In conventional practice, a lead is appointed, who in turn subcontracts many others to contribute to the project. This modus operandi extends to film crews, often composed of individuals who move fluidly between various projects, frequently operating as independent contractors engaged by larger institutions. These institutions act as intermediaries in the traditional system, skillfully knitting together a diverse tapestry of talents and roles. However, this approach invites reflection on its inherent limitations and begs the question: could a more innovative way to structure these creative collaborations exist? Could the intermediaries be replaced, or their role be diminished, allowing for more direct interaction and collaboration between the creative individuals? Could blockchain technology provide a toolset for this transformation?

Picture a scenario where a scriptwriter, imbued with the power of blockchain technology, uploads their script onto a public ledger, thereby securely declaring their creative rights. They can then offer these rights for sale to interested parties, inviting investments via this transparent, blockchain-based platform. The proposed process has the potential to engender a network of supply chains, diverging significantly from the traditional, centralized distribution systems prevalent today. A film conceptualized and birthed in this manner would navigate its path to consumers, who, in their act of viewing it, would contribute to a revenue stream. This revenue, rather than being concentrated in the hands of a few, could be equitably disseminated across the entire film supply chain through the blockchain. This proposed paradigm extends not merely to the rights holders but encapsulates everyone engaged in the creative and construction process of the film – a group that generally comprises a substantial number of individuals.

It was our belief that this innovative concept held promise not only for the film industry, but also for music and other creative sectors. The potential for disruption was palpable - leveraging blockchain technology to engender a more equitable, transparent, and collaborative creative industry. Our exploration of these concepts began in earnest around 2012 or 2013, and the subsequent year marked significant advancements in this space. Those acquainted with the blockchain landscape can attest to its dynamic, rapid-paced character – a realm where developments and updates emerge with breathtaking speed. This rapidity, while invigorating, also presents a formidable challenge; it demands continuous attention and engagement to keep abreast of each new development.

The continually evolving face of blockchain technology necessitates a keen understanding and a vigilant eye to stay informed about every development. A pivotal moment in the trajectory of blockchain technology occurred in 2014, with the introduction of the world's first non-fungible token (NFT), Quantum. Since this event, the interest and engagement with NFTs have soared dramatically. Various influential figures, such as musician Jay Z, who embraced the trend by altering his Twitter handle to reflect the Bored Ape NFT he acquired, have further fanned the flames of this rising trend. These influencers have leveraged their broad reach across numerous social media platforms, spreading the idea to millions of followers. This widespread surge in interest has captivated the curiosity of individual artists and celebrities and drawn the attention of various reputable organizations, such as the musical artist Aphex Twin and the globally recognized media outlet, *The New York Times*. Adding to this shift, revered auction houses like Sotheby's have also begun to acknowledge the significance of this new avenue, joining the exploration of these technologies. This development signals a notable shift in the broader industry's stance toward these technologies. It's remarkable to observe how what began as a deeply egalitarian concept has now found acceptance and involvement from institutions of such prestige and influence as Sotheby's. This transition highlights the far-reaching potential and transformative power of these digital assets and the blockchain technology that underlies them.

Economic View on the Decentralized Approach

To understand the unfolding events in the non-fungible tokens (NFT) landscape fully, especially in the context of its growing entanglement with larger institutions, it becomes crucial to incorporate a perspective informed by economic theory. The famous Coase theorem – a staple for anyone who has studied economics – provides a useful lens. This theorem postulates a relationship between marginal transaction costs and the size of a business entity. Specifically, it suggests that as marginal transaction costs rise, so does the size of the firm. Ronald Coase, the architect of this theorem, posited that a company forms an economic structure to mitigate these costs, primarily achieved through the orchestration of standardized contracts.

This economic perspective aids in comprehending the structural shift insti-gated by the decentralized approach, and the implications of this shift on the broader landscape of creative industries and beyond. This economic principle explains the size and dominance of large studios; it is financially logical to centralize the management of numerous contracts within a single institution given the prevailing high transaction costs. However, the advent of decentralized verification mechanisms and the implementation of smart contracts via blockchain technology have the potential to reduce these contract-associated costs drastically. This technological evolution naturally leads us to the question: is it feasible to establish an alternative economic structure that can compete with existing establishments like colossal stu-dios and dominant corporations within the music and wider creative indus-tries? These entities, in their current form, essentially act as value-extracting intermediaries within the creative economy, amassing power and resources through their role as aggregators. Could we pioneer a new path that chan-nels greater rewards to artists and producers? By delving into the eco-nomics at play and devising inventive mechanisms to manage contractual interactions in this space, we stand on the cusp of introducing substantial disruption to the existing system. We're not merely contemplating minor alterations, but rather a comprehensive restructure that challenges the pre-vailing dominance of large studios. Such a shift could lay the groundwork for amplified diversity and an expanded breadth of creative expression. Embracing a more decentralized approach has the potential to acknowledge and foster diverse forms of creativity, which may be otherwise marginalized or ignored within the constraints of the current centralized paradigm. This, in turn, could foster an environment that welcomes an extensive array of creative voices, encouraging innovation and novel expressions in the artistic landscape.

Creative Potential of Decentralized Autonomous Organizations (DAOs)

Transitioning from the discussion of blockchain-enabled decentralization in creative industries, it becomes pertinent to examine decentralized autono-mous organizations (DAOs). This innovation has been gaining traction in the blockchain community. DAOs, essentially, are organizations governed by rules encoded as computer programs called smart contracts. These open-source programs use blockchain technology to facilitate, verify, or enforce the negotiation or performance of a contract. DAOs are autonomous because they can operate independently of their creators once deployed. Emerging concurrently with NFTs, DAOs have steadily gained attention for their potential to redefine traditional organizational structures. These organizations, contrasting sharply with conventional corporate models, eliminate the need for a centralized authority. They embody the principles of democratized decision-making that align with the fundamentals of blockchain technology. An increasing number of Web 3.0 native music communities, such as Melody, are adopting this novel organizational framework, leveraging the unique advantages that DAOs offer. This includes an inherently democratic governance structure, where each member has a say in the decision-making process. Given their unique characteristics and potential, it can be hypothesized that DAOs, alongside NFTs, are well positioned to stimulate a significant shift in investment trends. By offering a decentralized, participatory organizational framework, DAOs permit a diverse range of contributors to have a say in an organization's operational and strategic decisions. This broadened inclusivity presents novel opportunities within the creative industry landscape.

Building upon the discussion of DAOs, I would argue that they potentially pose a more profound challenge to the prevailing market structures within the creative sectors than NFTs. The idea of a decentralized, democratic organization that can facilitate creative collaborations opens up a whole new realm of possibilities that could significantly reshape the landscape of the creative industry. A key aspect of the current DAO landscape is its intrinsic characteristics of token-mediated membership, financing, and governance activities. In a DAO, membership is usually token-based, meaning that holding a token represents a stake in the organization. This token-based system extends to the DAO's financing model, where fundraising and investment often take place through the issuance or trading of tokens. Furthermore, governance in a DAO, including decision-making and voting, is typically carried out using these tokens. This unique structure enables a level of transparency, inclusivity, and democracy seldom found in traditional organizations.

Looking ahead, the future of this field seems likely to revolve around effectively navigating the distribution of rights and finances across these decentralized operations. This task is undoubtedly complex, requiring careful consideration and strategic decision-making. Yet, the potential payoff is monumental. The exciting prospect to anticipate is the establishment of a decentralized governance system capable of providing authentic competition against the large intermediaries and aggregators within the creative industries. It is not just about contesting the hegemony of these entities but also about opening up the creative landscape to a diverse range of voices and talents. This new form of organization, by design, could foster inclusivity and equality, leading to a richer and more diverse creative ecosystem. The implementation of such a system could redefine the way value is created, distributed, and perceived within these industries, marking a significant shift in the way we conceive creative endeavors. Beyond the boundaries of creative industries, the potential applications of DAOs are vast and wide-reaching, including crucial sectors such as finance, public infrastructure, and education. For instance, envisioning the possibilities within the educational realm, we can explore an innovative approach to handling perennial challenges such as funding cuts.

Take the case of the United Kingdom, where music education programs frequently bear the brunt of budget reductions during economic downturns. This unfortunate trend highlights an area ripe for intervention and innovation. Could we harness the power of DAOs and NFTs to safeguard and ensure the continual provision of music education for future generations? The concept is intriguing. DAOs, built on blockchain technology, could enable the establishment of community-governed funds dedicated to supporting music education. Schools or educational institutions could issue NFTs representing pieces of artwork, performances, or other creative outputs from students. These NFTs, sold in the global marketplace, could generate funds to sustain the music programs, creating a novel, decentralized model of financing education. This exemplifies how blockchain technologies can play a transformative role, not only in redefining creative industries but also in other sectors, opening up new avenues of possibilities and shifting paradigms across traditional landscapes. Expanding the vision further, DAOs could potentially become instrumental in funding novel types of cultural institutions. It is a prevalent observation that numerous existing cultural establishments possess an elitist aura, subtly demanding specific modes of conduct from their patrons. These norms may inadvertently restrict a broader section of society from engaging with these institutions. Consequently, an intriguing question emerges – could we, through the use of DAOs, pioneer the creation of novel types of cultural institutions that are more universally accessible and less imposing? Such institutions could democratize cultural participation, breaking down the barriers associated with traditional, more elitist establishments. They could create spaces where a larger number of individuals feel welcomed and encouraged to engage with various forms of cultural expression, ultimately fostering a more inclusive cultural ecosystem. International organizations, such as UNESCO, are already exploring fascinating initiatives in this direction. They are investigating the potential of digital technologies to make cultural institutions more accessible to the public. Through their efforts, they are striving to unlock the benefits of culture for a broader demographic, recognizing the value of cultural participation in promoting social cohesion, personal development, and community engagement. Incorporating DAOs into this equation could further democratize access to culture, promoting a fairer distribution of cultural resources and opportunities, and fostering a more inclusive cultural landscape. This presents yet another domain where blockchain technologies, such as DAOs and NFTs, could have a transformative impact, challenging established norms, and paving the way for more equitable and inclusive future models.

In assessing the future implications of DAOs, I am particularly drawn to their potential for democratizing access to resources and opportunities that have traditionally been restricted due to geographical constraints or socioeconomic status. The inherent decentralized nature of DAOs offers the potential to redistribute power and resources more equitably across society. DAOs, essentially global entities operating beyond traditional boundaries, could serve as a driving force in mitigating the effects of geographical isolation, providing individuals, regardless of their physical location, with the ability to participate, contribute, and benefit from collective endeavors. This element of inclusivity is integral to the philosophy of decentralization and forms a cornerstone of DAOs' transformative potential. Moreover, the socioeconomic inclusivity offered by DAOs could be a game changer. Historically, economic resources and opportunities have often been unevenly distributed, skewed toward those with higher socioeconomic status. DAOs, by virtue of their transparent and open nature, could potentially challenge these longstanding disparities, facilitating a more equitable access to resources and opportunities. In essence, DAOs could initiate a profound shift in the way resources are accessed and distributed, leveling the playing field, and fostering an environment of equitable opportunities for all, irrespective of geographical location or social standing.

Embracing Decentralization for a More Equitable Future

In conclusion, the transformative potential of blockchain technology, particularly in the form of NFTs and DAOs, heralds a new era of decentralization within creative industries and beyond. The unique capacity of this technology to redistribute power and resources, lower transaction costs, and reimagine traditional hierarchical structures offers a tantalizing glimpse into a future where creativity and enterprise are democratized, and opportunities are more equitably distributed. While it is undeniable that we are still in the early stages of this blockchain revolution, the developments to date indicate a progressive trajectory. Case studies, such as the adoption of NFTs by artists and auction houses, and the burgeoning interest in DAOs among music communities, suggest a growing appetite for change and innovation within creative industries and the broader economic landscape. The application of blockchain technology and DAOs to sectors beyond the arts, such as civil infrastructure and education, holds tremendous promise for societal advancement. The potential to fund novel cultural institutions and guarantee continued access to music education, among other initiatives, could significantly enhance cultural diversity and inclusivity. However, as we forge ahead, it is imperative to approach this transition thoughtfully, with a clear understanding of the underlying economics and a steadfast commitment to ethical and equitable practices. We must ensure that the benefits of this transition reach beyond the confines of existing structures, extending to those who have traditionally been excluded. In this context, the advent of NFTs and DAOs is not just about introducing new technologies or disrupting established industries. It is, at its core, about reimagining the way we create, collaborate, and share value, in pursuit of a more inclusive, equitable, and diverse future. As we continue to explore the full extent of blockchain's transformative potential, let's ensure this vision remains at the heart of our endeavors.

8

Breaking the Fifth Wall: The Transformative Power of Blockchain in Virtual Music Performances

Kristof Timmerman

Royal Academy of Fine Arts Antwerp, Antwerp, Belgium

Introduction

Since the rise of the Internet, the commercialization of smartphones and the success of social media, our lives are increasingly shifting toward the digital. The COVID-19 crisis has only given another tremendous boost to this. Artists, too, increasingly dwell, wander, work, create, play, and host audiences in virtual worlds, some attempts more successful than others. For the nostalgic souls among us: this evolution is irreversible. Not to replace physical experiences, but to create new forms and tap into new audiences.

Since the pioneers of the late 1980s and 1990s such as Jeffrey Shaw, Chris Marker, Monika Fleischmann, and Char Davies, technology has made such a leap forward that an enormous potential of digital worlds has become accessible. A network of unexplored virtual environments emerges, the so-called metaverse. The metaverse concept refers to a collective virtual shared space that is created by the convergence of physical and virtual reality. It is a complex and evolving ecosystem that encompasses virtual worlds, augmented reality, virtual reality, online gaming, social platforms, and various other immersive digital experiences. The metaverse aims to provide a persistent, interconnected, and user-driven virtual environment. Blockchain can facilitate interoperability between different metaverse platforms, allowing musicians to extend their performances seamlessly across various virtual spaces. This interconnectedness has the potential to break down barriers and to encourage collaboration among artists and audiences from diverse virtual communities.

DOI: 10.1201/9781003458227-9

The Metaverse Playground

The term 'metaverse' first appeared in 1992. In the cyberpunk novel *Snow Crash*, American writer Neal Stephenson used the contraction of the words 'meta' and 'universe' to describe the successor to the Internet; a virtual environment like a massively multiplayer online game (MMO) populated by avatars and system daemons (Stephenson 1992). Just over a decade later, this speculative concept took concrete form for the first time with the online multimedia platform Second Life, in which residents build a parallel life in a virtual world. Since its launch in 2003, the number of visitors has grown steadily until it reached one million unique users in 2013.

Artists also found their way to Second Life. In 2009, the French film director and multimedia artist Chris Marker built a radically futuristic museum within the platform in which he exhibited his own photographic work, video installations, film clips, and other media work. The number of MMO-like platforms – e.g. Fortnite, Roblox, Minecraft – and artistic interventions within such environments have exploded in recent years. In combination with the evolution toward affordable technology, a very accessible world is gradually opening up for artists and their audiences.

A distinctive virtual reality platform, underpinned by the Ethereum blockchain, is Decentraland. This platform operates on blockchain technology that enables users to purchase, trade, and cultivate virtual land parcels using the platform's native cryptocurrency, MANA. Each parcel is tokenized as a non-fungible token (NFT), offering users decentralized ownership and control over their digital musical assets. Decentraland serves as a decentralized metaverse, empowering participants to shape their musical experiences and connect socially.

Although Decentraland has received widespread criticism for its technical bugs and the mostly empty nature of its virtual world, the platform remains an interesting case study. While specific implementations may vary, the principles of ownership, decentralization, and community engagement can inspire future developments in the evolving landscape of decentralized music and virtual reality experiences.

Unlike most concerts and artistic performances in traditional Western settings, virtual performances place the audience at the center of the artistic creation – they put the spectator in the driver's seat for their own, unique experience. By putting the viewer at the center of the narrative, XR creators strive to create an environment where the distinction between observer and actor becomes blurred. In VR, the viewer is not merely an onlooker but an integral part of the unfolding story. The immersive nature of XR technologies allows users to interact with and influence their surroundings, forging a more profound connection with the content.

Portals between the Real and the Virtual

To make these experiences valuable, it will be necessary to make all those involved – artists, performers, spectators – feel part of these virtual worlds. The portal, the access to this experience, plays a crucial role here. How can the transition between the real and the virtual be constructed in such a way that those involved feel part of the virtual? Concepts such as storytelling, interaction, presence, and immersion[1] are of great importance.

In the expansive landscape of information technology, a portal serves as a conduit to present intricate underlying functionality in a user-friendly manner (Ramanathan & Raja 2014). It acts as a gateway, offering a centralized point of access that simplifies navigation and enhances user experience. This notion is integral to the exploration of decentralized music, where blockchain technology, with its principles of transparency and decentralization, intersects with virtual environments to reshape contemporary music performances.

In the realm of science fiction, a 'portal' signifies a magical or technological gateway connecting distant locations separated by spacetime. While these portals remain a fantastical concept, in the context of decentralized music, the exploration leans more toward transitioning states of presence between reality and virtuality. I distinguish between spatial presence and social presence, following the model of M. Lombard and M.T. Jones. Where spatial presence is defined as 'the subjective experience of being in one place or environment, even when one is physically in another place', social presence is defined as 'the feeling of being socially present with another person in a remote location' (Lombard & Jones 2015).

The reality-virtuality continuum, spanning from our physical world (reality) to the entirely synthetic digital realm (virtual reality), provides the backdrop for understanding the interconnectedness of various states. This continuum challenges the binary perception of reality and virtuality, highlighting the infinite intermediate values between the two extremes. In this intricate web, we find the 'embodied' position of the audience. As Hornecker notes, experiencing virtual reality engages the entire body, providing a means to see and recognize objects and understand the world within the immersive environment (Hornecker 2011). This spatial embodiment positions individuals within a physical space, emphasizing the interconnected relationship between the material and immaterial, analogue and digital (Figure 8.1).

The representation of reality and virtual reality as opposites may suggest distinct, coexisting worlds. However, the continuum illustrates a nuanced perspective, acknowledging an infinite number of intermediate values between the binary extremes. The intertwining of reality and virtuality creates a complex web, influencing and changing each other in various ways.

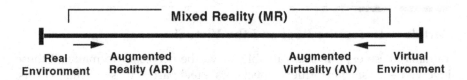

Reality-Virtuality (RV) Continuum

FIGURE 8.1
Reality-Virtuality Continuum (Milgram & Kishino 1994).

The concept of double negation or non-duality, prevalent in philosophies like Buddhism, aligns more closely with the experience in virtual reality, highlighting the interconnectedness of real, virtual, and latent spaces (Favero 2019).

Theatre of Cruelty

Now, consider extending this luminal state of being – existing between or within multiple realities – to the concept of breaking the fourth wall. Traditionally, the fourth wall acts as an imaginary barrier between the audience and the stage, a one-way mirror through which the narrative is observed without reciprocation. Breaking the fourth wall is a theatrical technique that involves the performer addressing or interacting with the audience, thereby disrupting that traditional separation between the world of the performance and the real world. This concept gained prominence in the context of Antonin Artaud's Theatre of Cruelty, a groundbreaking and revolutionary approach to theater that sought to shatter conventional boundaries and immerse the audience in a visceral and transformative experience.

The French playwright, actor, and theorist Artaud introduced the Theatre of Cruelty in the first half of the 20th century as a reaction against the perceived limitations of conventional theater. Artaud envisioned a form of theater that would go beyond mere entertainment, aiming to engage the audience at a primal, emotional level.

Breaking the fourth wall played a crucial role in realizing this vision. The performers in the Theatre of Cruelty were encouraged to confront the audience directly, challenging them to face their emotions and perceptions, in order to achieve a direct and intense engagement with the audience. Artaud believed in the power of the visceral and emotional impact of theater. By breaking the fourth wall, performers could elicit authentic emotional responses from the audience, transcending the confines of traditional narrative structures. It invited the audience to actively participate in the unfolding drama. This participation was not just intellectual but aimed at stimulating the senses and emotions, creating a collective experience that went beyond the boundaries of traditional spectatorship.

Breaking the Fifth Wall

Drawing a parallel from Antonin Artaud's groundbreaking approach to theater, breaking the fifth wall in the context of immersive experiences extends the concept of audience engagement even further. In immersive VR experiences, breaking the fifth wall implies placing the viewer or participant at the epicenter of the narrative with a heightened sense of agency. Just as breaking the fourth wall in traditional theater shattered the boundaries between performers and audience, breaking the fifth wall in immersive experiences dissolves the line between the virtual and the real. In this paradigm, the viewer, now often a participant or 'immersant', is not merely an observer but an active contributor to the unfolding story.

The immersive experience, by design, allows participants to navigate, interact, and influence the narrative trajectory. This newfound agency aligns with Artaud's vision of active audience participation, as breaking the fifth wall invites individuals to co-create the story, blurring the distinction between spectator and actor. As viewers become immersed in virtual worlds or augmented environments, breaking the fifth wall amplifies the emotional and sensory engagement. The sense of presence and interactivity enhances the overall experience, making it more profound and personal. Participants are not just witnessing events; they are shaping them, making choices, and directly impacting the course of the narrative.

This concept finds resonance in the evolving landscape of virtual and augmented realities, where creators are leveraging technology to empower participants with unprecedented agency. Breaking the fifth wall in immersive experiences signifies a departure from traditional modes of storytelling, embracing a dynamic where the participant is not just an audience member but an active co-author of the narrative. The transition from breaking the fourth wall in traditional theater, as championed by Artaud, to breaking the fifth wall in immersive experiences represents a continuum of audience empowerment. It encapsulates a shift toward a more participatory, engaging, and transformative form of storytelling, where the viewer's agency becomes a central element in the creation of the narrative.

In the realm of breaking the fifth wall in immersive experiences, the integration of blockchain and decentralization emerges as a pivotal component in enhancing the authenticity, security, and participant agency. Blockchain technology's decentralized nature ensures that the immersive environment operates without a single controlling entity, fostering a trustless and transparent ecosystem. Through the use of smart contracts, blockchain facilitates the creation of immutable rules, allowing participants to have a secure and verifiable impact on the narrative. This decentralized approach not only ensures data integrity and transparency but also empowers participants by providing ownership of virtual assets, contributing to a more democratized and user-centric immersive experience. By incorporating blockchain and decentralization, breaking the fifth wall transcends the boundaries of traditional storytelling, forging a dynamic and participatory relationship between the immersive environment, the creator, and the engaged participant.

Extending the concept of breaking the fifth wall to immersive experiences in contemporary music, the integration of blockchain and decentralization becomes a transformative force. In decentralized contemporary music, breaking the fifth wall signifies a departure from the traditional spectatorship model, where the audience is not merely a passive listener but an active participant in shaping the musical journey. In this immersive and decentralized realm, breaking the fifth wall in contemporary music expands beyond the physical and virtual spaces, creating a dynamic and collaborative experience that redefines the traditional boundaries.

Research: Concretizing a Speculative Model

Engaging in research about decentralized music within the metaverse inherently carries a speculative dimension, as it involves exploring uncharted territories at the intersection of technology, art, and virtual experiences. The metaverse, as a concept, is still evolving, and its full realization remains speculative itself. Researching decentralized music within this evolving digital landscape entails investigating the potential impact on how music is created, distributed, and experienced. The speculative nature lies in envisioning new paradigms of artistic expression, digital ownership, and collaborative musical environments that transcend current boundaries. As decentralized technologies like blockchain converge with the metaverse, researchers navigate unexplored terrain, seeking to understand how these innovations might revolutionize the music industry, redefine audience engagement, and reshape the very fabric of musical experiences within this emerging virtual realm. The speculative aspect invites researchers to envision and contribute to a future where decentralized music in the metaverse becomes not just a theoretical concept, but a transformative reality.

This exploration leads us to fundamental research questions: How can spectators, dispersed in various physical locations, feel virtually connected in the context of decentralized music performances? How can the presence and individuality of fellow 'players' be perceived and experienced? What strategies can be employed to make both the audience and performers feel truly present in the virtual world? How can decentralized music foster a sense of shared space, creating a virtual community where performers and audiences coalesce in a decentralized ecosystem?

The following two case studies are the results of research projects or a description of ongoing research, trying to formulate an answer to the research questions above.

Case Study 1: Empty Mind

In the research project 'Empty Mind', our objective was to explore and modify existing, open-source digital art platforms, with a keen artistic focus on interdisciplinary content – virtual art, music, dance, and spoken word (Timmerman and Vanoeveren 2022). This endeavor laid the foundation for a hybrid, digital art form that transcends traditional boundaries and opens new possibilities for artistic creation, experience, and distribution. The project, funded under the DARIAH Theme 2020–2021, brought together researchers and professionals from diverse disciplines, including ICT developers, a graphic design company, musicians, mocap specialists, and digital artists.

The output of 'Empty Mind' materialized as an audiovisual live performance featuring flutes (piccolo, flute, alto flute, and bass flute), live electronics, and live visuals within a virtual environment designed to be experienced online, on a monitor or a TV screen. Comprising six large movements that can be performed in any order, the project introduced a unique element of audience agency by allowing spectators to influence the performance's trajectory through an interactive UI-layer on top of a livestream.

This interactive layer empowered audiences to actively shape the performance experience. Participants could choose the order of movements by engaging with floating 3D objects representing each movement, and even follow their own movement traces on the screen. The composition's dynamic nature and responsiveness to audience input hinted at the potential for decentralized decision-making within the digital art realm (Figure 8.2).

Flutist Ine Vanoeveren performed in a motion capture suit, and her movements were transferred into a Unity environment, co-creating the virtual environment in real-time. The sound, both the dry flute signal and FX signal, integrated into Unity through a PureData-patch, influenced the virtual environment concurrently. This fusion of sound and movement showcased the collaborative processes inherent in digital art creation.

Wim Henderickx, the composer of 'Empty Mind', was inspired by the geometric figures of the American painter Agnes Martin and how she creates

FIGURE 8.2
Live performance of Empty Mind at the Royal Academy of Fine Arts Antwerp.

© Jayne Nattida Kanyachalao.

discretion on inward-ness and silence. The virtual rooms drew inspiration from Martin's work, incorporating idiosyncratic behavior into their design. The project's virtual assets, represented by abstract avatars, set the stage for potential future scenarios where these objects could become interoperable across different virtual worlds, akin to the discourse on in-game assets as non-fungible tokens (NFTs).

Transition to a VR Performance

The project has recently undergone a transformative phase, transitioning into a live VR performance for up to 20 spectators. This progression represents a significant advancement in the endeavor to break the fifth wall and, more importantly, positions the project on a trajectory that aligns with principles of decentralization, pointing toward potential integration with blockchain technology. The shift to a live VR performance introduces an immersive and participatory dimension, enabling the audience to actively engage with the virtual environment in real time. This departure from traditional observational roles toward a more interactive and dynamic experience is foundational to breaking down barriers between performer and audience (Figure 8.3).

FIGURE 8.3
The virtual scene of *Awakening*, Empty Mind Project.

The move to live VR performance lays the groundwork for future developments that resonate with decentralization and blockchain principles. As the VR experience becomes increasingly interactive, there emerges a heightened potential for decentralized decision-making within the digital art realm. The immersive nature of VR, coupled with blockchain's potential, offers the prospect of establishing a decentralized ecosystem where artistic assets and performances can transcend individual platforms.

The experience gained from transforming 'Empty Mind' into a live VR performance serves as a critical step toward exploring the integration of blockchain technology. The aim is to establish a decentralized framework that empowers creators and audiences alike, facilitating more fluid interactions and ownership of virtual assets.

Envisioning the future of 'Empty Mind', the prospect of interoperability for virtual assets across diverse VR worlds takes center stage. Virtual reality, paired with blockchain and NFTs, could propel these objects into a realm where they become tradable assets with distinct value in a decentralized ecosystem. VR's immersion, combined with blockchain's transparency and NFTs' uniqueness, opens avenues for ownership, exchange, and value creation beyond the immediate performance (Figure 8.4).

While currently operating within a centralized medium, the project's exploration of breaking the fifth wall and the potential interoperability of its objects foreshadows a future where digital art transcends platform constraints. 'Empty Mind' thus acts as an introduction and preparation for further research into blockchain and decentralization, anticipating a transformative shift in how digital art is created, experienced, and shared within interconnected and decentralized ecosystems.

FIGURE 8.4
The virtual scene of *Without desire*, Empty Mind Project.

Case Study 2: DISSOLUTION. Accumulation to the Absurd

Our life in the cloud seems less bound by limitations than the finite life in which we depend on our own body, living conditions, decisions of others, etc. We work online, watch video's online, shop, game, meet friends, gamble, visit festivals, listen to music, up- and download online. But what are the consequences of this virtual indulgence? What is the role of a live happening in an era where linear experience of events has been canceled out? And what digital traces do we leave behind?

Everyday thousands of servers are added somewhere around the globe. And numerous amounts of storage are taken by zombie profiles and inactive virtual rooms. The mass of virtual space clutter is almost as incomprehensive as the (un)limitless of the universe itself. And with the advent of blockchain technology, the challenges become even greater.

Although the integration of blockchain and the metaverse introduces unprecedented opportunities, it also raises more concerns about data consumption and the potential for data waste, serving as a potential pitfall in this technological landscape. Blockchain, with its decentralized and transparent ledger, relies on the verification and storage of vast amounts of data across a distributed network. This process, while ensuring security and immutability, can result in substantial data consumption. In the metaverse, where immersive experiences generate a continuous flow of data, the demand for storage and processing capabilities intensifies.

Data waste emerges as a concern when considering the substantial storage requirements for blockchain transactions and the voluminous data generated within the metaverse. Redundant or outdated information, coupled with the continuous influx of new data from virtual interactions, can lead to an inefficient allocation of resources. This not only impacts the scalability and performance of blockchain networks but also raises environmental concerns due to the energy-intensive nature of certain blockchain consensus mechanisms.

Mitigating data waste in the context of blockchain and the metaverse necessitates strategic design considerations, such as optimizing data structures, implementing efficient consensus algorithms, and exploring sustainable data storage solutions. As the metaverse continues to evolve, striking a balance between the immersive richness of virtual experiences and the responsible management of data resources becomes paramount to ensure the long-term sustainability and scalability of these innovative technologies.

> Is the virtual universe infinite? Can we continue to inexhaustibly exploit the virtual space by spewing never-ending trails of digital data? Is digital clutter the new space junk?

This ongoing project proposes a series of hybrid digital performances as a reaction to this unawareness of human influence on data and server consumption, by addressing the issue on a technological and artistic level as well as by implementing the data visualization into the artwork itself to increase awareness and conceptual understanding.

Experiencing Data

Inspired by the avant-garde compositions of Brian Ferneyhough, the project 'DISSOLUTION. Accumulation to the absurd' delves into the realms of centralized and decentralized digital waste within the context of blockchain technology. Ferneyhough's work, particularly 'Sisyphus Redux' (2011), serves as the musical muse, echoing Albert Camus' existential exploration of the absurdity of life – a theme central to the entire project.

> Acknowledging the truth will conquer it; Sisyphus, just like the absurd man, keeps pushing. When Sisyphus acknowledges the pointlessness of his task and the certainty of his fate, he is freed to realize the absurdity of his situation and to reach a state of contented acceptance.[2]

The immersive experience unfolds in an interactive virtual space, drawing inspiration from Ferneyhough's 'Carceri d'Invenzione', a musical cycle influenced by 18th-century artist Giovanni Battista Piranesi's etchings. The virtual world, akin to a 'wicked dungeon', will be accessible from days preceding the performance until its conclusion, immersing the audience in Ferneyhough's

FIGURE 8.5
Concept art for DISSOLUTION by Studio Plankton.

compositions and offering an enduring immersive experience, featuring poetic live interventions and multiple live performances (Figure 8.5).

These live performances will unfold within a physical cube, serving as an artistic installation and a portal between the physical and virtual performance realms. The performers will wear a motion capture suit, making it possible to create the virtual surroundings by their performative embodiment. Audiences can engage with the performances in both real life and the virtual space. However, this comes at a cost. While the virtual experience seems limitless, the underlying technological constraints become a central theme. The inclusion of data-intensive elements, such as an audiovisual livestream, necessitates carving out space for the livestream to function. While open-source platforms like Mozilla Hubs provide accessibility, they come with limitations, notably the constrained data that can be implemented, including that used by avatars to exist in the virtual space. Consequently, each performance will gradually deconstruct parts of the virtual space, ensuring sufficient data for the livestream and inducing permanent changes to the virtual environment.

The linkage to blockchain becomes evident as the project grapples with the need to maintain the continuity of the blockchain by storing the entire transaction history on a multitude of nodes. This struggle parallels the central theme of 'Dissolution' – the tension between the conqueror, representing action and engagement, and Sisyphus, embodying a seemingly meaningless task.

The attendance of live performances, both in-person and online, correlates with the metaphorical consumption of server capacity: Sisyphus pushing his eternal boulder, representing the drain on virtual resources. The increasing utilization hastens the depletion of these resources, leading to the dissolution and eventual cessation of the virtual space. A digital meter within the room will apprise visitors of their digital footprint, fostering awareness of their actions.

Prior calculations and communication will determine the daily audience capacity for live performances, crucial for sustaining performances throughout the festival's duration. Adherence to these limitations is the responsibility of the audience, as disregard may lead to the cancellation of the final live performances, denying an entire audience the live experience (Figure 8.6).

The project challenges the audience's responsibility, presenting a predetermined limit to live performance attendance. Disregarding this premise risks canceling subsequent performances and the eventual dissolution of the virtual experience. This intentional choice, mirroring Sisyphus' acceptance of his fate, forces contemplation on the consequences of our actions in both the real and virtual realms.

As a poignant conclusion, the artists grapple with erasing their digital traces by permanently closing the virtual room and destroying all artwork at the festival's end. This act encapsulates the project's ethos – an exploration of the ephemeral nature of virtual experiences and the difficult choices artists face in the digital age. The memories of those who witnessed it become the sole remnants, echoing Camus' acknowledgment of the absurdity of existence (Figure 8.7).

In envisioning the evolution of the Dissolution project, the incorporation of blockchain technology emerges as a transformative force, enriching its conceptual framework and surmounting challenges tied to centralization,

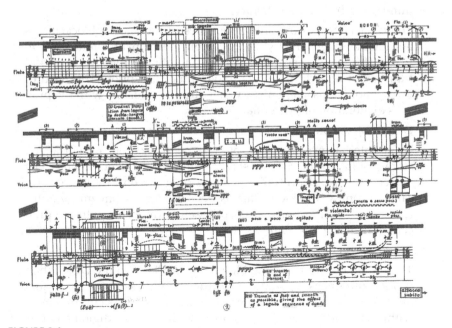

FIGURE 8.6
Score of Ferneyhough's 'Carceri d'Invenzione'.

FIGURE 8.7
Concept art for DISSOLUTION by Studio Plankton.

digital waste, and the ephemeral nature of virtual spaces. The integration of blockchain unfolds across several pivotal dimensions:

- Immutable Transaction History:

  The cornerstone of this integration lies in harnessing blockchain's immutable ledger. Every nuance, from participant interactions to live performances and virtual space alterations, finds a secure and transparent record through cryptographic encryption. This ensures an indelible transaction history that aligns seamlessly with the project's exploration of existential themes.

- Decentralized Storage:

  To counterbalance the risks of data centralization, decentralized storage solutions take center stage. Platforms like InterPlanetary File System (IPFS) or decentralized cloud storage become the bedrock for safeguarding voluminous data associated with livestreams and virtual space modifications. This approach harmonizes with the project's core tenet of decentralization.

- Tokenization of Digital Assets:

  The integration of non-fungible tokens (NFTs) into the Dissolution project introduces a paradigm shift in the representation of virtual assets. Artistic performances, poetry readings, and specific moments within the virtual space are bestowed with a unique digital identity. NFTs confer ownership, transferability, and even potential economic value, ushering in a novel intersection of art and blockchain.

- Smart Contracts for Performance Rules:

  Smart contracts emerge as the architects of automated and enforceable performance rules within the virtual space. These contracts navigate and enforce predetermined limits on live performance attendance, ensuring that the project's constraints are programmatically adhered to, eliminating the need for external oversight.

- Blockchain-Based Digital Footprint Meter:

  At the forefront of user engagement and environmental awareness stands the blockchain-based digital footprint meter. Empowered by smart contracts, this meter delivers real-time insights into participants' interactions within the virtual space. The transparency it fosters ensures heightened accountability and a nuanced understanding of the environmental impact of each participant.

- Decentralized Governance Model:

  The exploration of a decentralized governance model introduces an innovative layer of community engagement. Blockchain's architecture facilitates decentralized voting mechanisms, empowering participants to influence decisions related to alterations, performances, and the overall trajectory of the project. This communal approach amplifies the essence of community engagement.

- Closing the Virtual Room with Blockchain Event:

  In a crescendo, a blockchain-based event takes center stage to ceremoniously close the virtual room and erase digital traces at the festival's conclusion. This symbolic act, etched on the blockchain, signifies not just the culmination of the project but also the artists' unwavering commitment to embracing the ephemeral nature of the digital experience.

The integration of blockchain technology into the Dissolution project is not merely a technical augmentation; it is a profound exploration of the intersections between art, technology, and the evolving landscape of the virtual realm. This harmonious synthesis propels the project into uncharted territories, where decentralization and transparency redefine the boundaries of immersive artistic expression.

Conclusion

The exploration of blockchain technology for decentralized music within virtual environments, as illuminated by the research projects Empty Mind and DISSOLUTION, marks a profound paradigm shift in our understanding and interaction with contemporary music. These projects, driven by the ethos of breaking the fifth wall, extend beyond the traditional boundaries of music performance, challenging established structures and fostering a more inclusive, transparent, and artistically vibrant future within the metaverse.

The synergy between decentralized technologies and musical expression, exemplified through the creation of non-fungible tokens (NFTs), fundamentally transforms how musicians navigate the digital age. These tokens not only establish ownership and authenticity but also empower musicians to directly connect with their audience, redefining ownership dynamics in an era where the virtual and the real seamlessly intertwine.

This transformative journey echoes the essence of breaking the fifth wall, not merely dismantling barriers within music performance but actively engaging audiences in the co-creation, ownership, and appreciation of musical art in virtual spaces. As musicians pioneer this innovative approach, the fifth wall becomes a dynamic space co-shaped by performers and spectators alike, ushering in a democratic and participatory era that promises a richer, more engaging, and collectively crafted musical landscape.

Notes

1 Usually, one refers to immersion as the feeling that occurs in a situation where spectators (e.g., viewers, gamers) focus so much attention on medium content, and where the latter causes such 'involvement' (literally translated: 'engagement') that the audience ceases to notice things happening around them (Jennett et al. 2008). I distinguish between strategic immersion and narrative immersion. In strategic immersion, the individual is so absorbed in achieving a goal that the environment around him/her completely fades into the background (Moeller 2017). Narrative immersion is experienced when the user becomes so enthralled by a story that he/she experiences an irresistible urge to discover the plot of the story and cannot stop watching or playing (Mandal 2013).
2 Albert Camus, The Myth of Sisyphus (1942), chapter 4.

References

Favero, P. S. H. A journey from virtual and mixed reality to byzantine icons via Buddhist philosophy. *Anthrovision*, 7(1), 1–15, 2019.
Hornecker, E. The role of physicality in tangible and embodied interactions. *Interactions*, 18(2), 19–23, 2011.

Jennett, C., Cox, A. L., Cairns, P., Dhoparee, S., Epps, A., Tijs, T., & Walton, A. Measuring and defining the experience of immersion in games. *International Journal of Human-Computer Studies*, 66(9), 641–661, 2008.

Lombard, M., & Jones, M. T. Defining presence. In Lombard, M., Biocca, F., Freeman, J., Ijsselsteijn, W., Schaevitz, R. (eds) *Immersed in Media*. Zurich, Switzerland: Springer, 2015.

Mandal, S. Brief introduction of virtual reality & its challenges. *International Journal of Scientific & Engineering Research*, 304–309, 2013.

Milgram, P., & Kishino, F. A taxonomy of mixed reality visual displays. *IEICE Transactions on Information and Systems*, E77–D, 1321–1329, 1994.

Moeller, X.X. (2017). "Different types of immersion and how they work". Retrieved from: https://ispr.info/2012/06/28/different-types-of-immersion-and-how-they-work/

Ramanathan, Raja & Raja, Kirtana. *Handbook of Research on Architectural Trends in Service-Driven Computing*. Hershey: IGI Global, 2014.

Stephenson, Neal. *Snow Crash*. New York: Bantam Books, 1992.

Timmerman, Kristof & Vanoeveren, Ine. Empty Mind: an exploration towards an autonomous digital experience and aesthetics within a virtual live performance. In *Sixteenth International Conference on Tangible, Embedded, and Embodied Interaction (TEI '22)*. Association for Computing Machinery, New York, 1–6. 2022.

9

Hypermusic Experiment 0.9: Modeling, Mapping, and Prototyping the Future

Einar Torfi Einarsson

Iceland University of the Arts, Reykjavik, Iceland

Introduction

Embarking on a journey into the realm of music generation, the Hypermusic Experiment 0.9 proposes an innovative system that goes beyond traditional boundaries. It reimagines the creative process, introducing a novel mechanism and spectra interaction to generate *notated* music, ultimately aiming to explore an ever-evolving, fluid, nonlinear, decentralized and a participatory musical milieu, one that is continually shaped by its interactions – from internal processes and performer's interpretation to societal and cultural shifts.

The Hypermusic system envisaged initiates its process by generating notated/inscribed pages, termed partial-scores (as artifacts). These pages, laden with an assortment of musical graphics, are the basic units of our compositional system. Furthermore, they aim to function as nonlinear, decentralized, and multiple, signifying an infinity of possible musical pieces, unending and ongoing. From its inception, this system is a fusion of the digital and physical realms, a blend of the virtual and the real. It doesn't merely start; it exists in a continuum. In this sense, it furthermore seeks to align with differential ontology.

This chapter aims to elucidate this system that aims to operate as an infinite notation-machine by tracing the creative path that led to its inception and shedding light on the rationale behind its unique functionalities. Moreover, the architecture of the system will be delineated and its future as a decentralized autonomous organization (DAO) explored that promises an intricate interplay of differential ontology, musical creation, and performer empowerment.

Before proceeding I want to stress the significance of notation and how it is viewed here as a crucial assembly component, functioning as a nexus for interpretation and experimentation, and a bridge between various planes, moving beyond the rigidity of traditional notation, yet preserving the interpretive space vital for musical creation. Historically, notated artifacts have

DOI: 10.1201/9781003458227-10

acted as touchstones of human intellect, emotion, and cultural expression, offering glimpses into sociocultural, philosophical, and technological epochs (Chanan, 1994; Magnusson, 2019). Within music, notation is instrumental in transmitting, interpreting, and evolving musical ideas. Scores become living entities, stimulating and challenging successive generations of musicians.

As the digital era evolves, notated artifacts continue to find relevance in new avatars. Digital notation, like e-books, digital art, screen scores, animated notation, or simply music scores on PDFs, marries the essence of traditional notation with modern potentialities (Craig, 2019, 2023). Technologies such as AR and VR will offer immersive experiences that intertwine physical and digital notations in innovative ways.

As raw audio music generation through AI is upon us, where any kind of music can be generated with a single prompt (Agostinelli et al., 2023), it becomes critical to renew and challenge our relationship with musicking and its core components such as notation. Notations are 'codings' intrinsically future-facing and operate as relational tools always positioned between agents, an element of 'interstrata', such as the performer-audience, composer-performer, or computer-human dynamic. Notation seen as such advocates for a culture of making, process, potentials, and transformation through intermediary spaces, where different flows, codes, and strata intersect (Deleuze & Guattari, 1987). Within the ambit of the Hypermusic Experiment 0.9, the system merges the rich historical legacy of notation with its future potential. This digital-physical hybridity not only reinforces the value of notation but propels also it into the future, inviting us to imagine new ways of interacting with these culturally significant objects (be it human and/or post-human interaction).

Differential Ontology, *Desiring-Machines*, Hypermusic, and Other Background

In some of my compositional endeavors in the past I have explored the application of differential ontology to music or as I like to call it: continuing the real into the music domain. I have done this in different ways in different pieces. Here, I will detail three approaches I've termed 'multipieces', or multiplicity compositions. I will explore their ties to differential ontology and demonstrate how they lay the foundation for the Hypermusic Experiment 0.9.

Desiring-Machines

The exploration of implementing differential ontology into music was most notably developed in my piece *Desiring-Machine* (Einarsson, 2012), a piece originally written for 24 musicians and 2 conductors and makes various use of a concept by the same name developed by Deleuze and Guattari. This piece, as well as others which will be discussed here, presents a critique on the idea of wholeness, fixity, representation, and identity, and aims to operate as a multiplicity, on local and global levels, and therethrough explore a differential ontology of the 'work'. This constitutes, partly, what I mean by multipieces and resonates also as a critique on the conception of the musical work as a whole and a fixed object that developed in the 18th century through the empowerment of the score, but could doubtless be traced to earlier conceptions (Goehr, 2007). But the main impetus here was the ontology put forth by Gilles Deleuze and Felix Guattari, which affects the compositional approach in different ways. *Desiring-Machines* can be performed and assembled in various open-ended ways: each instrumental part and any combination of parts can be performed as a piece on its own (with or without conductor(s)), resulting in a postfix title: partial-object 0.xxxx. Thus, the piece is in fact a *multipiece* in the sense that there is no single instance capable of representing it, as it consists of 24 solos, 276 duos, 2024 trios, 10626 quartets, 42504 quintets, 134596 sextets, .., 2704156 duodectets, etc. I call this the global assemblage/multiplicity. Through this aspect the piece is never a whole piece; i.e., the piece does never present itself as a single fixed object, we only ever can perceive it partially. Each performance is merely an open window onto that ever incomplete 'whole-less' activity which is the only identity of *Desiring-Machines*.

> In desiring-machines everything functions at the same time, but amid hiatuses and ruptures, breakdowns and failures, stalling and short circuits, distances and fragmentations, within a sum that never succeeds in bringing its various parts together so as to form a whole.

> **(Deleuze & Guattari, 1983)**

As there is, of course, a single version for 24 instruments and one/two conductors I needed to establish a multiplicity on the local level as well. The *local* assemblage/multiplicity strives to create a dynamic and unpredictable interplay between the conductor, performers, and the material itself. There I employ and invent techniques that assure that each performance produces difference, most important of which are the following intertwined techniques: (1) decoupling (prescriptive notation), (2) difference-repetition (multiple pathways), and (3) nonlocalizable conducting-moment (Einarsson, 2015a).

Through the technique of (1) decoupling, physical components of players are separated from each other and physical actions prescribed. For instance, the left and right hands of string players are given their own distinct parts. This means that the movements of both hands – or even fingers, hands, and mouths, when applied to various instruments – don't necessarily work in tandem for a specific end result. Instead, they can be seen as independently moving forces, gaining independent materials and working

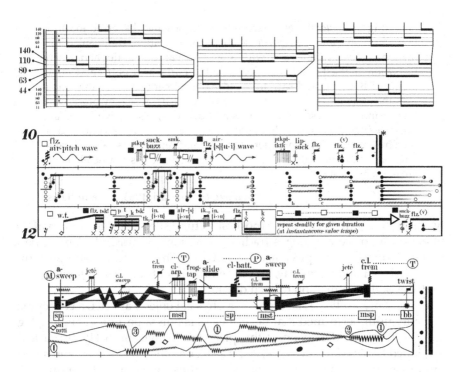

FIGURE 9.1
Desiring-Machines, fragments from the conductor's part (above, tempi patterns), and flute and violin parts demonstrating multiple paths and various repeating lengths.

toward an unpredictable sonic outcome. This approach results in rhythmic and dynamic independence within each instrumental part through the use of prescriptive notation (Einarsson, 2012). Furthermore, decoupling is also employed between the performers and conductor(s), resulting in an independent part for the conductor(s). Moreover, the conductor's part and the instrumental parts are designed to repeat, but they are of different lengths, and, importantly, continuously different lengths. This means that as they repeat, they constantly meet each other's movements differently, creating a dynamic interplay (Figure 9.1).

This dynamic interplay of various lengths, sizes, and content, between conductor(s), performers and materials, is the main functioning of the (2) difference-repetition, which in turn secures that the conducting moment emerges as a nonlocalizable communication at all times (3). Thus these elements and the piece itself aim to converge with Deleuze and Guattari's outline of desiring-machines:

> Desiring-machines are the following: formative machines, whose very misfiring are functional, and whose functioning is indiscernible from their formation; chronogeneous machines engaged in their own assembly,

operating by *nonlocalizable* intercommunications and dispersed localiza-
tions, bringing into play processes of temporalization, fragmented formations, and *detached parts*, with a surplus value of code, and where
the whole is itself produced alongside the parts, as a part apart or, as
[Samuel] Butler would say, 'in another department' that fits the whole
over the other parts; machines in the strict sense because they proceed by
breaks and flows, associated waves and particles, associative flows and
partial objects, inducing – always at a distance – transverse connections,
thereby *producing selections*, detachments, and remainders, with a trans-
ference of individuality, in a generalized schizogenesis whose elements
are the schizzes-flow.

(Deleuze & Guattari, 1983, my emphasis)

By emphasizing difference, in a (post-)structural sense, and the return of the
different, the piece challenges traditional notions of musical identity, be it
within the piece or the piece itself as a whole. The conductor and performers, in their dynamic interplay, become embodiments of pure difference, constantly evolving in relation to each other.

But the score itself is a fixed object, a physical object/artifact, a conceptual
virtuality until performed that nevertheless is only a part of something bigger. And here we must connect this piece to the concept of Hypermusic as
developed by de Assis (de Assis, 2022) as it combines, assembles, and super-
imposes multiple materials of various natures, musical and non-musical.
Hypermusic as conceived by de Assis is a multidimensional musical practice
that intersects sonic events with a virtual constellation of texts, images, ideas,
and cultural references, transcending traditional boundaries to create richer,
more complex musical experiences (de Assis, 2022). The whole is always a
part of another assemblage. The Hypermusic Experiment 0.9 is an endeavor
to further develop this connection.

Grapher Morphogenetics IIb

Another approach is explored in the piece *Grapher morphogenetics IIb*
(Einarsson, 2023), where a step into the digital realm provided a different perspective on the 'whole-less' activity of the ~~work~~ (now under erasure). Written
for a browser environment (screen score) and solo to any amount of string
instruments and conceived as a multipiece, both as (1) having multiple versions graphically, i.e., every time they are opened in a browser new graphics
are produced, and as (2) how they are performed/interpreted (various durations, techniques discretion, etc.). Here, the differential ontology is reflected,
differently, in the ongoing aspect which is captured by the animated streaming of lines that are constructed in real-time using different frames of randomization (see snapshot in Figure 9.2). These moving lines (flows) are the
notations; they are never ending and thus escape any structural beginning
and end. Furthermore, the lines are placed within a parametric notational

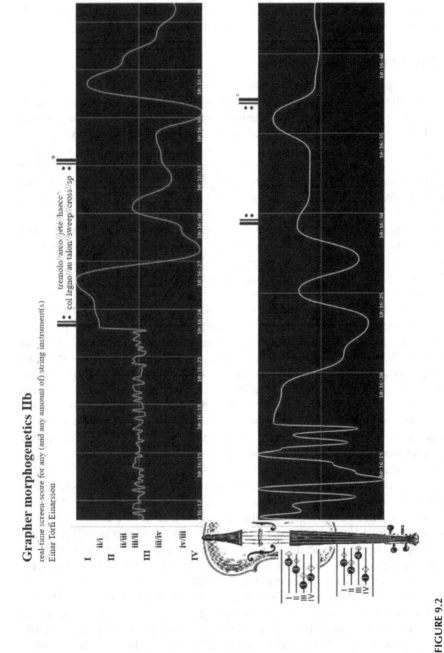

FIGURE 9.2

A snapshot from the *Grapher morphogenetics IIb* score, (a moment that might never return).

space (prescriptive notation) indicating movement in designated areas on the instrument(s); again the technique of decoupling is employed; i.e., the left and right hands are here engaged as independent, unforeseen, interplay of forces/movements. Various additional instrumental techniques are outlined but are implemented on performer's discretion.

Underdetermined Figures

The third piece I want to outline is *Underdetermined figures* (Einarsson, 2015/2018) where a specific field notation is developed and network of multiple paths employed that bring various forces into interaction. The piece is a multipiece (multiplicity composition) that is designed for any combination and type of instruments. It is also based on prescriptive notation of physical parameters. These notations are not specific to any single instrument or group but aim to combine ambiguity and specificity in notation. The notation should maintain instrumental ambiguity while being specific in its emerging instructions. The piece worked with the concept of proto-objects (Schwab, 2015), which are shapes or figures that depend on context and are not yet identifiable. Transcribing this concept into a musical context it becomes a 'proto-score', which is a score that requires a specific context to become an actual score and music. The proto-score remains in a state of virtuality, entangled in multiple pathways, awaiting specific contexts to actualize into music (obviously an element of all scores but here it is amplified structurally). It does not prescribe a sonic identity but instead opens up a field of possibilities, much like Deleuze and Guattari's concept of the virtual (Deleuze & Guattari, 1987). This virtuality, filled with potential connections and inclusions, resonates with the Deleuzian-Guattarian idea that identity is not fixed but is a continuous process of becoming through differences. Just as Deleuze and Guattari argue that entities are constituted by a myriad of relations and differences, the piece is never singular but is always open to multiple interpretations and performances. Each performance, with its unique context and interpretation, becomes a new becoming, a new difference.

This multipiece revolves around 100 such figures, as seen in Figure 9.3, that are read according to certain guidelines, but the duration, order, instrumentation, and presentation format are all open-ended, giving performers a lot of discretion. Each figure is placed within a field or parametric space. This space has different circular areas representing numbers (see Figure 9.3), and when a figure is placed in this space, it can be read in multiple ways to indicate changes in values, which are then assigned specific physical parameters that operate as instructions for performers. For example, the parameters for string instruments include force or pressure of action (indicated by F in Figure 9.3), location on the instrument (L), number of active fingers (A), and spread of fingers or bow division (S), and each parameter has multiple starting points (e.g., F^x, F^y) and multiple pathways, and a specific spectrum

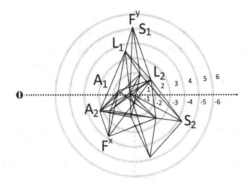

FIGURE 9.3
A figure from *Underdetermined figures*.

while 'moving' (Einarsson, 2015b). Furthermore, the field notation is divided into two halves by a zero line, which indicates a change in nature of the parameters; e.g., force (F) becomes inwardly directed when it is below the zero line, i.e., not as pressure asserted outward onto instruments, but ranging from imagination to muscle/ligament tensions (see Einarsson, 2015b, for a more detailed delineation).

When such figure is actualized or read by a performer, an interplay of specific forces is activated, or emerges, and the interaction of these forces can result in complex outcomes and interpretations; moreover, the parameters can be seen as a set of forces that might clash or cancel each other out, making the piece open to unpredictability and experimentation by and through

> summoning forces. […] making the invisible forces visible in themselves, drawing up figures with a geometrical appearance but that are no more than forces – the forces of gravity, heaviness, rotations, the vortex, explosion, expansion, germination and time.
>
> **(Deleuze & Guattari, 1994, p. 182)**

Planes, Aesthetico-Epistemic, and Hypermusic

What these three multipieces have in common is an interplay of three main planes (tri-planes): conceptual plane (knowledge), performative plane (the concrete sensory production, aesthetic), and technical plane (means and methods). These multipieces could therefore be seen as complex arrangements of aesthetico-epistemic components (de Assis, 2022, p.53), emphasizing the intricate interplay between aesthetic properties and knowledge components within musical works. These are important aspects of Hypermusic as conceived by de Assis that emphasizes the multidimensional and virtual nature of musical works. What is envisaged with the Hypermusic Experiment 0.9 is a shift, where the conceptual plane shifts into the performative/concrete plane, or, put differently, the *actualization* of some of the virtual elements present in these works. The differential ontology explored through these pieces is only an approximation to these conceptual worlds as the 'bridge' (the technical plane) is, in a sense, incapable and representational (which only makes an incomplete image). Performance instances of these scores only actualizes them briefly (like appearing/disappearing windows), but with new technology being able to *perform* them as code, nonstop, these conceptual worlds would no longer be only conceptual; they become concrete, as these planes become more porous and variously flowing into each other. Of course, a new conceptual plane opens up, new virtuality, whenever the performative plane reaches into the previous conceptual plane, and in that sense, these multipieces, these scores outlined above are scores awaiting to become codes performed by computers, triggering a new set of tri-planes and coming closer to 'recasting' the real (Morrison, 2015).

Outline of a Prototype: Hypermusic Experiment 0.9

The multipieces discussed so far can be viewed as (proto)models for important functional aspects of the Hypermusic Experiment 0.9 system. *Grapher Morphogenetics* provides or prepares the dynamic *window* onto that ever incomplete, ongoing, production, that 'whole-less' activity; while the *Desiring-Machines* provides the schizzes-flows, multiple paths, and the necessity of structural difference techniques (e.g., decoupling, spectrum from prescriptive notation to descriptive notation), as well as the value and power of a fixed object with virtual dimensions, but now as a network of partial-scores (artifacts). *Underdetermined figures* provides the interplay of forces, virtuality as possibility spaces, and an intermediary space or 'thinking' space for the system (where similar fields could be constructed and employed with randomized dots and lines drawn between them to create infinite version of multidimensional parametric movements). Thus, the outputs of the Hypermusic Experiment 0.9 system will be in heterogeneous forms and formats, i.e., various live/real-time formats as well as various fixed formats of artifacts (partial-scores, indicating a fragment, a break, from something larger, namely process or flows). The generated partial-scores will emphasize the aesthetico-epistemic qualities of their making by allowing the tri-planes to flow into each other, where graphics (multifunction of inscription/material/technique/instruction and metaphoric interpretability), text (the language of theory, concepts and poetry), and performance come into contact with each other, and where performance is conceived as manifold: human and machinic, performer (human/post-human), and/or composer (yielding possibly other partial-scores).

And when it operates on them, when it turns back upon them (se rabat sur elles), it brings about transverse communications, transfinite summarizations, polyvocal and transcursive inscriptions on its own surface, on which the functional breaks of partial objects are continually intersected by breaks in the signifying chains, and by breaks effected by a subject that uses them as reference points in order to locate itself.

(Deleuze & Guattari, 1983, p. 47)

Hypermusic Experiment 0.9 serves as a venture into the realm of musical notation, meticulously constructed at the confluence of differential ontology and computational design. Its core components are the input parameters, the infinite notation-machine (with all its sub-machines), the subsequent partial outputs, as well as the various feedback loops (see diagram, Figure 9.4). This system is not merely a passive recorder, or reorder, of musical thought but must be considered as an active participant in the very act of musical creation.

The system strives to be a hybrid of physical/digital and conceptual/performative dimensions; the outputs, both digital and physical, are the breaks in the ongoing digital flow, points of discontinuity that lead to new connections, flows, and formations (Deleuze & Guattari, 1983). The physical objects, i.e., the partial-scores, will thus have various invisible threads linking them to the ongoing digital/machinic performance of the system, and each physical performance can be fed back into the system, transformed, in various forms and formats to further influence the system's production.

The notation-machine approaches notation as an open-ended graphical problem rather than a staff notation that conventionally employs representational symbols for precise durational values and pitch. It will, however, employ noteheads and curves, of various sizes, shapes, and colors, but here we emphasize molecular forces instead of molars (even though the system will be equipped to fluctuate between and/or superimpose such qualities on its surfaces), and give certain level of autonomy to 'cells' (and, as with biological cells, they might not express all their genes all the time). What follows is an outline of this system, its architecture and functional components. At this stage the focus is on the design rather than technical details as the system is still in development.

System Architecture

The inception of the musical notation process starts with user-defined inputs. These parameters serve as initial conditions, setting the stage for the infinite notation-machine's subsequent operations. Here, basic elements like the amount of pages, amount of instruments, type of instruments, morphology type, complexity types and levels, and other spectra can be adjusted. However, these are only variables partially informing the notation-machine, which is a multidimensional production, rendering, always to a certain degree,

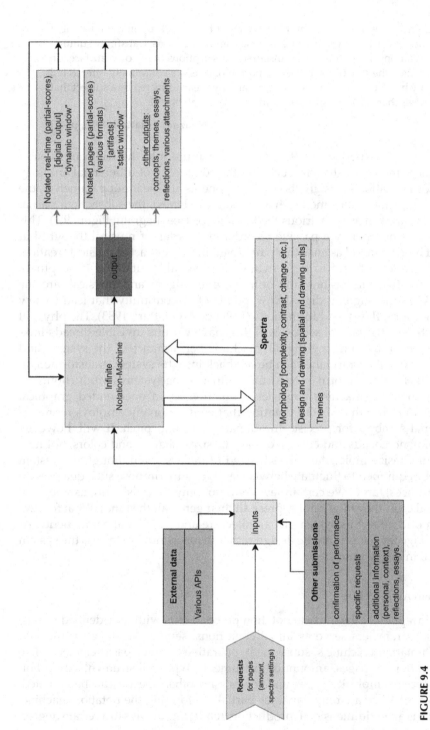

FIGURE 9.4

Diagram of the basic components of the Hypermusic Experiment 0.9 system.

unforeseen results. Furthermore, not all parameters can be adjusted and the available ones can also be randomly determined. Other inputs are foreseen to be implemented, such as post-performance submissions ranging from facts (dates and names, etc.) to reflections as well as other type of inputs that are not user-defined such as various external data flow that the system can 'listen' to through various APIs. In this way the system, as a multipiece and an instance of Hypermusic, becomes a network of multidimensional and multifarious aesthetico-epistemic components.

At the heart of the system lies the infinite notation-machine. Drawing inspiration from Deleuze's concept of the machinic, the notation-machine examines how disparate elements connect to produce a novelty (Deleuze & Guattari, 1987). It promotes a rhizomatic model, favoring nonlinear, multifaceted connections that embrace continual change. This machinic perspective challenges static identities and rigid classifications, advocating for multiplicity and transformation. It seamlessly integrates processes, drawing units, spectra, and solves various graphical problems by means of scalable vector graphics (SVG). This machine continuously operates, generating endless musical possibilities that interact with the given input parameters. How the interaction of the spectra works and the general operation of the notation-machine is delineated below.

Post-processing within the notation-machine, the outputs manifest in the form of (1) partial-scores (PDF pages of various dimensions) and (2) dynamic and evolving graphic notations inspired by the *Grapher morphogenetics IIb* through real-time 'windows', variously defined, ready to be interpreted and experimented with, by human or post-human entities.

Spectral Interactions in the Notation-Machine

> Deleuze maintains a dimension of order that operates randomly through discontinuous junction that is comprised of divisions, and also determined sections. In Deleuze, the nature of order is, then, semi-random. Furthermore, the connected elements do not signify and are not homogeneous. In other words, they are nonsignifying and heterogeneous. What is found assembled in an ordered section are mobile stocks of information that fit into a system of points and drawings, a nondiscursive, transcursive kind of writing, according to Deleuze and Guattari, which forms a pastiche with Simondonian translation in order to locate a process straight out of the real.
>
> **(Sauvagnargues, 2013, p. 129)**

In this quote, Sauvagnargues captures many important aspects of the operation of the notation-machine, such as the semi-randomness filtered through divisions, and nonsignifying elements assembled to form a transcursive writing. The idea of spectral interaction within the notation-machine reflects, in many respects, the physical world's interference patterns, where waves,

be it light or sound, superimpose to create new patterns, sometimes ampli-
fying and at other times cancelling each other out. What follows is how the
spectra is defined and envisaged to interact and function by taking the 'middle road between order and disorder' (Sauvagnargues, 2013).

Within the notation-machine are various spectra (Figure 9.5) that can be
categorized thus:

Morphology: this amounts to form, structure and its dynamics, informing both the design and content, globally and locally. Within this category operate six spectra of complexity (complex vs. simple); contrast
(seamless vs. contrasting); change (static vs. gradual vs. eruptive); fixity
(indeterminate vs. determinate); geometry (linear vs. nonlinear); and
information (descriptive vs. prescriptive).

Design and drawing: this category is divided into spatial units and drawing cells, both informed by various morphology spectra.

Themes: consisting of list of concepts, they might influence, e.g., textual
material as a layer within the score, performance notes, and/or affecting the parameters of certain spectra.

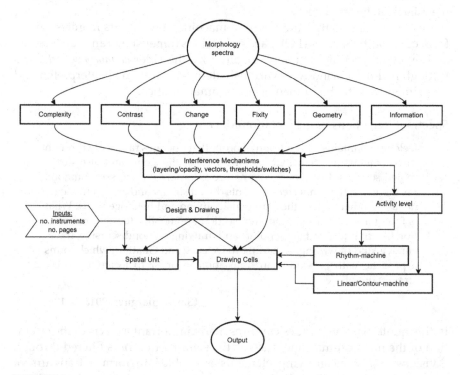

FIGURE 9.5
The notation-machine's flowchart.

It is important to notice that the morphological spectra can influence each other by being superimposed, overwritten, or canceled out. Three main mechanisms of spectral interference are employed:

- Layering and opacity: just as in graphic design or digital art, each spectrum is visualized as a layer. The intensity, or amplitude, of its influence is related to its opacity. So, one spectrum can be 'faded' in the presence of a stronger, more opaque one, representing the overwriting mechanism. For example, fixity-spectrum shifting toward 'determinate' would push that layer into the foreground and decrease the opacity of the indeterminate layer, until hidden.

- Vector influence: using vector mathematics, each spectrum is represented as a vector in a multidimensional space. The resultant when all spectra are combined would give the final output, allowing for superpositions and cancellations.

- Thresholds and switches: certain thresholds where if spectra overlap beyond a certain point, they cancel each other out or trigger a new, unexpected outcome.

The spectra influence and inform the design and drawing's spatial unit (see Figure 9.5): As the notation-machine operates with a two-dimensional canvas or paper formats (width × length) for the partial-scores, the initial step is to determine these dimensions (per request). This is the first step; it is randomly determined and sets the frame for other factors. The second step is informed by morphology: geometry spectrum (linear vs. nonlinear) and divides this canvas into subframes or spaces, and is furthermore informed by the following inputs and spectra:

- number of instruments (which can be fixed, open, or randomized as per request),

- complexity (determining the numbers of layers per instrument as spatial division of the canvas-area for that instrument, or superimposed layers within a given subframe, called sub-layer(s) with various degree of opacity),

- number of pages (informed also by morphology:contrast and :change spectra in regard to how similar the pages are per request).

All of these can be randomized and the resulting partial-score approached by any instrumental force (solo to x-number).

Once the spatial unit concludes their frame design, the drawing cells take over. Their function is to draw graphics into these frames using vector graphics (SVGs), and are divided into (1) rhythmic activity degree (horizontal divisions, rhythm-machine), and (2) linear/contour activity degree (vertical variation, contour-machine) within given subframe. These are further influenced by morphology spectra on a local level.

These drawing cells are constantly running but are not always employed directly or inscribed onto the pages. They are thus smaller machines within the overall notation-machine, dynamic entities, defined by what I call meta-random functions, in-between order and disorder. For example, the linear/contour-machine generates constant values or variables (defined as percentage of a given frame), but does that through various, autonomous, behavioral patterns, e.g., through meta-random loops (see Figure 9.6).

In Figure 9.6b we see two instances of 2,000 points being generated within the meta-random loop;[1] notice that they exhibit a great variety of patterns, with some fields being very short-lived and others being long-lived. The randomization of parameters for each distribution also adds to the variability and extremity of the values. The parameters of different random distributions (here, as an example, Uniform, Gaussian, and Exponential) are also controlled by various spectra, which in turn influence the behavior of the cell. This is similar to a biological cell expression that is not always being read, and can change its expression when other behavior or 'genes' are activated (Sheetz & Yu, 2018), which happens here through the influence of spectra settings. Furthermore, this cell activity can be sampled through different resolutions depending on the spectra settings; for example, low-complexity and high seamless settings would sample the activity with low resolution, aiming for few dots and smooth curves being drawn within a given frame.

This is all part of the ongoing 'performance' of the system propelled by the differential ontology. This also resonates with Bolognini's *Sealed Computers* series (Bolognini, 2012), as these 'cells' exist not as fixed entities but as endless possibilities, forever changing and never fully realized. However, this drawing cell's expression is eventually connected to the rhythm-machine which also runs continuously in a similar vein but when connected they distribute the values (as points) horizontally and vertically within a given (sub) frame, drawing noteheads onto points, curves between them and/or various other symbols. Based on the complexity level, these can have many layers superimposed within frames that are defined either as descriptive (using traditional clefs) or as prescriptive (using physical spaces), or indeed both superimposed (e.g., if that spectra is in balance). For instance, see Figure 9.7, where frames have been generated with high linear geometry setting and low complexity resulting in two curves superimposed in one subframe. Various clef-spaces (g/f-clef, bow-clef, valve-clef) define the activity within and could all be present (like in this example), enabling performer's discretion, or they could have different level of opacity (e.g., more determinate). The various spectra further influence their range and behavior, in terms of linearity, activity, transformation, variety, etc.

Examples of extremes: When considering the drawing cells alone we can predict certain outcomes of various extremes, such as very small canvas with

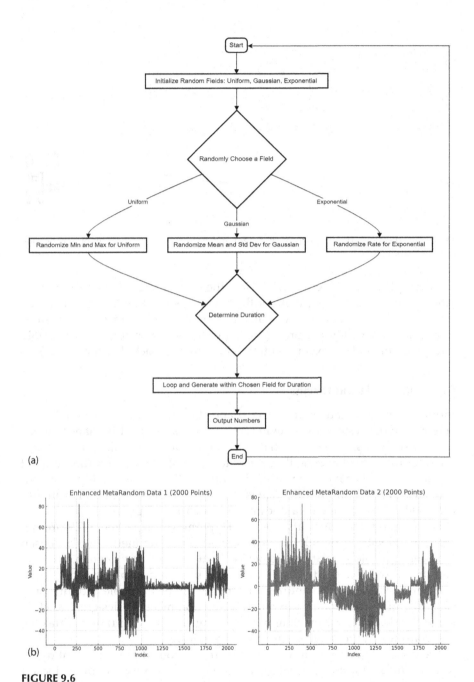

FIGURE 9.6
(a, b) Example of a (6a) meta-random loop flowchart; random distribution (various types, e.g., Uniform, Gaussian, and Exponential), within random parameters, for random duration; 6b: two plots showing different outputs of 2,000 index points.

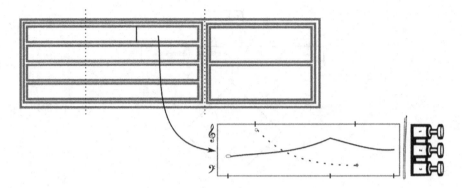

FIGURE 9.7
Demo of a division of a canvas (upper image) and various subframe definitions using clef-spaces (lower image).

high complexity and high activity. Here the system might have to adjust the size of the graphics (e.g., line width) to make sure they fit into the given frame/space, but these kind of outcomes are of high interest as they afford a specific challenge to performers/composers, which in turn need to apply interpretation and/or experimentation in their approach (D'Errico, 2018).

Design Rationale and Discussion

Input parameters and interactions shape the outputs and eventually the behavior of the system. By allowing both humans and post-humans to influence these inputs, the system challenges and redefines traditional boundaries, offering a novel avenue that caters to contemporary and future musical sensibilities. This also emphasizes decentralization of authorship and control. However, a built-in challenge is necessary as the system is also an infinite multipiece, i.e., not a blank-canvas scorewriter program.

The partial-scores' formats used in Hypermusic Experiment 0.9 are not arbitrary, albeit semi-randomly determined. They are meticulously chosen to foster a symbiotic relationship between human and post-human, physical and digital worlds. The formats function as breaks, possible obstacles even, and never as streamlined entities; they might not be printable and thus only exist digitally. This is a research-based notation-machine designed to challenge and destabilize prevailing practices, urging 'users', or rather partakers, to reconsider and reimagine music's boundaries.

The decision to adopt prescriptive notation is rooted in its inherent dynamism. Unlike traditional musical notations, prescriptive notation doesn't merely depict frequencies and durations, i.e., fixed sonic results. It illustrates the movement of forces, the collisions, and is open to accidents and unforeseen results. This format celebrates movement over static frequencies.

The 'how' of this notation revolves around unique spaces, focusing on mapping instrumental dimensions rather than adhering to fixed pitches and precise note-values (Einarsson, 2017, 2015/2018; Kanno, 2007).

We have outlined a system that integrates the diverse spectra into a coherent notation-machine. The crucial aspect is to fine-tune the interactions, ensuring that the outcomes, even when unpredictable, are fruitful for engagement, although in a challenging way. Experimentation, iterative adjustments, and feedback from performers/composers/musicians are pivotal in continuing and refining this system. As it develops with and through those who engage with it, or participate, it must be noted that the submissions, outputs, and requests are intended to be (1) archival in nature, i.e., gathering various versions, information 'particles', artifacts, forming constellations and growing the network of the ~~work~~, and (2) affecting the behavior of the system through feedback loops. This calls for a comprehensive computational operation that ideally aligns itself with the differential ontology explored by the multipiece.

Implementing Hypermusic Experiment 0.9 as a DAO: Empowering Performers through Decentralization

Decentralized autonomous organizations (DAOs) have not only redefined digital ownership and decentralized governance but have also paved the way for collective participation and empowerment. When Hypermusic Experiment 0.9 aligns with a DAO framework, as its trajectory, it promises an intricate interplay of differential ontology, musical creation, and performer empowerment.

The essence of a DAO, with its fluidity and absence of a central authority, parallels the principles of differential ontology which emphasizes dynamism, becoming, and difference. When Hypermusic Experiment 0.9 operates within this decentralized context, it promotes a collective and dynamic creativity, echoing the infinite prospects of the infinite notation-machine.

Building upon the ethos of indeterminate music, prescriptive notation, and collaborative works, the DAO framework can foster a paradigm where every performer or entity does not just engage but becomes an integral co-creator. This evolution finds its roots in musical developments like indeterminate music, open scores, and proportional notation, where performers have substantial autonomy, enabling them to shape and co-create pieces (Nyman, 1999), and also in research projects like MusicExperiment21 where performance is redefined and goes beyond interpretation into experimentation (de Assis, 2018).

In the DAO-driven Hypermusic Experimental system, every performer is a shaping participant and a co-author (partaking 'owner'), investing not just their creativity but also influencing the system's trajectory through the further development of the submission/request system. This democratization of ownership and creation aligns seamlessly with the advancements in music that prioritize performer autonomy, co-authorship, and co-creation, but importantly, it propels it beyond the current situation as those elements become more concrete.

The Potential of Smart Contracts: Dynamic Evolution of the System

For the development of the submission part of the system smart contracts offer a dynamic layer of engagement (Zeilinger, 2018). Imagine a performer releasing new functionalities or modifying existing ones by merely submitting a documented performance (or annotated partial-score which elements the system can archive and learn to integrate). These contracts can act as catalysts, with each performance potentially redefining the system's landscape.

Furthermore, the system's adaptability extends beyond human interaction. Through advanced algorithms, it can 'listen' to societal data, such as social trends or environmental metrics, and integrate this information into its processes, forming human-environment-cultural hybrids as active agents within the work. This continuous data intake will also ensure that the musical outputs remain relevant and resonant with contemporary contexts.

Data Solutions and Future Considerations

To build the Hypermusic Experiment system as a DAO, a comprehensive design is essential. It requires a robust mechanism to generate partial-scores, store them, and manage the influx of external data. Integrating with a solid file system such as the interplanetary file system (IPFS) would ensure decentralized storage that also aligns with the conceptual dimensions being explored, enabling sustainable and accessible network of partial-scores and other data. In the ever-evolving DAO space driven by differential ontology, each partial-score undergoes a transformative journey, constantly reshaped by its interactions within the decentralized network. This is the ideal environment for a multipiece 2.0.

The convergence of Hypermusic Experiment 0.9 with a DAO framework brings forth several exciting possibilities. Yet, specific considerations remain:

- Governance and Ownership Model: creating an equitable model that balances individual creative freedoms with collective decisions.
- Incentivization and Tokenomics: introducing mechanisms to reward performers and contributors.

- Scalability and Adaptability: ensuring that the system evolves with changing societal contexts and technological advancements (such as integrating AI and VR on several structural levels).
- Interoperability and Integration: seamlessly integrating with diverse digital infrastructures and data sources.

Melding Hypermusic Experiment 0.9 with a DAO framework signifies a future where technology, philosophy, and art converge. It champions a vision where performers are not just interpreters but active co-creators, influencing and being influenced in a dynamic, decentralized musical cosmos.

Envoi

The Hypermusic Experiment 0.9 presents a radical reimagining of music generation. By intertwining notation, randomness, interactivity, physical and digital dimensions, and societal context, it pushes the boundaries of our understanding of works of music. It embodies a concept of music that is not bound by linear time, but rather exists simultaneously in multiple temporalities and formats, ideally suited as a DAO. This novel approach aligns with the ontological perspectives espoused by Deleuze and Guattari as well as Timothy Morton's concept of Hyperobjects – which respectively influenced de Assis' concept of Hypermusic – as it presents music as a fluid, dynamic entity that is continuously evolving and interacting with the world we live in (Morton, 2013; de Assis, 2022). Furthermore, the system aims for transcursive writing exemplified by the flow of semi-random functionalities and spectra interactions, where the connected elements do not signify but ceaselessly assemble possibilities, where the process of reading, interpreting, and experimenting with various breaks of these flows (the partial-scores) continually produces different signification. In doing so, Hypermusic Experiment 0.9 paves the way for a new kind of musical experience, one that is rich, participatory, and deeply connected to the reality of our lived experiences.

Note

1 Each value on the y-axis corresponds to a randomly generated number, and its position on the x-axis (the index) indicates the order in which it was generated.

References

Agostinelli, A. et al. *MusicLM: Generating Music from Text* (2023). https://doi.org/10.48550/arXiv.2301.11325

de Assis, Paulo. "HYPERMUSIC: New Musical Practices at The Crossroads of Music, Art and Thought", in *New Paradigms for Music Research*, edited by Adolf Murillo et al. (Spain: University of Valencia Press, 2022).

de Assis, Paulo. *Logic of Experimentation* (Belgium: Leuven University Press, 2018).

Bolognini, Maurizio. *Machines: Conversations on Art & Technology* (Italy: Postmedia Books, 2012).

Chanan, M. *Musica Practica: The Social Practice of Western Music from Gregorian Chant to Postmodernism* (London: Verso, 1994).

Craig, Vear. "The Digital Score Project: Review of Ongoing Research into Digital Score Creativity and Digital Musicianship (2022–23)", *TENOR Conference Proceedings*, 2023.

Craig, Vear. *The Digital Score: Musicianship, Creativity and Innovation* (UK: Routledge, 2019).

Deleuze, Gilles, & Guattari, Felix. *A Thousand Plateaus: Capitalism and Schizophrenia* (Minneapolis: University of Minnesota Press, 1987).

Deleuze, Gilles, & Guattari, Felix. *Anti-Oedipus: Capitalism and Schizophrenia* (Minneapolis: University of Minnesota Press, 1983).

Deleuze, Gilles, and Félix Guattari. *What is Philosophy? Translated by Hugh Tomlinson and Graham Burchell* (London: Verso, 1994).

D'Errico, Lucia. *Powers of Divergence* (Belgium: Leuven University Press, 2018).

Einarsson, Einar Torfi. "Desiring-Machines: In between Difference and Repetition, Performer and Conductor, Cyclones and Physicality, Structure and Notation." *Perspectives of New Music* 53(1), 5–30 (2015a). https://doi.org/10.1353/pnm.2015.0006

Einarsson, Enar Torfi. *Desiring Machines* (Netherlands: Deuss Music, 2012).

Einarsson, Einar Torfi. *Grapher Morphogenetics 2b* (self-published score, 2023). http://einartorfieinarsson.com/grapher2b/

Einarsson, Einar Torfi. *Underdetermined figures* (self-published score, 2015/2018).

Einarsson, Einar Torfi. "Proto-scores: Explorations of Ambiguous Specificity", *(Research Catalogue)*. 2015b. https://www.researchcatalogue.net/view/186304/221229

Einarsson, E. T. "Re-Notations: Flattening Hierarchies and Transforming Functions", in *Dark Precursor: Deleuze and Artistic Research* edited by Paulo de Assis et al. (Belgium, Leuven University Press, 2017).

Goehr, Lydia. *The Imaginary Museum of Musical Works: an Essay in the Philosophy of Music* (UK: Oxford University Press, 2007).

Kanno, Mieko. "Prescriptive Notation: Limits and Challenges" *Contemporary Music Review* 26(2), 231–254 (2007).

Magnusson, Thor. *Sonic Writing: Technologies of Material, Symbolic, and Signal Inscriptions* (UK: Bloomsbury, 2019).

Morrison, Margaret. *Reconstructing Reality: Models, Mathematics, and Simulations* (UK: Oxford University Press, 2015).

Nyman, M. *Experimental Music: Cage and Beyond* (Cambridge: Cambridge University Press, 1999).

Morton, Timothy. *Hyperobjects: Philosophy and Ecology after the End of the World* (Minneapolis, USA: University of Minnesota Press, 2013).

Sauvagnargues, Anne. *Deleuze and Art* (UK: Bloomsbury, 2013).

Sheetz, M., & Yu, H. *The Cell as a Machine* (UK: Cambridge University Press, 2018).

Schwab, M. (2015). Proto-objects (Research Catalogue). https://www.researchcatalogue.net/view/186304/219199

Zeilinger, M. Digital Art as 'Monetised Graphics': Enforcing Intellectual Property on the Blockchain. *Philosophy Technology* 31, 15–41 (2018). https://doi.org/10.1007/s13347-016-0243-1

10

Decentralized Transindividual Collaborative Experimental Musicking

Kosmas Giannoutakis

Rensselaer Polytechnic Institute, Troy, NY, USA

Introduction

The concept of decentralization has recently attracted much attention due to the proliferation of technical infrastructures that supposedly enhance this aspect in many important areas of our society. In order to assess the impact of these technologies on music and society, it is crucial to frame the discussion by addressing the ideological and historical lineages of technological automation and their relation to dominant forms of power. Such investigation is pivotal for conceptualizing the horizons of possibility for future endeavors that experiment with alternative modes of music-making.

If we adopt an anthropocentric worldview, we observe that technical innovations automate processes that require human labor and/or are beneficial to human intentions. By automating, we typically understand the making of something more efficient in relation to an intended outcome. Following the etymological understanding of the Greek word *automatos* (*autos* 'self' + *matos* 'strive hard, desire with fury'), we can think of the process of technization as the transfer or surrender of a minuscule but intense amount of human agency to nonhuman constructs.[1] Therefore, technical objects[2] maintain a very special relationship with us, extending and enhancing our individual and collective activities as it has been analyzed in relational anthropological (Gell, 1998) and philosophical (DeLanda, 2016) accounts. Technical objects afford specific opportunities that define possible sets of actions, ultimately shaping and delineating the boundaries of our social reality.

By highlighting this understanding, it becomes obvious that all technologies partake in various forms of decentralization. The vitalist forces[3] that are manifested as human agency and located in the embodied mind are outsourced and distributed over networks of nonhuman actors.[4] This tendency has been observed in all human cultures as well as in animal species with various degrees of intensity. In the recent history of humanity, Western culture has evolved with the premise of an unconditional technization, achieving

DOI: 10.1201/9781003458227-11

cultural and geostrategic hegemony while driving the planet to a new geological epoch described as the Anthropocene.

Navigating the Political and Economic Landscape of Western Musics

Political Economies of Music

Musics that have been practiced in the Western world have been heavily influenced by technological developments. In his book *Noise: The Political Economy of Music* (1985), Jacques Attali explains how music functions as a prophet for sociopolitical developments and discerns four stages that characterize socioeconomic modes of music production. In *Sacrificing*, Music was practiced as oral tradition and functioned as the antithesis to the chaos and noise of nature. The primary music technologies in that period were handcrafted acoustic instruments that could accompany and support singers and choruses, for example, during performances of ancient Greek tragedies and comedies. These technical objects, which are abundant to date, function by outsourcing the musical labor of the sound-producing human organs to artifacts that consist of organic parts of deceased animals and plants and inorganic materials such as metals, ceramics, and plastics.[5], [6] In the ancient Greek world, wider sociopolitical transformations were musically reflected in the attenuation of epic poetry by solo performing rhapsodists and the prevalence of lyric poetry and drama often performed by a number of musicians, facilitated by the invention and use of diverse musical instruments (West, 1992).

During the Renaissance, the visual technologies of music notation and printing press enabled a rudimentary commodification of music, which later led to the proliferation of musical works, sheet music, music publishers, public concerts, music venues, music journalism, polyphonic musical instruments, and large instrumental ensembles. Musicians achieved financial independence from the church and the courts of the nobility by becoming specialists as instrumentalists, conductors, composers, singers, and critics. During this period, which is designated as *Representing* by Attali, the modern notion of the musician and the musical work was established and began to regulate the musical practice. According to Lydia Goehr:

> The musical work-concept found its regulative function within a specific crystallization of ideas about the nature, purpose, and relationship between composers, scores, and performances. This crystallization shaped and continues to shape a standard or 'establishment' interpretation of the work-concept and of the practice it regulates. It continues also to motivate our classification of examples of musical works.
>
> **(Goehr, 1992)**

A notable mythologization and mystification occurred during this period, namely the spread of the ideology of 'autonomous' art and music, in which artists and musicians were now free to choose and determine the themes, forms, and conduct of their artistic and musical practices. This ideology is exemplified in the concept of the genius artist that purports the significance of a divine solitary individualism as the locus of artistic and musical excellence. While this myth still guides contemporary artistic and musical practices, it is imperative to attend to the de-constructionist and de-mystificatory inquiries that have been undertaken by critical and new musicology. The myth of the genius artist serves to idealize and glorify the subjectivity of the middle class in Western and Central Europe, affirming the cultural and political dominance established by the bourgeoisie through capitalist activities in the recently established democratic nation-states. Janet Wolff notes:

> individualism of the liberal-humanist thought associated with mercantile capitalism and with the bourgeoisie confirmed and reinforced the aesthetic ideology of the artist as sole and privileged originator of the cultural work.

> **(Wolff, 1987)**

While these developments are considered instrumental for the decentralization of political and cultural power from aristocratic elites to the urban bourgeois, the majority of the human population that did not have the characteristics of the middle class, including the default gender, race, ethnic, and national identities, were not enjoying any of the new privileges associated with the nation-state status quo. Such understandings are the culmination of a rich intellectual tradition that was put forth by Karl Marx and Friedrich Engels, who introduced dialectical materialism and the theorization of class struggles, followed by the critique of the Enlightenment ideologies by the Frankfurt school, leading to post-modern/post-structural analyses within contemporary feminist, queer, decolonial, and intersectional perspectives.

As industrialization intensified during the end of the 19th and the beginning of the 20th centuries, new conditions emerged that reconfigured the geopolitical and cultural landscape. In this era, which was first theorized by Benjamin (1968)[7] and is designated by Attali as *Repeating*, musicians and music technologists are concerned with the fidelity of their artifacts. Musical performances are evaluated according to the resemblance of 'masterful' recordings, which are meticulously produced, mixed, and crafted in the recording studio. Listeners are predominantly absorbed in the process of acquiring the resources that allow them to purchase recordings, while the music industry produces far more recordings that can be listened to in one's lifetime. As a result, the musical works become shorter since the stockpiling of recordings facilitates a distracted and consumeristic mode of listening. Along the same line, Adorno and Simpson (1941) has argued for a regressive development of music, in which melodies are being evaluated not in relation to other musical structures within the musical work but according to their recognizability, which is facilitated by the recording and reproduction apparatuses. According to Mowitt (1987), electronic and digital media have intensified the reproducibility of music, which has led to a 'radical priority of reception', a phenomenon that is exemplified in the development of the phenomenological theory of reduced listening by Schaeffer (2017) and the subsequent reductive asocial objectification of sound by Smalley (1986) and Chion (1982).[8]

The dominant socio-politico-economic configuration of state capitalism created the conditions for the proliferation of the music industries that automated music production, dissemination, and consumption to unprecedented degrees. In particular, the music industries found a way to scale up the musical relevance of folk cultures, which was considered low-brow by the previous representational political economy of music. The repetitional logic of the 20th century had different priorities and politics, valorizing musicians and music genres by measuring their success with record sales, Billboard chart performance, and concert ticket and merchandise revenue. Meanwhile, it had no taboos for uplifting the cultural and musical significance of marginalized and historically oppressed communities. For example, African-American musics, such as Blues, Jazz, Soul, Hip Hop, Rap, R&B, and Black EDM, among many others, became highly popular and influential while capturing the musical imagination of the international youth to date. The nexus of technologies that induced repetitive musicking began to bring about and continue to do so, a decentering of the Eurocentric middle-class subjectivity and its eclectic musical taste as the measure of musical virtue while establishing new regimes of musical normativity based on Americano-centric popular idioms.

Digital Economy

The fourth stage in Attali's analysis, which was more anticipated rather than analyzed when formulated in 1977, bears the name *Composing*. Some essential features which are described in this forecasted political economy are that 'the musician plays primarily for himself, outside any operationality', 'a negation of the division of roles and labor', and 'a new form of socialization, for which self-management is only a very partial designation'. In her Afterword to Attali's book, musicologist Susan McClary argued for the recognition of 'new movements [that] seem to herald a society in which individuals and small groups dare to reclaim the right to develop their own procedures, their own networks'.

With the Internet's advent and the digital economy's founding, many musicians have started experimenting with alternative ways of engaging their musical audiences. These include publishing and live-streaming their music on online audio and media distribution platforms, creating educational, memetic, and viral content for their social media profiles, winning the support of online users around the globe who become micro-donors, subscribers, and patrons, and selling physical copies of their music and personalized merchandise. These practices have succeeded in establishing sustainable careers for some musicians. However, they operate under the regime of a grim hyper-evolved neoliberal capitalism that has generally been referred to as Web 2.0.[9] Various aspects of it have been highlighted as digital capitalism (Schiller, 1999), cognitive capitalism (Moulier Boutang, 2012), agnotological capitalism (Betancourt, 2015), surveillance capitalism (Zuboff, 2015), platform capitalism (Srnicek, 2017), and Corporate Platform Complex (Terranova, 2022). In this virtual realm, major technology corporations that endured the dot-com bubble at the beginning of the millennium, such as Google, Amazon, Microsoft, and Meta (formerly Facebook), have accumulated substantial infrastructural and social capital, evolving into transnational monopolies. These entities now exert control over and manipulate the online social sphere, resulting in unforeseen political, economic, and environmental ramifications. Their revenue is generated by offering online services to users, who are required to create profiles and willingly share personal information. The companies use proprietary algorithms to gather and analyze this data, creating customer profiles that are then sold to third-party advertising firms.

The Rise of Blockchains

Bitcoin was born during the financial crisis of 2008 by the mysterious figure of Satoshi Nakamoto. It emerged from the cypherpunk mailing list, consisting of an online community of technologists and hackers advocating for information privacy and protection from state and corporate surveillance. Their ideology was rooted in libertarianism and anarchism with lineages to the Austrian school of economics that understands social phenomena through the lens of individualistic intentions and behaviors. Soon, it was realized that the underlying technology, namely Blockchain,[10] is a powerful tool that can be utilized to subvert the web hegemony of big tech. The basic problem was that libertarian and right-wing tendencies were encoded in the open-source code of the technology (Golumbia, 2016), with the result of creating new power centers (De Filippi, 2019) and attracting and eventually saturating the blockchain spaces with opportunists, scammers, criminals, crypto bros, California ideologues, investors, arbitrageurs, and speculators.

According to Swartz, blockchains entail two conflicting social imaginaries, what she describes as *digital metalism* and *infrastructural mutualism*. The view on metalism 'embraces a theory of money in which the only truly sound money is one backed by a commodity like gold, which derives its intrinsic value from the market' (Swartz, 2018). The mutualist perspective 'affords a cooperativist vision of a money technology and therefore society' that is concerned with the freedom not of the markets but of information.

The argument that Blockchain technology or Distributed Ledger Technology (DLT)[11] more broadly can and should be adopted and explored by the Left for communitarian, mutualist, socialist, and egalitarian purposes has been articulated by many thinkers and scholars (Massumi, 2018; Alizart, 2020; Malabou, 2020; Terranova, 2022; Quaranta, 2022; Catlow & Rafferty, 2022; Dávila, 2023).

Decentralization in the Arts and Music

Blockchains and DLTs have the potential to bring about post-capitalist economies for the arts and music, as has been envisaged by Attali and desired by a majority of artists and musicians who strive for survival in the current socio-economical landscape. Toward that aim, important experimentations have been undertaken, and progress has been achieved, especially in the area of decentralized autonomous organizations (DAO).[12] Alternative governance methods that seek to overcome the tyranny of the majority, such as quadratic, reputation, conviction, and delegative voting, Holographic Consensus, and liquid democracy, are currently in the testing phase, with very promising preliminary results (Hellström, 2022) (Li et al., 2023).

Numerous visual and media artists have embraced Blockchains, DAOs, and NFTs[13] as mediums for creative experimentation, collectivization, and activism. Apart from blockchain-based art projects made by solo artists, community-building projects are being built by core groups of a few artists who establish technical infrastructures that support the conduct of innovative artistic experiments, enabling additional artists to join the collective in subsequent stages. Typically, such groups have a wider mission, which they attempt to achieve by exploiting different affordances of the technology. For instance, the Furtherfield organization strives for eco-social change and utilizes Quadratic Voting on the Blockchain to engage its community and create a stronger sense of agency.[14] Another example is the collective Creeps & Weirdos, which has been experimenting with such collaborative processes since 2012. They have developed a collaborative painting practice, which they term 'visual conversations', that resembles the surrealist technique of 'exquisite corpse', with the basic difference that the whole history of a painting is visible. This practice consists of endless strips of digital canvases, which are accessed through an online platform by multiple artists who sequentially continue the paintings in a stigmergic fashion.[15]

The music industry has recognized the impact of these technological advancements and has made efforts to adjust to the decentralized landscape (Chalmers et al., 2021). Various proposals have emerged, aiming to enhance managerial and administrative tasks, such as royalty management efficiency, connectivity between musicians and fans, and piracy mitigation. As a product of state capitalism, the music industry seeks to incorporate blockchains into its framework for further value extraction and accumulation. Yet, it fails to recognize the untapped potential of alternative, sustainable, and egalitarian economies that could benefit musicians and bring about novel musical practices.

Besides practicing music as a business, creative musicians face a different kind of problem that prevents them from adapting to the incipient decentralized terrain. Conventional musicians remain closely tied to the historical subjectivities shaped by prior political economies and are reluctant to experiment with new technologies that destabilize the relationship networks that support their old-fashioned creativity. For the musicians who retroclusively operate under the representational political economy, the feature of disintermediation that DLTs promote endangers the privileged and gatekeeping positions they have achieved throughout their careers.

For musicians, it is imperative to leave aside the nostalgia of the glorious past and renounce the patronalistic patronage of the state, as well as the hollow fantasies of a prosperous rise to stardom. By relying less on their citizenship status, they can start cultivating a netizen subjectivity, as web nomads who are able to create and experience music indiscriminately with anyone they can encounter in the global digital stack.[16] If musicians do not actively engage in the post-humanization process by assembling with decentralized technical infrastructures, they face the risk of extinction in potential futures. These could involve scenarios such as neo-feudalism, illustrated by hyper-enslavement under a technocratic elite that speciates itself through the assimilation of advanced technologies like Artificial Intelligences, nanotechnologies, DLTs, and biotechnologies. Alternatively, they may become vestigial in the face of a 'Fully Automated Luxury Communism' (Bastani, 2019), which realizes a post-scarcity economy characterized by widespread prosperity. Therefore, apart from the involvement in decentralizing their artistic practices, musicians should be informed by and contribute to the wider discourses on post-humanism, which questions anthropocentrism by exploring and critiquing the implications of the blurring boundary between humans and technology.

The following section elaborates on two projects currently in progress, aiming to experimentally reconsider and redesign two types of musical practices: one associated with electroacoustic music and another involving live coding as transindividual[17] collaborative practices.

Experiments in Distributed Musicking

Transindividual Electroacoustic Music Composition

Experimentations on open-form in the field of electroacoustic music have produced various pieces that engage the creativity of multiple composers and can be better described as compositional processes. One famous example is John Cage's 'Williams Mix' (1952), whose score instructs how to cut and splice sounds recorded on tape. Henri Pousseur's 'Scambi' (1957) stands out as another significant piece, comprising 32 sound segments characterized by four parameters (Relative Pitch, Speed, Homogeneity, and Continuity) that describe their starting and ending conditions. These pieces can be actualized multiple times by composers who are interested in re-composing historical works of electroacoustic music. With the advent of the Internet, various web-based platforms enabled a 'reactive' approach to collaborative composition, such as the FMOL project, which received more than 1,100 brief pieces by around 100 composers (Jordà and Wust, 2001). Collaborative composition frameworks for electroacoustic music composition that implement synchronous and asynchronous features have also been proposed in educational studies (Biasutti and Concina, 2021).

These practices follow the logic of modularity and composability, namely, the provision of small compositional units that are shared within a community and can be combined in a variety of ways. While such practices are rare in the field of instrumental and electroacoustic music composition, they have the potential of actualizing a transindividual approach to the composition of new music. Similar approaches can be found in the field of music production, for example, Charles Holbrow's Fluid Music Software Framework, which '[includes] the construction of a massive, open repository of music production Techniques that sound designers, producers, and composers can use to share malleable sound worlds without reimplementing complex music production processes' (Holbrow, 2021).

In 2021, with composer and researcher Juan Carlos Vasquez, I conducted a study investigating the applicability of DLT infrastructures to collaborative music composition processes (Giannoutakis & Vasquez, 2022). The core principle of our approach involves breaking down the collaborative composition process into distinct units or modules, termed contributions, where composers can engage in two types: segments and revisions. A segment, defined as a tentative musical idea created using a DAW program with a duration between 1 and 60 seconds, comes in three types: Opening Segment (OS), Intermediary Segment (IS), and Closing Segment (CS). An Opening Segment is exclusively linkable from the right, making it suitable only for the beginning of a composition. In contrast, an Intermediary Segment is versatile, allowing linkage from both left and right and enabling it to continue any other segment anteriorly or posteriorly seamlessly. A Closing Segment, reserved for serving as the coda, can only be linked from the left. A Root Segment (RS), which can be an Opening, Intermediary, or Closing Segment, involves submission without links to other segments. A Root Segment acts as the initial segment, offering a starting point for the potential development of a new composition nexus. In terms of the meta-structure, a composition nexus denotes the emergent arborescent structure encompassing all interlinked segments. Composers have the flexibility to create various segment types and append them to existing composition nexuses or initiate a new one using a Root Segment.

A preliminary composition denotes a trajectory from an Opening Segment (OS) to a Closing Segment (CS) within a composition nexus. These compositions can be extracted from the nexuses so that multiple revisions can be made by different composers. A revision contribution involves modifying the compositional parameters of a tentative composition, involving alterations such as editing audio clips, inserting sound effects, adjusting gains, and overall mixing, with all changes requiring commentary within the DAW file. A revision contribution can be submitted as open, allowing further revisions by other composers, or as final, permitting no further revisions. A final revision contribution is recognized as a completed composition and is made available for public listening.

We have introduced a novel protocol called Proof of Creative Contribution (PoCC) that enhances and validates the contribution process based on the compositional effort invested by the composers in the system. The protocol includes explicit rules: (1) a submitted contribution can only be linked to one other contribution, (2) only Root Segments do not provide a link, and (3) two contributions by the same composer cannot be linked. Submitted contributions are collected in a pool, awaiting validation. Once a specific amount (e.g., 10) of contributions accumulates, a composer is declared the block creator through the consensus protocol. The block creator is responsible for recording the pool's segments on the blockchain and broadcasting the updated composition field to the network. This cycle, known as an epoch, repeats indefinitely, enabling the evolution of multiple compositions simultaneously.

We've introduced a pointing system to measure the contribution value for each composer and designate the composer with the highest value to record the composition data on the blockchain. The composer with the highest contribution value becomes the validator-leader In each epoch. This mechanism rewards composers who invest compositional effort and are appreciated by the community through the continuation of their segments. Selected block validators are motivated to ensure fairness and transparency in the process, as their artistic work is at stake.

We conducted a four-month simulation study involving the researchers as composers to evaluate the collaborative model's creative potential and test the consensus protocol's properties. In the initial phase, we created ten pseudonyms inspired by five male and five female historically prominent figures (byron, shelley, goguen, basho, voltaire, hypatia, lovelace, hopper, boulanger, derbyshire).[18] Both composers had to adopt one of these identities before submitting a new segment. With this model, we completed 8 epochs and generated 71 segments, each having an average duration of 10.3 seconds. Throughout the process, we observed the formation of four prospering and three underdeveloped nexuses, resulting in a total of 20 preliminary compositions. The average duration of these preliminary compositions was

46.3 seconds. Notably, the model tends to produce shorter compositions, but as more epochs pass, longer pieces may emerge. We did not engage in any revisions, leading to a perceptible fragmentation in many of the preliminary compositions, with noticeable sonic transitions from segment to segment.

In each epoch, a single pseudo-composer with the highest contribution value was designated as the leader responsible for recording the data on the blockchain. The highest contribution value was fairly distributed among the pseudo-composers, supporting the diversification property of our PoCC protocol. It's worth noting that during the composition process, we did not track the contribution values of the pseudo-composer but assigned pseudonyms according to aesthetic attributes.

The PoCC protocol attempts to monitor the contribution value in a manner reminiscent of academic citation or the way Google's PageRank algorithm organizes websites based on their referential significance. The more recent DAO-based projects SourceCred[19] and Coordinape[20] experiment with novel ways of valuing contribution and reputation and should be considered for future research. Our simulated PoCC protocol is quite limited, with a number of security flaws, such as Sybil attacks and Denial of Service (DDoS). Several essential aspects required for practical implementation by a community of electroacoustic music composers have not been modeled or simulated in the current analysis. The main objective of this project is to generate research interest in decentralized musicking and stimulate inventive experimentation that entangles creation, collaboration, and communalization while launching a discussion about coordination technologies in music and their ethics and politics.

Transindividual Live Coding

Digital artifacts have a fluid and ambivalent ontology while 'they become increasingly editable, interactive, reprogrammable, and distributable' (Kallinikos et al., 2013). Their technological determinism and instrumentality can be subverted by creative practices that use computer code to generate aesthetic outcomes encompassing visual, musical, choreographic, and poetic expressions. When these processes are presented to an audience in real time, whether on-site or online, it is often denoted as live coding. However, the live coding community is reluctant to give absolute definitions of its creative practice. As it is described in the live coding user's manual, '[l]ive coding is a performance practice that operates as an adventure and exploration, deliberately rejecting fixed definitions, remaining heterogeneous in nature, continually challenging its self-understanding through the practice of writing and rewriting – defining and redefining – as a public performance' (Blackwell et al., 2022).

Numerous practices, techniques, and software applications have been developed that explore various possibilities of music co-creation with computer code. Almost exclusive emphasis has been given to just-in-time interactions, as live coding is a time-based performance for situated or virtual audiences.[21] The laptop ensemble 'powerbooks_unplugged' has since 2003 developed highly collaborative live coding tools for their practice (Rohrhuber et al. 2007). Their system, which has been distilled as the SuperCollider extension library 'Republic', allows snippets of code, called codelets, to be circulated and modified by all ensemble members during a performance. Their system has also been applied to educational contexts, making the 'reuse and adaptation of code lines by other participants easier, more likely to work immediately, and thus more rewarding and enjoyable' (Campo, 2014).

The digital materiality of live coding facilitates reusability and collaboration (Blackwell et al., 2014) and can also be extended to longer timeframes, a prospect that has not been investigated thoroughly yet. This would involve manipulating and exchanging code snippets that exceed the time limits of a live performance or a workshop. A systematization of a live coding collaboration practice that facilitates the exchange of code snippets (codelets) as digital commons over the internet can be facilitated through a tailored DLT that registers and protects all the contributions while allowing the community to be organized in novel and experimental ways.

The first step toward exploring the transindividuation of live coding is to investigate the aesthetic significance of this remix-based practice. For over a year, I have been conducting a simulation study involving the reappropriation of SuperCollider Tweets (SCTweets). SCTweets are code snippets that used to have a maximum length limit of 140 characters (currently 280) and are shared on the social media platform Twitter (currently X).[22] The tweets are meant to be copied and pasted to the native SuperCollider programming environment. Once executed, they produce music pieces of various degrees of duration, sonic intensity, and complexity. This custom started around 2009 when Dan Stowell started tweeting tiny snippets of musical code using SuperCollider. Around that period, *Wire Music* magazine published the sc140 album, which consisted exclusively of SCTweets.[23] Since then, many composers and computer musicians have taken the challenge of exploiting all kinds of shortcuts and syntactic sugar that the SuperCollider language provides in order to produce complex musical textures and sounds. The body of the SCTweets is an invaluable resource of diverse computer music that can be appropriated for educational and artistic purposes.

In my experimental music practice, the SCTweets are modified to facilitate their live manipulation. I have developed various techniques such as mixing, tweaking, self-/hetero-modulation, feedback, and modulation coupling, which erode the repetitive and latticed musical structures that are typical in algoraves[24] and introduce non-linearities that result in unexpected, chaotic sonic behavior with a liquid and organic character. In a live coding session, the sonic contribution of each codelet to the overall performance is tracked and calculated as the accumulated sonic energy of the signal. This proposed metric can be used to estimate the contribution value for each cited composer in actual performances and the overall reputation value for all participants in the ecosystem. A problem arises when a live coder miscodes a block of code, resulting in the explosion of its sonic energy. Such hiccups in live coding performances are not rare. Additionally, this metric fails to capture listening attention, which can be higher in sounds with low energy. Therefore, additional metrics have to be invented and experimented with to measure fair estimates of communal contribution during a live set.

Engaging in this live coding practice, I have collaborated with the interdisciplinary artist-researcher Aaron Juarez, who applies similar techniques to live coding visuals, presenting over 13 public performances.[25] Furthermore, I have made over 35 live stream performances,[26] often collaborating with fellow live coders. My goal is to build an international community that is accustomed to this practice and, in a subsequent step, attempt to organize our collaborative activities through decentralized technical infrastructures.

Playing often with other musicians' creative code, one develops preferences and becomes infatuated with specific SCTweets, akin to the emotional attachment instrumentalists develop for specific works of their instrument's repertoire. Hence, while my sonic aesthetics typically lean toward continuous flows of heterogeneous sonorities, what I refer to as *liquid noise*, various aesthetic expressions can be realized through this approach. This is a crucial point since this practice can be perceived as an attempt to homogenize the practice of live coding, especially with the proposal for integrating DLT infrastructures. The first argument against such critique is that this practice is very versatile and all-encompassing, allowing diverse live coding aesthetics to emerge. The second argument is that if such a practice is successful and attracts many members of the live coding community, it will prompt other approaches to elevate their collaborative mechanics by applying novel DLTs tailored to their specificities, eventually rendering them more dynamic and sustainable.

Ecosystemic Integration of Various Computer-Based Music Practices

In terms of modular contributions that can be combined and remixed in infinite ways, we can imagine various computer-based music practices that can be reconfigured in a decentralized fashion. Areas such as instrument and interface design, Musical XR, auditory display and sonification, AI-based music generation, and sound installation can discretize and systematize the creative contributions of their practitioners and utilize decentralized technical infrastructures to organize their community-wide activities.

The prospect of an ecosystemic integration of various computer-based music practices resonates with Brian Massumi's proposal of an *economy based on affective intensities*. In his post-capitalist manifesto, Massumi[27] stipulates 14 speculative strategies[28] that aim at 'the invention of an anarcho-communist alter-economy' and 'actively ward away' the capturing and accumulative tendencies of neoliberal capitalism that is fostered by the nation-state. He advocates for 'a directly aesthetic form of value' that has 'an improvisational edge' and 'comprises such sub-surplus-values as zest, beauty, wonder, and adventure'. My proposal for grounding the locus of value on electroacoustic music segments and creative code snippets that have an immediate aesthetic effect (affect) is corroborated by Massumi's insights.

There is a multitude of features that can be ascribed to the monitored forms of value in the proposed projects. In a tokenization scheme, where digital tokens are linked to the registered contributions, properties like fungibility or non-fungibility, transferability or non-transferability, and deflationary or inflationary dynamics[29] must be thoughtfully selected and synthesized based on the communities' inclinations. These tokens are only applicable within a community, particularly for implementing non-majority-based voting mechanisms for political governance. These could include decisions concerning the very structure of the DAO and implementations of the technical infrastructure as it is practiced in most current DAOs.[30] Furthermore, such tokens can be utilized for the allocation of external funds as well as for curating concerts, presentations, and exhibitions. The degree of liquidity, e.g., how quickly the digital tokens can be exchanged for services or other forms of value, will determine the economic dynamics of the communities. For example, mutual credit[31] mechanisms could be implemented to induce future anticipations and drive creativity forward. Any of these experiments should be conducted with excellent knowledge of the undergoing research on collaborative economies and peer production so that the pitfalls of accumulative and power law dynamics[32] are avoided.

When a computer music community (e.g., with a focus on live coding) establishes a functional operational status, it can start interfacing with another community (e.g., with a focus on electroacoustic music) by identifying and monitoring reciprocal contributions. These flows will require a different monitoring mechanic that satisfies both communities. We can think of an organic, bottom-up process where all communities develop bartering rhizomes with each other, establishing a vivid network of creative exchange. Then, the network as a whole can devise mechanisms for unitization, inventing an integral value to represent the ecosystem. This value could be used in exogenous economies to bring external value into the creative music environment. In Massumi's proposal, this overarching current is called *Occurency*, which 'would fulfill the threefold function of money', namely store of value, unit of account, and medium of exchange.

Conclusions

Technologies can be understood as external carriers of human agency that partake in the decentralization process of the human. In the Western world, as technologies are advancing uninhibitedly, they reconfigure our social reality at an accelerating pace. Western musical traditions have incorporated and sonically mirrored the principles of the political economies in which they exist, such as adhering to representational logic in the 18th–19th centuries and embracing repetitive doctrines in the 20th century. In the 21st century, new conditions have emerged with the Corporate Platform Complex regulating our social, economic, and political lives while surveilling, extracting, and accumulating value globally. While blockchains have been corrupted by the neoliberal regime, they still offer mechanisms of autonomous collectivization that small artistic and activist communities can utilize.

Decentralized technical infrastructures such as blockchains wield significant power by automating the tasks involved in social coordination and organization, as well as facilitating the manifestation of political intentions. This material form of social labor can be parallelized with the affective modes of sociality that are communed through music and sound. These two aligned streams can converge by aestheticizing (audifying, sonifying, musifying) the currents of value and valorizing the expressive musical flows that can circulate in the digital sphere. Coupled with an egalitarian ethos, such more-than-human assemblages can be manifested as transindividual subjectivities that can navigate post-capitalist futures.

The premise of decentralization lies in the decentering, warding away, and diverting of the hyperpositive toxicity of neoliberal capitalism and fostering an influx of autonomous communities that can connect rhizomaticaly and cooperate consensually and equitably. This constitutes the primary thesis of Massumi, and it is also articulated by Terranova, who advocates for 'reprogramming the internet away from recent trends toward corporatization and monetization' and 'seek[ing] a new political synthesis that moves us away from the neoliberal paradigm of debt, austerity, and accumulation', while 'organiz[ing] cooperation and produc[ing] new knowledges and values'.

Various experimental musical practices can be rethought and redesigned as decentralized, transindividual, and collaborative, taking advantage of Blockchains and DLTs' new possibilities. Each practice entails a different integration level with such technologies, with practices invented in previous politico-economic milieux being less compatible. For example, sheet-based acoustic music composition is conceivable to work under such circumstances. However, it would be substantially impractical since the process of writing sheet music, rehearsing, performing, and organizing concerts with attendees in real venues is too cumbersome to benefit from technical decentralization. This is the case because such activities need to be recorded and digitized, increasing the required technical expertise, time, and cost. On the other hand, creative practices that occur primarily in the digital sphere, such as live coding, can fit seamlessly into a DLT-based framework. What can be anticipated is that novel forms of musicking could emerge that take full advantage and explore the whole space of affordances the technologies of decentralization offer.

The prospect of computer musicians redesigning their experimental practices with a transindividual and collaborative outlook by leveraging the capabilities of decentralized technical infrastructures needs to be further investigated. The two presented projects offer just a first glimpse of a radical transformation of musicking that, if fully pursued, will likely advance novel musical aesthetics and potentially configure new subjectivities for the musician. It is up to contemporary musicians to embrace the radical futurity of the transindividual subject and commit to the emancipatory politics of post-capitalist and critical post-humanist discourses.

Notes

1 The verbs *transfer* and *surrender* imply a prioritization of human subjectivity. It is crucial to note that a side of such processes is subconscious, machinic, and vitalist, outside of human desire and rational control.

2 This definition of technical objects aligns with Bernard Stiegler's, who perceives them as the 'intergenerational support of memory, which, as material culture, overdetermines learning (apprentissages) and mnemonic activities' (Stiegler 2010). In this context, I consider them to encompass not only material entities but also various mental constructs, including ideas, concepts, theories, and numbers.

3 I am adopting a Bergsonian (Élan vital) and Deleuzian understanding of a metaphysical vitalism.

4 This depiction highlights an individualistic perspective. Collective human agency is manifested socially through its technical diffusion in non-human constructs such as language, social hierarchies, political forums, religious institutions, and mass media.

5 For example, melodic instruments automate the labor of the vocal tract, and percussion instruments outsource the labor of synchronicity generated by other organs in the body. Regular rhythms are correlated to the autonomic nervous system (heart and lungs), and irregular figurations to the movements of the self-determinant muscular body. Although musical instruments and technical objects, in general, are designed with features that enable specific automations, they can combine expressive tropes of other organs and have the potential to be misused and employed in unconventional ways to undermine their intended purpose or achieve new and unexpected outcomes.

6 Certain musical instruments in history have involved the abuse of living animals, such as the cat organ (Katzenorgel in German) and piganino (Schweineorgel), as detailed by French composer Jean-Baptiste Weckerlin in his 1877 work, *Musiciana. Descriptions of Rare or Bizarre Inventions.*

7 In his seminal essay 'The Work of Art in the Age of Mechanical Reproduction' published in 1935, Walter Benjamin analyzes the impact of industrial technologies that enabled the extensive reproduction of works of art, putting an emphasis on the newly at the time developed art practices of photography and film.

8   For an English translation of Michel Chion's *Guide des objets sonores*, refer to John Dack's and Christine North's version *Guide to Sound Objects* (2009), which is publicly available at Monoskop wiki (https://monoskop.org/images/0/01/Chion_Michel_Guide_To_Sound_Objects_Pierre_Schaeffer_and_Musical_Research.pdf).

9   The term Web 1.0 describes the early phase of the Internet when users could only read and download content from websites. In Web 2.0, users could additionally write and upload content under the auspices of Big Tech. Web 3.0 is currently under development and entails the ability for users to own their content.

10   Blockchain technology is an ingenious coalescence of various digital technologies developed over the past 30 years, including the internet, peer-to-peer networks, asymmetric cryptography, digital signatures, data structures, and proof of work. Information of societal importance, such as financial transactions, reputation scores, healthcare records, votes, and logistics data, is recorded in data structures known as 'blocks', which are securely linked through cryptography. These records are stored in databases, referred to as the ledger, with copies distributed across multiple computers worldwide. These computers, known as nodes, maintain the ledger's accuracy and security by adhering to a consensus protocol, ensuring the network's integrity.

11   Blockchain is commonly regarded as a specific subset within the broader DLT universe, employing a distinct data structure composed of a chain of hash-linked blocks of data.

12   Decentralized autonomous organizations (DAOs) are purpose-driven entities that streamline their administrative processes using algorithmically encoded and enforced smart contracts. These organizations operate without a central authority, and their members participate in governance through voting.

13   NFTs (non-fungible tokens) are ownable unique digital assets that can be sold and traded.

14   https://www.furtherfield.org/culturestake/.

15   https://dada.art/home.

16   One of the very few musical projects that explore decentralized musicking is the project *Holly+* by the composer, artist, and vocalist Holly Herdon, developed in collaboration with musician and technologist Mat Dryhurst. For an analysis of this project, see Martin Zeilinger's contribution to this volume.

17   According to Gilbert Simondon (2017), the transindividual is an intermediate state in the individuation process, represents the dynamic, relational dimension where individuals are interconnected and interdependent within a collective or social context. It characterizes a phase where individuals are not yet fully separated but are actively evolving and becoming.

18   The male historical figures are taken from Cardano's roadmap (https://roadmap.cardano.org/en/). The female figures were pioneers of science, mathematics, computation, music composition, and electronic music.

19   https://sourcecred.io/.

20   https://coordinape.com/.

21   Kirkbride includes an excellent review on live coding collaboration in his PhD dissertation (2020).

22 After the acquisition of Twitter by Elon Musk, many creative coders migrated to the Mastodon network.

23 https://www.thewire.co.uk/audio/tracks/supercollider-140.1.

24 Algorave refers to the live coding of dance music, typically occurring in clubs and underground venues.

25 We perform as the artist duo Serendipitous Liquidators (www.serendipitousliquidators.art).

26 These performances are live-streamed and archived on my YouTube channel (www.youtube.com/@giannoutakis). This platform is a major actor in the current capitalist landscape, and the employment of its services is a temporary measure until communal DLT-based alternatives surface. At present, there exist video hosting decentralized platforms such as odysee and DLive that have garnered a far-right user base. Alternatively, there is the PeerTube platform that uses peer-to-peer technology but lacks the necessary tools to manage videos effectively.

27 Brian Massumi took on the task of translating Attali's book *Noise: The Political Economy of Music* into English from the original French.

28 These are presented in the thesis number 94.

29 For an analysis of the properties of digital tokens, see *Token Economy* by Shermin Voshmgir (2020).

30 Massumi is proposing the evolution of DAOs to DPOs (distributed programmable organization) that 'potentially dispense[s] with the vocabulary of the contract altogether' and 'give way to a more rhizomatic architecture'.

31 Mutual credit is an ethical form of borrowing and lending through mutual agreement within a community.

32 In simple terms, power law dynamics refer to the 'rich get richer' phenomenon.

Bibliography

Adorno, Theodor W., and George Simpson. "On Popular Music." *Zeitschrift für Sozialforschung* 9, no. 1: 17–48, 1941.

Alizart, Mark. *Cryptocommunism*. Wiley, 2020.

Attali, Jacques. *Noise: The Political Economy of Music*. Vol. 16. Manchester University Press, 1985.

Bastani, Aaron. *Fully Automated Luxury Communism*. Verso Books, 2019.

Benjamin, Walter. "Art in the Age of Mechanical Reproduction." In *Illuminations*, edited by Hannah Arendt, 217–251. Schocken Books, 1968.

Betancourt, Michael. *The Critique of Digital Capitalism: An Analysis of the Political Economy of Digital Culture and Technology*. Punctum Books, 2015.

Biasutti, Michele, and Eleonora Concina. "Online composition: Strategies and processes during collaborative electroacoustic composition." *British Journal of Music Education* 38, no. 1: 58–73, 2021.

Blackwell, Alan F., Emma Cocker, Geoff Cox, Alex McLean, and Thor Magnusson. *Live Coding: A User's Manual*. MIT Press, 2022.

Blackwell, Alan, Alex McLean, James Noble, and Julian Rohrhuber. "Collaboration and learning through live coding (Dagstuhl Seminar 13382)." In Dagstuhl Reports, vol. 3, no. 9. Schloss Dagstuhl-Leibniz-Zentrum fuer Informatik, 2014.

de Campo, Alberto. "6.7 Republic: Collaborative Live Coding 2003–2013." In A. Blackwell, A. McLean, J. Noble, & J. Rohrhuber (Eds.), *Collaboration and Learning through Live Coding*, 152–153, Schloss Dagstuhl – Leibniz-Zentrum für Informatik, 2014.

Catlow, Ruth, and Penny Rafferty, eds. *Radical Friends: Decentralised Autonomous Organisations and the Arts.* Torque Editions, 2022.

Chalmers, Dominic, Russell Matthews, and Amy Hyslop. "Blockchain as an External Enabler of New Venture Ideas: Digital Entrepreneurs and the Disintermediation of the Global Music Industry." *Journal of Business Research* 125: 577–591, 2021.

Chion, Michel. *La musique électroacoustique. No. 1990.* Presses universitaires de France, 1982.

Dávila, Joshua. *Blockchain Radicals: How Capitalism Ruined Crypto and How to Fix It.* United Kingdom: Watkins Media, 2023.

De Filippi, Primavera. "Blockchain Technology and Decentralized Governance: The Pitfalls of a Trustless Dream." In *Blockchain Technology and Decentralized Governance: The Pitfalls of a Trustless Dream. Decentralized Thriving: Governance and Community on the Web 3.0*, edited by De Filippi, P., 3, 2019. HAL Archives-ouvertes: ffhal02445179.

DeLanda, Manuel. *Assemblage Theory.* Edinburgh University Press, 2016.

Gell, Alfred. *Art and Agency: An Anthropological Theory.* Clarendon Press, 1998.

Giannoutakis, Kosmas, and Juan Carlos Vasquez. "Collaborative Electroacoustic Music Composition on the Blockchain." In *ICMC 2022 Conference Proceedings*, 2022, 10–15.

Goehr, Lydia. *The Imaginary Museum of Musical Works: An Essay in the Philosophy of Music.* Clarendon Press, 1992.

Golumbia, David. *The politics of Bitcoin: Software as right-wing extremism.* University of Minnesota Press, 2016.

Hellström, Erik. "Fair Voting System for Permissionless Decentralized Autonomous Organizations." 2022.

Holbrow, Charles Joseph. "Fluid Music: A New Model for Radically Collaborative Music Production." Ph.D. diss., Media Lab, Massachusetts Institute of Technology, 2021.

Jordà, Sergi, and O. Wust. 2001. "A System for Collaborative Music Composition over the Web." In *12th International Workshop on Database and Expert Systems Applications*, pp. 537–542. IEEE.

Kallinikos, Jannis, Aleksi Aaltonen, and Attila Marton. "The Ambivalent Ontology of Digital Artifacts." *MIS Quarterly* 37: 357–370, 2013.

Kirkbride, Ryan Philip. "Collaborative Interfaces for Ensemble Live Coding Performance." PhD thesis, University of Leeds, 2020.

Li, Chao, Runhua Xu, and Li Duan. "Liquid Democracy in DPoS Blockchains." In *Proceedings of the 5th ACM International Symposium on Blockchain and Secure Critical Infrastructure*, pp. 25–33. 2023.

Malabou, Catherine. "Cryptocurrencies: Anarchist turn or strengthening of surveillance capitalism? From Bitcoin to Libra." Trans. Robert Boncardo. *Australian Humanities Review* 66: 144–155, 2020.

Massumi, Brian. *99 Theses on the Revaluation of Value: A Postcapitalist Manifesto.* University of Minnesota Press, 2018.

Moulier Boutang, Y. (2012) *Cognitive Capitalism.* Polity Press, Cambridge.

Mowitt, John. "The Sound of Music in the Era of Its Electronic Reproducibility." In R. D. Leppert & S. McClary (Eds.), *Music and Society: The Politics of Composition, Performance and Reception,* 173–197, Cambridge University Press, 1987.

Quaranta, Domenico. 2022. *Surfing with Satoshi: Art, Blockchain and NFTs.* Postmedia books.

Rohrhuber, Julian, Alberto de Campo, Renate Wieser, Jan-Kees Van Kampen, Echo Ho, and Hannes Hölzl. "Purloined Letters and Distributed Persons." In *Music in the Global Village Conference (Budapest),* 2007.

Schaeffer, Pierre. *Treatise on Musical Objects.* University of California Press, 2017.

Schiller, Dan. *Digital Capitalism: Networking the Global Market System.* MIT Press, 1999.

Simondon, Gilbert. *On the Mode of Existence of Technical Objects.* Univocal Publishing, 2017.

Smalley, Denis. "Spectro-Morphology and Structuring Processes." In *The Language of Electroacoustic Music,* 61–93. Palgrave Macmillan, 1986.

Srnicek, Nick. *Platform Capitalism.* John Wiley & Sons, 2017.

Stiegler, Bernard. *For a New Critique of Political Economy.* Polity, 2010.

Swartz, Lana. "What was Bitcoin, What Will It Be? The Techno-Economic Imaginaries of a New Money Technology." *Cultural Studies* 32, no. 4: 623–650, 2018).

Terranova, Tiziana. *After the Internet: Digital Networks between Capital and the Common.* Vol. 33. MIT Press, 2022.

Voshmgir, Shermin. *Token Economy: How the Web3 reinvents the internet.* Vol. 2. Token Kitchen, 2020.

West, Martin Litchfield. *Ancient Greek Music.* Clarendon Press, 1992.

Wolff, Janet. "The Ideology of Autonomous Art." In R. D. Leppert & S. McClary (Eds.), *Music and Society: The Politics of Composition, Performance and Reception,* 1–12, Cambridge University Press, 1987.

Zuboff, Shoshana. "Big other: Surveillance Capitalism and the Prospects of an Information Civilization." *Journal of Information Technology* 30, no. 1: 75–89, 2015.

Glossary

This glossary is intended to be a comprehensive resource. It covers key technical, philosophical, and music-related terms that are essential to understanding the context and content of this book. In particular, it focuses on terms at the intersection of blockchain technology, music, and artificial intelligence. It aims to enhance the readability and usefulness of the book, ensuring that readers have the essential definitions to fully engage with its content.

Agency (human, non-human, posthuman): Agency denotes the ability of individuals or entities – be they human, non-human, or posthuman – to operate autonomously and make independent choices. Within the human scope, it highlights the capability of individuals to impact and shape their surroundings. Non-human agency extends this concept to animals, plants, or even inanimate objects, recognizing their ability to cause effects in the world. Posthuman agency expands further to include technological or artificial intelligences, suggesting that future entities may possess the ability to make decisions and impact their surroundings beyond traditional biological constraints. *[term used in chapters by Giannoutakis, Łukawski, O'Dair, Timmerman, Zeilinger]*

Assemblage: The concept of assemblage within the context of artistic and philosophical discourse is complex and multifaceted. Originating from the work of Gilles Deleuze and Félix Guattari, this term derives from the English translation of their concept of 'agencement'. This French term refers to processes of grouping, arranging, organizing, and fitting together heterogeneous materials, emphasizing processuality rather than stabilized collections or material arrangements. It's important to note that the concept critically differs from the French term 'assemblage', which implies stabilized arrangements of different component parts. Assemblages are dynamic entities that fluctuate and change over time. They can be understood as complex constellations of objects, bodies, expressions, codes, qualities, and territories that come together under specific conditions and for varying periods. Therefore, assemblages are always in a state of construction and reconstruction, operating through processes of de- and reterritorialization according to intensive coding processes. These processes repurpose objects and desires and can be triggered by both human and non-human agents. This understanding of assemblages is crucial for appreciating their application in various fields, including art, social theory, and philosophy, highlighting the fluid and ever-changing nature of relationships among disparate components within a given assemblage. *[term used in the chapters by de Assis, Einarsson, Giannoutakis, Łukawski, Zeilinger]*

Artificial Intelligence (AI): Artificial intelligence (AI) is a term coined in the 1950s, which has been applied to a range of different technologies. In its broadest sense, AI refers to a computer program that can perform tasks typically requiring human intelligence. These tasks include learning, problem-solving, decision-making, understanding natural language, and audio-visual perception. AI technology ranges from simple algorithms capable of solving specific tasks to complex machine learning and deep learning systems that can learn from data, adapt to new situations, and perform multifaceted functions. *[term used in the chapters by de Assis, Giannoutakis, Łukawski, O'Dair, Zeilinger]*

Blockchain: Blockchain is a system for recording transactions or data across a network of computers in a way that ensures the security, transparency, and immutability of the data. Each record, grouped into 'blocks', is linked sequentially to previous blocks, forming a chain. This chain is stored across multiple computers making the blockchain secure, ensuring no single entity can alter the record without consensus of the network. Blockchain's key features include its resistance to data modification, its ability to provide a transparent transaction history, and its potential to eliminate the need for trusted third parties in many processes. This technology underpins cryptocurrencies like Bitcoin, but its applications extend to various fields such as supply chain management, voting systems, and secure healthcare data management. *[term used in all chapters]*

ChatGPT: ChatGPT is an advanced artificial intelligence program developed by OpenAI that specializes in generating human-like text responses based on the input it receives. "GPT" stands for "Generative Pre-trained Transformer." The "Generative" part of GPT indicates its ability to create text, "Pre-trained" signifies that it has been initially trained on a large dataset before being fine-tuned for specific tasks, and "Transformer" refers to the deep learning model architecture it uses, which is effective for processing and generating natural language. Models used by ChatGPT belong to a broad category of Large Language Models that aim to facilitate natural and intuitive interaction between humans and computers. These models are trained on a diverse dataset of text from the internet, allowing them to generate responses that can mimic human writing styles across various subjects and contexts. ChatGPT can perform a wide range of tasks, from answering questions and participating in discussions, writing essays and composing poetry, to writing usable computer code. *[term used in the chapters by Łukawski, O'Dair, Zeilinger]*

Creative Economy: The creative economy, as discussed in the context of Web3 and blockchain technology in music, encompasses the intersection of art, culture, technology, and economics, leveraging innovations like non-fungible tokens (NFTs) and blockchain to redefine value creation and exchange in the creative sectors. This economy transcends traditional financial metrics, incorporating social, environmental, and experiential values to assess the broader impact of creative works and their distribution. Through the lens of Web3, the creative economy not only includes the monetary value generated by artists and creative works but also emphasizes the importance of social equity, environmental sustainability, and the unique experiences that creative content offers. This approach challenges conventional value systems, advocating for a more holistic understanding of worth in the creative industries, from music to art and beyond, facilitated by the decentralized and transparent nature of blockchain technology. *[term used in the chapters by Mulligan, O'Dair]*

Cryptocurrencies (e.g., Bitcoin, Ether): Cryptocurrencies are digital or virtual currencies that use cryptography for security and operate on decentralized networks based on blockchain technology. Bitcoin and Ether are prominent examples, serving as digital money that facilitates secure, transparent, and peer-to-peer transactions without the need for central authorities like banks. Cryptocurrencies can be used for a wide range of applications, from simple transfers of value to complex financial contracts, thanks to the programmable nature of some platforms like Ethereum. They represent a new form of asset and payment system, aiming to make financial transactions more accessible, efficient, and resistant to censorship. *[term used in the chapters by Drubay, Giannoutakis, Łukawski, Mulligan, O'Dair, Tessone, Timmerman, Zeilinger]*

Cybernetics: Cybernetics is a field of study that explores the systems of control and communication in living beings and machines. It focuses on how systems self-regulate through feedback loops and how they can be controlled or made more efficient. Originating in the mid-20th century, cybernetics applies across various disciplines, including biology, engineering, and computer science, to understand and enhance the functioning of complex systems. It investigates the structure, constraints, and possibilities of systems that process information and respond to their environments, aiming to uncover universal principles of organization and adaptation applicable to both technological and biological systems. *[term used in the chapter by Łukawski]*

DAOs (Decentralized Autonomous Organizations): DAOs (decentralized autonomous organizations) are blockchain-based entities that operate without centralized control, governed by rules encoded as smart contracts. These digital organizations are run by a collective of members who make decisions in a democratic fashion, often through token-based voting mechanisms. DAOs aim to democratize business operations and decision-making processes, enabling transparent, efficient, and secure collaboration among stakeholders. They are used for a variety of purposes, including managing collective investments, operating decentralized applications (dApps), and organizing community projects. DAOs represent a shift toward a more open and participatory model of organizational governance and resource management. *[term used in the chapters by Drubay, Einarsson, Giannoutakis, Mulligan, O'Dair, Zeilinger]*

Decentralization: Decentralization refers to the distribution of power, authority, or resources away from a central location or governing body. In the context of technology, particularly blockchain and Web3, decentralization involves spreading out the control and management of networks, applications, and data across multiple nodes or participants to reduce reliance on a single point of failure or control. This approach enhances security, promotes transparency, and fosters greater user participation in governance. Decentralization challenges traditional centralized systems by enabling more democratic and equitable decision-making processes and facilitating peer-to-peer interactions without intermediaries. *[term used in all chapters]*

Decentralized Creative Networks (Łukawski): Decentralized creative networks, introduced by Adam Łukawski in his chapter of this book, are envisioned as blockchain-based post-human social networks where artists and AI agents collaborate to develop and exchange composable artistic processes. These networks enable transparent and interoperable contributions, allowing artists to build upon each other's work for various artistic endeavors, such as composing music or generating digital art. *[term used in the chapter by Łukawski]*

Decentralized Music: Decentralized music is a term manufactured for this book's title to propose an overarching conceptual and philosophical rethinking of musical creation, distribution, and ownership through technological management of digital musical interactions, processes, and networks without central authorities. This approach encourages viewing music as a participatory and collaborative art form, fostering direct connections within a community-driven ecosystem. In its various forms and notions, Decentralized Music exists thanks to blockchain's decentralized, secure, and transparent nature. Smart contracts and non-fungible tokens (NFTs) enable artists to directly connect, maintain ownership, and ensure the authenticity and provenance of their works. This approach not only facilitates novel artistic collaborations and distribution methods but also challenges traditional notions of agency, inviting a reevaluation of creative practices in the digital realm. Decentralized Music represents a shift toward a more equitable and innovative musical ecosystem, leveraging blockchain to expand the possibilities of musical expression and collaboration.

Digital Humanities: Digital humanities is an interdisciplinary domain that merges digital technologies with the diverse fields of the humanities, such as literature, history, arts, philosophy, and cultural studies. It utilizes computational techniques for the analysis, synthesis, and presentation of humanistic data, enabling activities like digital archiving, database creation for academic research, and visual mapping of cultural and historical trends. The objective of digital humanities is to enhance conventional humanities practices, making research more accessible, collaborative, and analytically profound. It also critically reevaluates and broadens the theoretical frameworks of humanities scholarship by incorporating digital advancements, prompting scholars to investigate new methods for generating, sharing, and interpreting the wealth of humanistic knowledge. *[term used in the chapter by de Assis]*

Digital Scarcity: Digital scarcity is the practice of deliberately limiting the availability of digital assets to create rarity and uniqueness in a realm where duplication is typically effortless and infinite. This principle plays a pivotal role in the blockchain and cryptocurrency sectors, especially evident in non-fungible tokens (NFTs), where uniqueness is guaranteed through cryptographic techniques. The assignment of unique codes or the issuance of limited editions elevates the value of digital artworks, collectibles, and virtual items, akin to the scarcity found in physical assets. This concept disrupts conventional views on digital value and scarcity, fostering innovative ownership, exchange, and valuation methods for digital content. *[term used in the chapter by Zeilinger]*

Distributed Database: A distributed database is a database configuration where data is stored across various locations or nodes instead of a single central site. This structure enables users to access and manage data from multiple points within a network, improving the system's dependability, availability, and operational efficiency. Designed to facilitate data sharing across numerous computers, distributed databases ensure continuous operation, even if one node encounters issues. This setup is crucial for decentralized systems like blockchain, supporting data security, integrity, and consensus without needing a central overseeing authority. It enhances system scalability and offers robust protection against data loss or failures, making it a key component in modern, resilient database architectures. *[term used in the chapter by O'Dair]*

Double-spending problem: The double-spending problem is a digital currency issue where the same funds can be spent more than once.

This challenge arises because digital information can be easily replicated. Blockchain technology, as used in cryptocurrencies, solves this problem by ensuring each transaction is uniquely recorded in a way that prevents duplication. *[term used in the chapter by O'Dair]*

Eco-friendly Consensus Methods (Proof of Stake): Eco-friendly consensus methods, such as Proof of Stake (PoS), are approaches used in blockchain technology to validate transactions and maintain network security with minimal environmental impact. These methods focus on reducing the need for extensive computational work and energy consumption that characterize traditional Proof of Work (PoW) systems. In PoS, the right to validate transactions and create new blocks is granted to participants based on the quantity of cryptocurrency they agree to lock up as security, or 'stake'. This system not only encourages less energy use but also aims to improve network scalability and security. As a result, Proof of Stake and similar methods are gaining traction among blockchain projects looking to be more environmentally friendly and efficient. *[term used in the chapters by Drubay, O'Dair, Tessone, Timmerman, Zeilinger]*

Ethereum blockchain: Ethereum blockchain is a decentralized platform known for its smart contract functionality. It allows developers to build and deploy decentralized applications (dApps) and use its native cryptocurrency, Ether (ETH), for transactions. Ethereum's blockchain is programmable, enabling complex agreements and automated transactions without intermediaries. *[term used in the chapters by Drubay, Łukawski, O'Dair, Timmerman, Zeilinger]*

Feature Engineering (in Machine Learning): Feature engineering is the technique of transforming raw data into structured, relevant variables that better inform machine learning models. It involves selecting the most informative attributes, creating new variables from existing data, and modifying or removing data points to enhance model accuracy and efficiency. This step is critical in the development of predictive models, as it directly impacts their ability to learn from the data and make accurate predictions. *[term used in the chapter by Łukawski]*

Fractional Ownership: Fractional ownership is a model where multiple parties can share and divide ownership of a high-value asset, such as real estate, artwork, or digital assets like NFTs. This approach allows individuals to own a part of the asset, making it more accessible and affordable to invest in expensive items. In the context of digital assets and blockchain, fractional ownership is facilitated through smart contracts, enabling people to own fractions of a unique digital item, democratizing access to investments and ownership in the digital and physical world. *[term used in the chapter by Drubay]*

Fungible Token: A fungible token is a type of digital asset that is interchangeable with others of the same type, meaning each token has the same value and properties as another identical token. This makes them ideal for use as a medium of exchange or a store of value, similar to traditional currencies (for instance, 1$ equals 1$). Examples include cryptocurrencies like Bitcoin and Ether. *[term used in the chapters by O'Dair, Tessone]*

Generative Artificial Intelligence: Generative AI refers to artificial intelligence algorithms designed to create new content, including text, images, audio, and video, by learning patterns and features from existing data. These AI models can generate original, creative outputs that mimic human-like creativity. *[term used in the chapter by Zeilinger]*

Generative Art: Generative art is a creative practice where artists use autonomous systems, such as algorithms, to generate artwork. These systems can include computer programs, mathematical formulas, or rules-based processes, which determine the outcome of the art piece, often resulting in works that are unpredictable or infinitely variable. The artist's role shifts from creating a singular work to designing the process that generates the art, exploring the interplay between control and chance. *[term used in the chapters by Drubay, Łukawski, O'Dair, Zeilinger]*

Governance Tokens: Governance tokens are digital assets in blockchain platforms that grant holders voting rights on decisions within a decentralized project or organization. These tokens are used to democratize decision-making processes, allowing token holders to influence the direction and policies of the project, such as protocol updates or resource allocation. Governance tokens embody the principle of distributed control, enabling a community-led approach to management and changes within blockchain ecosystems. *[term used in the chapter by O'Dair]*

Hyperobjects (Morton): The concept of 'hyperobjects' was introduced by philosopher Timothy Morton, referring to vast, intangible entities that are so large and complex that they transcend specific locations, times, and understandings. Examples of hyperobjects include climate change, nuclear materials, or the internet. They are characterized by their omnipresence across time and space, affecting all aspects of life while being difficult to grasp fully or address through traditional means. Hyperobjects challenge human perception and societal structures, forcing a reevaluation of our interaction with the world and highlighting the interconnectedness of all things. *[term used in the chapters by de Assis, Einarsson, Łukawski]*

Hypermusic (DeAssis): Hypermusic, as developed by Paulo de Assis, is an expanded concept of music that incorporates a multimodal array of elements beyond mere auditory experiences. Drawing from Timothy Morton's concept of hyperobjects – entities vastly distributed in time and space – it includes not just sound but also texts, images, ideas, and cultural references, forming a complex web that mirrors the interconnected and relational nature of the contemporary musical world. *[term used in the chapters by de Assis, Einarsson, Łukawski]*

Interoperability (Blockchain): Blockchain interoperability refers to the ability of different blockchain systems to communicate, share information, and conduct transactions with each other seamlessly. This allows for the exchange of data and assets across various blockchain networks, enabling them to work together in a coordinated and integrated manner. *[term used in the chapters by Einarsson, Łukawski, O'Dair, Timmerman]*

Intra-actions (Barad): Intra-actions, a term coined by an American feminist theorist and physicist Karen Barad, redefines the traditional notion of interactions. Unlike interactions that presuppose separate entities coming together, intra-actions suggest that entities emerge through their relations, emphasizing that distinctions between objects and their agencies are not pre-established but rather are co-constituted. This concept challenges conventional metaphysics of individualism, proposing a more entangled approach to understanding phenomena, where the boundaries and properties of things materialize within the phenomenon itself, reshaping how cause and effect, agency, and existence are viewed. *[term used in the chapters by Łukawski, Zeilinger]*

Large Language Model (LLM): A Large Language Model (LLM) is an advanced AI system designed to understand, generate, and interact with human language at scale. Built using deep learning techniques, LLMs analyze vast amounts of text data to learn language patterns, grammar, and context, enabling them to produce text that mimics human writing or speech. These models are used in various applications, including chatbots, translation services, content creation, and more, offering nuanced and contextually relevant responses or content based on the input they receive. *[term used in the chapters by de Assis, Łukawski]*

Live Coding: Live Coding is a performance art and technique where artists write and modify code in real-time to create music, visuals, or both, often in front of an audience. This practice emphasizes improvisation and interaction, blurring the lines between coding, composition, and execution. It involves various programming languages and environments, showcasing the creative process as part of the performance. Live coding not only highlights the artistic potential of coding but also fosters a dialogue between the performer, the code, and the audience, making technology an integral part of the creative expression. *[term used in the chapter by Giannoutakis]*

Machine Learning: Machine Learning is a subset of artificial intelligence (AI) that enables systems to learn and improve from experience without being explicitly programmed. It involves algorithms that parse data, learn from that data, and then apply what they have learned to make informed decisions. Essentially, it's the process of teaching computers to learn patterns and structures within data, enabling them to perform tasks such as prediction, classification, and decision making based on their learning. *[term used in the chapters by Łukawski, O'Dair, Zeilinger]*

Metastability (Simondon): Metastability, as conceptualized by Gilbert Simondon, refers to a state of dynamic equilibrium where a system maintains balance amid the potential for transformation. Thus, the system is neither completely stabilized nor completely destabilized; it exists and operates in a permanent attempt to stabilize its unstable component parts. This condition allows for the coexistence of multiple, potentially conflicting, states without defaulting to a fixed state of stability. In Simondon's philosophy, metastability is crucial for understanding processes of individuation, where entities evolve from indeterminate, pre-individual potentials to more structured forms. This concept emphasizes the importance of internal and external interactions in the emergence of new structures and forms of organization, highlighting the processual and transformative nature of being. *[term used in the chapter by de Assis]*

Metaverse: The Metaverse is a collective virtual shared space, created by the convergence of virtually enhanced physical reality, augmented reality (AR), and the internet. It represents a highly immersive virtual world where users interact with a computer-generated environment and other users. This concept encompasses digital spaces that are made more lifelike by the use of virtual reality (VR) or AR, suggesting a future where digital and physical realities blend, offering new spaces for interaction, economy, and entertainment. *[term used in the chapters by Łukawski, O'Dair, Timmerman]*

MIDI Format: The MIDI Format, an acronym for Musical Instrument Digital Interface, is a technical standard that allows musical instruments, computers, and other electronic equipment to communicate, control, and synchronize with each other. It enables the sharing of musical information, such as notes, rhythms, and instrument sounds, in a digital format that can be easily manipulated and reproduced. MIDI has been fundamental in music production, composition, and live performance since its introduction in the 1980s, allowing for complex musical arrangements to be created and performed using electronic devices. *[term used in the chapter by Łukawski]*

Micro-ontology: Micro-ontology refers to a detailed and specific framework within the broader field of ontology, focusing on the categorization and relationships of very specific concepts or entities within a narrow domain. It aims to provide precise definitions and structure to small, often complex segments of knowledge, facilitating clear understanding, communication, and processing of detailed information. Micro-ontologies are particularly useful in fields that require granular data analysis and interpretation, such as specialized areas of science, technology, and digital humanities. *[term used in the chapter by de Assis]*

Musical work: Traditionally, a musical work is considered a unique creation of art expressed through sound and composed by an individual or a group. It is often documented and communicated through written musical notation or recording, serving as a blueprint for performances. This definition emphasizes the work's autonomy, fixed identity, and the composer's original intent, treating the composition as a tangible, immutable object that exists independently of its performances. *[term used in the chapters by de Assis, Einarsson, Łukawski, Zeilinger]*

Musical ~~work~~ (de Assis): The reimagined view of a musical work, challenging its conventional boundaries, as proposed by Paulo de Assis in his book *Logic of Experimentation* (2018). The concept views musical work not as a fixed entity but as an ongoing process of configuration, experimentation, and re-composition. This perspective emphasizes the fluidity and transformative potential of music, advocating for a dynamic interaction between performers, listeners, and the work itself. The strikethrough of 'work' signifies a departure from the classical paradigm of the musical work, which however is still graspable and operating 'in the background'. The concept of 'musical ~~work~~' enables new approaches to music materials proposing an ever-changing experience shaped by creative performative acts. *[term used in the chapters by de Assis, Einarsson]*

Non-Fungible Tokens (NFTs): Non-fungible tokens (NFTs) are uniquely identifiable data units that can store information such as a certificate of authenticity, a record of ownership of a digital asset. Unlike cryptocurrencies, each NFT has a distinct value, which makes it non-exchangeable on a one-to-one basis with other NFTs. Central to NFTs is the use of smart contracts, which automate the enforcement of agreements, including the transfer of ownership and the execution of specific conditions tied to the NFT. This technology underpins the creation, purchase, and sale of digital art, collectibles, and other unique assets, offering a new way to authenticate and transfer digital ownership securely. *[term used in the chapters by de Assis, Drubay, Giannoutakis, Łukawski, Mulligan, O'Dair, Tessone, Timmerman, Zeilinger]*

On-Chain / Off-Chain (blockchain): On-chain refers to transactions and data recorded directly on a blockchain, ensuring transparency and immutability. Off-chain, in contrast, denotes activities happening outside the blockchain, offering faster transactions and reduced costs. While on-chain transactions are publicly verifiable on the distributed ledger, off-chain transactions rely on other methods for validation and recording, potentially enhancing privacy and scalability. Integrating on-chain and off-chain operations can optimize blockchain networks for efficiency and performance. *[term used in the chapters by Drubay, Łukawski, O'Dair, Tessone, Zeilinger]*

Ontogenesis (Simondon): Ontogenesis, often synonymous with ontogeny, describes the development and growth of an organism from the earliest stage to its mature form. This process encompasses all transformations starting from a single cell (such as a zygote) through to the formation of structures and functions within an adult organism. It includes both the physical and the biological aspects of growth, differentiation, and morphogenesis. Ontogenesis is a fundamental concept in developmental biology, illustrating how genetic and environmental factors interact to shape the life cycle of living beings. The concept has been appropriated and repurposed for science and technology by French philosopher Gilbert Simondon. His innovative approach is primarily detailed in his seminal work, *L'individuation à la lumière des notions de forme et d'information* ('Individuation in light of the notions of form and information'), published in 1958. Simondon's concept of ontogenesis diverges from traditional notions by focusing on the processes and dynamics that give rise to individual entities, rather than viewing individuals as pre-determined or static entities. Simondon argues that the process of individuation is fundamental to understanding ontogenesis. Individuation is the process through which a pre-individual reality (a metastable state containing potential energy and tensions) differentiates into distinct individuals or forms. This contrasts with views that consider individuals as primary or given. This view implicitly criticizes Aristotelian hylomorphism with its clear cut separation of form and content. For Simondon, individuation is always incomplete, meaning that the individual is always in relation to the pre-individual from which it emerged and remains partly undifferentiated. Simondon's rethinking of ontogenesis has had a profound impact on philosophy, particularly in the fields of technology studies, media theory, and the philosophy of science. His work challenges us to consider the dynamic, relational, and processual nature of being, emphasizing the unfolding of potentialities into individuated forms through interaction with their environments. *[term used in the chapter by de Assis]*

Partial-Scores (Einarsson): Partial-scores, as conceptualized in Einar Torfi Einarsson's chapter of this book, represent notated or inscribed pages that are the foundational units of a novel compositional system. These artifacts, laden with musical graphics, serve as non-linear, decentralized, and multiple representations, indicating an infinite possibility of musical compositions. They emerge from a system that merges digital and physical realms, aiming to explore fluid, non-linear, and participatory musical environments. Partial-scores symbolize a departure from traditional musical notation, embracing a dynamic and ever-evolving approach to music creation and interpretation. *[term used in the chapter by Einarsson]*

Performative Transactions (Łukawski): Performative transactions, as defined in Adam Łukawski's chapter of this book, are specialized artistic interactions that integrate both human creativity and AI contributions within a collaborative framework. In performative transactions, creative processes are embedded into others in contractual agreements managed by smart contracts, ensuring the seamless execution and integration of various artistic contributions. They facilitate transparent and collaborative creation, allowing artists to define the terms under which their work can be utilized by others, promoting a culture of shared innovation and artistic development without the need for centralized oversight. *[term used in the chapter by Łukawski]*

Proof of Creative Contribution (PoCC): Proof of Creative Contribution (PoCC) is a blockchain protocol to validate and enhance the collaborative music composition process within decentralized frameworks, discussed by Kosmas Giannoutakis in his chapter of this book. PoCC quantifies the compositional effort of contributors in a system, governed by explicit rules and managed through a consensus mechanism. This protocol ensures fairness and transparency in collaborative artistic endeavors, rewarding composers based on the community's appreciation of their segments. PoCC represents a significant step toward reimagining decentralized musicking, stimulating research, and experimentation in creative collaboration and communalization, and initiating discussions on the coordination technologies' ethics and politics in music. *[term used in the chapter by Giannoutakis]*

Proof of Stake: Proof of Stake (PoS) is a consensus mechanism used by blockchain networks to validate transactions and create new blocks. Unlike Proof of Work (PoW), which requires miners to solve complex mathematical problems, PoS allows validators to participate in the consensus process based on the quantity of cryptocurrency they hold and are willing to 'stake' as collateral. This method is considered more energy-efficient than PoW, as it does not require extensive computational work. Validators are chosen to create new blocks based on their stake, promoting security and energy efficiency in the network. *[term used in the chapters by Drubay, O'Dair, Tessone]*

Proof of Work: Proof of Work (PoW) is a consensus algorithm used in various blockchain networks to validate transactions and add new blocks to the chain. In PoW, miners compete to solve complex cryptographic puzzles. The first miner to solve the puzzle gets the right to add a new block to the blockchain and is rewarded with cryptocurrency. This process requires significant computational effort and energy, ensuring security and preventing fraudulent activities by making it computationally infeasible to alter the blockchain without controlling a majority of the network's mining power. *[term used in the chapters by Drubay, Giannoutakis, O'Dair, Tessone]*

Prompt / Prompting / Prompt Engineer: In the context of AI and creative technologies, 'prompt' refers to the input given to an AI model to generate a response or output. 'Prompting' is the process of crafting these inputs to guide the AI toward producing specific or desired results. A 'Prompt Engineer' specializes in designing and refining prompts to optimize the AI's performance, ensuring that the generated content meets the intended criteria or purpose. This role is particularly significant in fields where AI generates text, images, or other creative outputs, requiring a deep understanding of the AI's functioning and creative problem-solving skills to achieve the best results. *[term used in the chapters by Einarsson, Zeilinger]*

Set Theory (music): Musical set theory provides concepts for categorizing musical objects and describing their relationships. It applies to both tonal and atonal music across any equal temperament tuning system, highlighting the theory's flexibility. The theory deals with sets and permutations of pitches and pitch classes, which may be ordered or unordered. These can be analyzed through musical operations such as transposition, melodic inversion, and complementation. Additionally, the methods of set theory extend to rhythm analysis, showcasing its comprehensive application in music theory. *[term used in the chapter by Łukawski]*

Smart Contracts: Smart contracts are self-executing contracts with the terms of the agreement directly written into lines of code. They utilize blockchain technology to automate the execution of contractual terms, facilitating, verifying, and enforcing contract negotiations and performances without intermediaries. Smart contracts can also imbue digital artifacts, such as digital art, with complex, self-governing behaviors, making these items programmable and capable of semi-autonomous enforcement of rules. This innovation introduces a new level of interactivity and functionality to digital objects. *[term used in the chapters by de Assis, Einarsson, Giannoutakis, Łukawski, O'Dair, Tessone, Timmerman, Zeilinger]*

Token: A token in the context of blockchain technology represents a unit of value issued by a project or organization. It can serve various functions, from acting as a digital asset or currency within a specific ecosystem, facilitating transactions, to representing ownership or access rights to assets or services. Tokens can be programmable, meaning they can include smart contracts that enable complex behaviors, such as automatic dividend distribution or access management. They are stored and transferred on blockchain networks, ensuring security, transparency, and immutability of transactions. *[term used in all chapters]*

Transduction (Simondon): Transduction is a concept introduced by French philosopher Gilbert Simondon. It refers to a process of energetic transfer that establishes a new dynamic structure by reorganizing and transferring information across different domains. Simondon introduces the notion of transduction to describe how individuation operates. Transduction is the fundamental operator in ontogenesis, a process by which an entity evolves from a pre-individual state to become progressively more structured and differentiated. Transduction highlights how change and development occur through internal resonances and adjustments within a system, rather than by external influence, emphasizing the dynamic interplay between potential and realization in the emergence of new forms and structures. It is a mechanism of transformation that can be applied to various levels of reality, from physical to psychic and collective. *[term used in the chapter by de Assis]*

Transindividual (Simondon): The term 'transindividual' in Simondon's philosophy refers to the process and state that transcends both individual and collective dimensions. It signifies a phase where individuals are interlinked through shared experiences, knowledge, and the collective pre-individual potentials that exist within them. This concept emphasizes the dynamic relationality and ongoing processes of individuation, where individual and collective boundaries are not fixed but are continuously formed and reformed through interactions. The transindividual highlights the interconnectedness of beings and their co-evolution within a shared milieu. *[term used in the chapter by Giannoutakis]*

Transformational Theory (Lewin): Transformational theory in music, developed by David Lewin, focuses on relationships between musical objects rather than the objects themselves. It employs mathematical groups to model musical transformations for both tonal and atonal music analysis. The theory emphasizes the process of transforming one musical object into another, such as changing a C major chord to a G major through a 'Dominant operation'. Lewin's approach shifts from analyzing the static composition of musical objects to exploring the dynamic intervals and movements between them. *[term used in the chapter by Łukawski]*

Turing-completeness: Turing-completeness refers to a system's ability to perform any possible calculation or solve any computational problem, given enough time and resources. It's based on the concept of a Turing machine, an abstract machine proposed by Alan Turing. This machine can, in theory, simulate any computer algorithm. A programming language or a computational system is Turing-complete if it can do everything a Turing machine can do. This means it can theoretically solve any problem that can be computationally described, assuming there are no limitations on memory or execution time. *[term used in the chapter by Łukawski]*

Virtual and Augmented Realities: Virtual and augmented realities refer to immersive digital experiences. Virtual reality (VR) creates a completely digital environment, isolating the user from the physical world. Augmented reality (AR) overlays digital information onto the real world, enhancing but not replacing the user's perception of their surroundings. Both technologies are used in various applications, including entertainment, education, and healthcare, offering interactive and enhanced experiences by blending the digital and physical realms. *[term used in the chapters by de Assis, Drubay, Timmerman]*

Virtual (computation): In the context of computation, 'virtual' refers to a representation or simulation of a real-world process, object, or environment on a computer system. It denotes elements that are not physically present but are made to appear or function as though they are real through software emulation or simulation. This concept is widely applied in areas like virtual reality, where immersive digital environments simulate physical presence in real or imagined worlds, and in virtual machines, where an operating system runs as if it were installed on a physical computer. *[term used in the chapters by de Assis, Drubay, Einarsson, Giannoutakis, Łukawski, O'Dair, Timmerman, Zeilinger]*

Virtual / Actual (Deleuze): In Gilles Deleuze's philosophy, the virtual and the actual are two interrelated dimensions of reality. The virtual is a realm of capacities that have not yet been actualized or materially realized in the concrete world. Nonetheless, they are real in a potent and generative sense, containing all possible outcomes or forms that something might take within a given context and assemblage. The actualization process is the transition from the virtual to the actual, where these potentialities become manifested in the world as tangible entities or events. This concept challenges traditional notions of reality and potentiality, emphasizing becoming and transformation over static and perennial being. *[term used in the chapters by de Assis, Einarsson, Giannoutakis]*

Web3: Web3 represents the next phase of the internet, focusing on decentralized networks and blockchain technology. It aims to create a user-owned internet, where individuals have control over their data, identities, and transactions. Web3 leverages cryptocurrencies, decentralized finance (DeFi), and non-fungible tokens (NFTs) to facilitate peer-to-peer interactions without central authorities. *[term used in the chapters by de Assis, Drubay, Łukawski, O'Dair]*

Web 3.0: Often confused with Web3, Web 3.0 refers to the semantic web and the evolution of web utilization and interaction. It emphasizes machine-readable information and data connectivity through technologies like AI and natural language processing, aiming to make the internet more intelligent and intuitive in understanding human requests. *[term used in the chapters by Giannoutakis, Mulligan]*

Index

Pages in *italics* refer to figures and pages followed by "n" refer to notes.

Taylor & Francis
Taylor & Francis Group

Printed in the United States
by Baker & Taylor Publisher Services